Culture and Customs of the Czech Republic and Slovakia

**Recent titles in
Culture and Customs of Europe**

Culture and Customs of Spain
Edward F. Stanton

Culture and Customs of Germany
Eckhard Bernstein

Culture and Customs of Italy
Charles Killinger

Culture and Customs of the Czech Republic and Slovakia

CRAIG CRAVENS

Culture and Customs of Europe

GREENWOOD PRESS
Westport, Connecticut • London

Library of Congress Cataloging-in-Publication Data

Cravens, Craig Stephen, 1965–
    Culture and customs of the Czech Republic and Slovakia / Craig Cravens.
        p. cm.—(Culture and customs of Europe)
    Includes index.
    ISBN: 0–313–33412–9
    1. Czech Republic—Civilization. 2. Slovakia—Civilization. 3. Czech Republic—Social life and customs. 4. Slovakia—Social life and customs. I. Title. II. Series.
    DB2035. C73 2006
    943.7—dc22   2006012035

British Library Cataloguing in Publication Data is available.

Library of Congress Catalog Card Number: 2006012035
ISBN: 0–313–33412–9

First published in 2006

Greenwood Press, 88 Post Road West, Westport, CT 06881
An imprint of Greenwood Publishing Group, Inc.
www.greenwood.com

Printed in the United States of America

The paper used in this book complies with the
Permanent Paper Standard issued by the National
Information Standards Organization (Z39.48–1984).

10 9 8 7 6 5 4 3 2 1

To Charles Townsend
Bohemist extraordinaire

Contents

Series Foreword

THE OLD WORLD and the New World have maintained a fluid exchange of people, ideas, innovations, and styles. Even though the United States became the de facto leader and economic superpower in the wake of a devastated Europe after World War II, Europe has remained for many the standard bearer of Western culture.

Millions of Americans can trace their ancestors to Europe. The United States as we know it was built on waves of European immigration, starting with the English who braved the seas to found the Jamestown Colony in 1607. Bosnian and Albanian immigrants are some of the latest new Americans.

In the Gilded Age of one of our great expatriates, the novelist Henry James, the Grand Tour of Europe was de rigueur for young American men of means, to prepare them for a life of refinement and taste. In a more recent democratic age, scores of American college students have Eurailed their way across Great Britain and the Continent, sampling the fabled capitals and bergs in a mad, great adventure, or have benefited from a semester abroad. For other American vacationers and culture vultures, Europe is the prime destination.

What is the New Europe post–Cold War, post–Berlin Wall in the new millennium? Even with the different languages, rhythms, and rituals, Europeans have much in common: they are largely well educated, prosperous, and worldly. They also have similar goals and face common threats and form alliances. With the advent of the European Union, the open borders, and the euro and considering globalization and the prospect of a homogenized Europe, an updated survey of the region is warranted.

Culture and Customs of Europe features individual volumes on the countries most studied and for which fresh information is in demand from students and other readers. The Series casts a wide net, inclusive of not only the expected countries, such as Spain, France, England, and Germany, but also countries such as Poland and Greece that lie outside Western Europe proper. Each volume is written by a country specialist, with intimate knowledge of the contemporary dynamics of a people and culture. Sustained narrative chapters cover the land, people, and brief history; religion; social customs; gender roles, family, and marriage; literature and media; performing arts and cinema; and art and architecture. The national character and ongoing popular traditions of each country are framed in historical context and celebrated along with the latest trends and major cultural figures. A country map, chronology, glossary, and evocative photos enhance the text.

The historied and enlightened Europeans will continue to fascinate Americans. Our futures are strongly linked politically, economically, and culturally.

Preface

CZECHS AND SLOVAKS never tire of pointing out that Prague lies to the west of Vienna and is closer to Dublin than Moscow. The Czech Republic and Slovakia lie at the very center of Europe, yet because of their forty-year imprisonment behind the iron curtain, westerners associate the two countries with eastern rather than western Europe. On the other hand, nowadays one often reads in the Czech and Slovak press about a "return to Europe," which suggests the two countries are not as central to Europe as they might wish. In fact, the fortunes of the Czechs and Slovaks at the crossroads of Europe have been uneven, and the numerous and subsequent invasions by Hapsburgs, Nazis, Soviets, and western tourists have more than once threatened the two countries with extinction. Today, they are shaking off the smothering cloak of Communism and forging full steam ahead into the twenty-first century. With the smooth integration of the two countries into the European Union in 2004, it appears that their continuing existence is assured for the time being.

The Czech Republic and Slovakia have separate histories as well as numerous linguistic differences, but they do have common links that go back a long way. Moreover, the fates of the two nations have been intimately bound with the rest of Europe through a network of cultural and historical ties. This region was the birthplace of Antonín Dvořák, Leoš Janáček, Franz Kafka, the religious reformer Jan Hus, and the father of modern psycho-analysis Sigmund Freud. In the fourteenth century, Prague was the seat of the Holy Roman Empire, and today it is a bustling tourist center abuzz with self-styled "bohemians." Slovakia by comparison has yet to be discovered. Until 1918 its history and culture were more closely associated with that of Hungary than western Europe. The Communists tried to industrialize the region, but it remains a country of rural beauty and enduring traditions.

After a brief exposition on the geography, language, and population of the two countries, a historical overview will set the stage for the subsequent chapters on different aspects of contemporary Czech and Slovak culture of today, but just as anywhere else in Europe the past looms large in the Czech and Slovak cultural imagination, especially the forty years of Communist rule from 1948 to 1989. Although the Czechs do indeed have the highest per capita beer consumption in the world, and Czech and Slovak fashion models have stunned the world with their unrivaled beauty, this book tries to go beyond the stereotypes and clichés and present the cultural achievements of the two nations.

I dedicate this book to Professor Emeritus Charles Townsend of Princeton University, mentor and friend whose unmatched interest in and enthusiasm for this region of the world is rivaled only by his partiality to Pilsner.

Chronology

500 BC	Celtic tribes settle Bohemia and Moravia and are joined later by Germanic Marcomans.
100–50 BC	Celtic tribes settle in east Moravia (present-day Slovakia).
6th century	Slavs settle alongside Germanic tribes in Bohemia.
8th century	Tribe of Czechs settles in central Bohemia.
800	Přemyslid Dynasty is founded.
863	Byzantine brothers Cyril and Methodius bring Christianity to Moravia.
870	Prague Castle is founded.
905	Nomadic Magyar (Hungarian) tribes occupy East Moravia (Slovakia) and rule area for over 1,000 years, until 1918.
1000	The multi-ethnic Hungarian Kingdom, which included east Moravia (Slovakia), is founded by King Stephen of the Arpad dynasty.
1031	Bohemia and Moravia permanently join together as the Czech crown lands.

1346–78	Reign of Charles IV and Golden Age of the Czech crown lands.
1415	Church reformer Jan Hus is burned at the stake.
1419	First defenestration of Prague. Hussite era begins.
1620	Battle of White Mountain. Imperial Austrian army and Catholic mercenaries defeat the Czechs.
1740–80	Reign of enlightened ruler Empress Maria-Theresa. Relaxation of Austrian rule.
1790s	Beginning of Czech National Revival, which lasts throughout the nineteenth century.
1843	Codification of a standard written Slovak language.
1914–18	Assassination of Imperial to successor to Austro-Hungarian throne, Archduke Francis Ferdinand, and start of World War I.
1918	Czechoslovakia is founded.
1938	Munich Agreement is signed, ceding the Sudetenlands to Germany
1939	Nazis take over Prague. Slovakia becomes a German satellite
1942	Slovak national uprising.
1945	Allies liberate Czechoslovakia.
1948	Communist Party assumes power, and Czechoslovakia becomes a Soviet satellite.
1967–68	Prague Spring reform movement.
1968	Warsaw Pact troops invade Prague on August 21, ending the Prague Spring.
1977	Human rights Charter 77 is drawn up after arrest of band, the Plastic People of the Universe.
1984	Jaroslav Seifert wins the Nobel Prize for Literature.
1989	Velvet Revolution: Communist government resigns in November, and Václav Havel is elected President of Czechoslovakia.

1993   Velvet Divorce: On January 1, the Czech and Slovak
        Federated Republic peacefully separates into the Czech
        Republic and the Slovak Republic.

2004   The Czech and Slovak Republics enter the European
        Union.

Czech Republic. Cartography by Bookcomp, Inc.

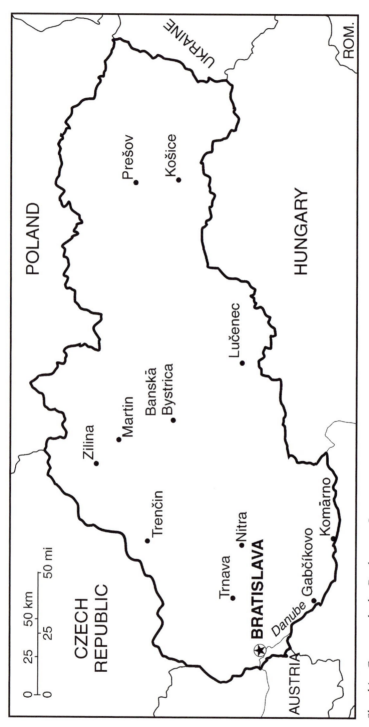

Slovakia. Cartography by Bookcomp, Inc.

1

Land, People, and History

We playwrights, who have to cram a lifetime or an entire historical era into a two-hour play, can scarcely understand this rapidity ourselves. And if it gives us trouble, think of the trouble it must give to political scientists, who spend their whole lives studying the realm of the probable and have even less experience with the realm of the improbable than playwrights do.

—Václav Havel[1]

Whoever wants to live in Central Europe must never sober up.
—Czech writer Bohumil Hrabal[2]

CZECHS AND SLOVAKS

ON JANUARY 1, 1993 CAME the final breakup of Czechoslovakia into the Czech and Slovak Republics. The "Velvet Divorce," as it was called, was unexpectedly amicable, and many Czechs and Slovaks were of the opinion it should not have come about at all. Truth be told, however, the Czechs and Slovaks had never considered living together until Tomáš Garrigue Masaryk (1850–1937), Czechoslovakia's first president roped together the two nations to create the First Czechoslovak Republic in 1918 after the collapse of the Austro-Hungarian Empire. But in the end, despite fundamental similarities in language and culture, the Czechs and Slovaks never really managed to create a common national Czechoslovak identity. The Czech writer and broadcaster Benjamin Kuras says of the Czechs and Slovaks:

In the Central European [c]ontext, the Czechs always tended to regard everybody else as underdeveloped peasants of whom only the Slovaks were civilizable—and only if they wanted to live with Czechs, behave like Czechs, and be grateful to Czechs for having once rescued them from national annihilation at the hands of the Hungarians. Now that the ever so ungrateful Slovaks have decided to go it alone, the Czechs have written them off, too, and consigned them into that vague, uninteresting, indistinguishable mass of East European peasantry.... The Slovaks themselves approach everyone with suspicion, assuming everyone is there to rip them off, because they know that everyone has already

Town Hall and the Týn Church on the Old Town Square in Prague. The square is the heart of Prague's Old Town. It dates from the late twelfth century when it was Prague's central marketplace. Courtesy of Getty Images/Photodisc.

ripped them off, and everyone owes them something. And by everyone, they mean everyone.[3]

The Land

Due to the Czech Republic and Slovakia's 40-year enforced residence behind the Iron Curtain (1948–1989), most westerners consider the two nations part of Eastern Europe. The fact is that they lie at the very heart of Europe. The capital of the Czech Republic, Prague, actually lies to the west of Vienna, and nearer Dublin than Moscow. The Czech Republic is bordered by Germany to the west, Poland to the north, Slovakia to the east, and Austria to the south. It covers 30,450 square miles (slightly smaller than South Carolina) and has a population of around 10 million.[4] The Czech Republic is made up of two geographical areas—Bohemia in the west and Moravia in the east. Bohemia is fundamentally a plateau surrounded by several sets of mountains. The Šumava Mountains lie to the southwest along the German border, the Bohemian Forest Mountains to the west, the Ore Mountains (Krušné hory) to the northwest, and the Giant Mountains (Krkonoše) to the north, along the Polish border. The Moldau (Vltava) is the republic's longest river (267 miles), and the mountaintop Sněžka, its highest peak (5,256 feet). Moravia comprises relatively flat lowlands with a few mountain ranges: the White Carpathians (Bílé Karpaty) and the Javorníky in the east, and the Beskydy and Jeseníky Mountains in the north.

Slovakia is bordered by the Czech Republic to the northwest, Poland to the north, Ukraine to the east, Hungary to the south, and Austria to the southwest. The country's most remarkable feature, and its greatest tourist draw, is its mountain ranges. The two most renowned are the High Tatras (Vysoké Tatry) to the north along the Polish border and the Low Tatras (Nízké Tatry) in central and eastern Slovakia. The highest peak is the 8,707-foot Gerlachovský štít in the High Tatras. Two smaller ranges forming part of the Tatras are the Malá Fatra and the Veľká Fatra. Another popular region for outdoor enthusiasts is Slovenský Raj, literally Slovak Paradise, an area of exceptional natural beauty, and of rare flora and fauna. There are few other places in the world where it is possible to encounter within such a small area such an enchantingly varied landscape—meadows, chasms, canyons, gorges, plateaus, caves, and waterfalls. The only lowland region in Slovakia lies to the southwest, along Hungary's border, and is the country's main agricultural area. The lowland region is where the country's longest river, the Váh (269 miles), joins the Danube.

POPULATION

In 2003 the population of the Czech Republic was estimated at 10,249,216 with a slightly negative population growth, that is, more deaths are being recorded than births (9.01 births and 10.74 deaths per 1,000). Life expectancy is 72 for men and 79 for women. The country is quite homogeneous, with 95 percent of the population ethnic Czechs and Moravians. Minorities include Slovaks (3.1%), Poles (0.6%), Germans (0.5%), Silesians (0.4%), Romany (0.3%), and Hungarians (0.2%). The capital is Prague, comprising an estimated 1.2 million inhabitants, but an additional 300,000 work in the city without having established residency. Prague has been called variously the "City of a Hundred Spires," "Golden Prague," the "Paris of the Twenties in the Nineties," and the "Heart of Europe."[5]

Slovakia has a population of 5,430,033 with slightly more births being recorded than deaths (10.1 and 9.22 per 1,000). Life expectancy is about 70 for men and 78 for women. Slovakia has more ethnic minorities than the Czech Republic; according to the 1996 census, 85.7 percent of the population was Slovak, and Hungarians made up 10.6 percent. Other minorities include Romany (1.6%), Czechs, Moravians, and Silesians (1.1%), Ruthenians and Ukrainians (0.6%), Germans (0.1%), and Poles (0.1%). Bratislava is the nation's capital with an estimated population of 430,000—the highest population density in Europe. In the past under various regimes, Bratislava has also been known as Pressburg (to the Germans and Austrians) and Pozsony (to the Hungarians).

THE CZECH AND SLOVAK LANGUAGES

Although the Czechs and Slovaks have separate and distinct national languages (Czech and Slovak), the two tongues are remarkably similar; in normal conversation, for example, a Czech will understand 99 percent of Slovak speech, and visa-versa. Nevertheless, because of differing grammatical structures, the two are considered distinct languages. They belong to the Indo-European family of languages and hence belong to the same family as English, French, German, and Spanish. Within this group, they reside in the subgroup referred to as Slavic, which includes Polish, Russian, Ukrainian, Belarusian, Bulgarian, and Serbo-Croatian, which are further divided into south, east, and west Slavic.

Czech and Slovak employ a variation of our Latin alphabet with some additional symbols above certain letters, called "diacritical marks." Above some consonants you will find a "háček" or "little hook." The letter "s," for example, is pronounced just like our "s," but "š" is pronounced like our "sh" in "ship." The letter "z" in Czech and Slovak sounds like our "z," but with a háček "ž" comes out as the English "zh." As you can see, Czech and Slovak use a letter and a diacritical mark to designate sounds that we have in English but which we designate with a combination of letters. One sound that exists in no other language in the world but Czech, however, is the notorious "ř," which sounds like a combination of a rolled "r" and "zh," as in Dvořák.

The other diacritic looks like an accent mark, but it actually indicates the length of the sound produced. The "čárka" can appear over any vowel and simply indicates that this vowel is voiced longer than an unmarked one. The difference may seem trivial, but often a single length mark is the sole distinguishing feature between two words with completely different meanings. The word *češka,* for example, means "Czech woman," whereas *čéška*—with a long "é"—means "patella" or "kneecap." One can imagine the referential confusions possible.

As with most other European languages, Czech and Slovak have borrowed many words from English, especially in the areas of business *(byznys)* and computers *(komputery).* For its part, Czech has contributed a couple of words to English. The Czech writer Karel Čapek coined the word "robot" in his 1920 drama *Rossum's Universal Robots,* which quickly entered most languages of the world. And the word "pistol" comes from the Czech *píšt'ala,* meaning "pipe" or "whistle."

Czechs are extraordinarily sensitive about spelling and grammar, and bad spelling is often taken as a sign of bad intelligence. A large part of schooling is taken up by dictation exercises and memorizing the notorious *vyjmenovaná slova* or exception words. This may be due to the fact that the modern Czech language is a somewhat artificial construction created in the nineteenth century (see section titled "The National Revival," below), and Czechs are still quite protective of it. A Czech language hotline in Prague takes over 10,000 calls a year.

HISTORY

The earliest settlers in the region of today's Czech Republic and Slovakia were Celtic tribes known to the Romans as *Boii,* hence the word "Bohemia." The first Slavs settled in the region in the fifth and sixth centuries, having migrated from the northeast. The first independent Slavic state arose in the south of today's Moravia as a counterbalance to the nomadic Avars invading from the east. Led by the Franconian merchant Samo, the Slavs freed themselves from Avar domination. After Samo's death in 658, present-day Moravia became the center of the Great Moravian Empire, which lasted until 906 and included Bohemia, Moravia, and parts of today's Slovakia, Poland, Germany, and Hungary.

In 863, the Great Moravian leader Rostislav (846–869) decided his denizens required the earthly and otherworldly benefits of Christianity, and in response to a request, Emperor Michael III of Byzantium dispatched two missionaries, the brothers Cyril and Methodius, to Moravia. Before their departure, Cyril, a linguist, philosopher, and diplomat, devised a written alphabet for the Slavic language called "Glagolitic" (during this early period, all Slavic languages were nearly identical). The alphabet was based on the Slavic dialect spoken in their hometown on the Balkan peninsula and was composed of a mixture of Greek and other eastern letters. Cyril's followers created the simpler Cyrillic alphabet from Glagolitic, which is still used by Russia, Bulgaria, Serbia, Ukraine, and Belarus.

The Rise of Bohemia

Hungarians and Germans destroyed the Great Moravian Empire around 907, causing two major cultural shifts: the seat of the central European Slavs moved to Bohemia, and the Czechs became cut off from the Slovaks for the next 1,000 years. Prince Bořivoj presided over the new Czech state. He is the first historically documented member of the Přemyslid Dynasty, which lasted from 870 to 1306. Bořivoj was baptized by Methodius and moved his seat to Prague around 885. According to legend, Bořivoj's decision to be baptized was fairly pragmatic. Once on a visit to a Moravian prince, he was forced to sit beneath the dinner table and dine with other pagan guests since only Christians could sit at the table. When Methodius explained to Bořivoj the manifold advantages and opportunities offered by Christianity, he had himself immediately baptized and returned to Bohemia with priests of the Slavic rite.[6]

The next most renowned ruler of Bohemia is another Přemyslid by the name of Prince Václav, or Wenceslas in English, who was eventually canonized for his lifelong devotion to the church. Wenceslas was murdered by his brother and successor Boleslav I at a mass in 935 and was beatified as the patron Saint of the Czech lands. Wenceslas was not a warrior, and it was eventually his continual appeasement of the Germans that led his brother to take his life. Today he is a controversial figure, but most Czechs consider him a symbol of the essential "goodness" of the Czechs. His statue sits at the top of Wenceslas Square in Prague. The Přemyslids remained on the throne for more than four centuries, and in 950 Bohemia became an independent kingdom within the Holy Roman Empire.

The Přemyslid dynasty reached its zenith under Otakar II (1253–1278) when military conquests stretched Bohemia all the way to the Adriatic. In 1278, however, Rudolf of Hapsburg killed Otakar. Bohemia and Moravia were plundered and occupied for five years, and all the southern territories were lost.

Prague endured years of foreign occupation and invasion. Things eventually calmed down, and through various marriages and alliances, the Czech kingdom became an administratively sovereign state within the Holy Roman Empire.

Charles IV

The Přemyslid line died out in 1306 and was succeeded by the House of Luxembourg. The zenith of Bohemia's medieval glory came under Charles IV who was crowned King of the Czech lands in 1346 and is known as *otec vlasti* or the "Father of the Homeland." He spoke and wrote Czech, Latin, German, French, and Italian and is the only Czech to ever be elected Holy Roman Emperor. When Charles came to Prague, the castle was in ruins; he set about reconstructing the castle along with the entire city, summoning Europe's foremost architects and transforming Prague into one of medieval Europe's preeminent cultural and commercial centers. It was also King Charles who founded in 1348 the first university in Central Europe, Charles University, which was meant to follow the grand examples of the universities in Paris and Bologna.[7]

The Mattias Gate is the main entrance to the Prague Castle. Built in 1614, it is one of the earliest Baroque structures in Prague. The figures represent battling Titans. Courtesy of Getty Images/Photodisc.

The Hussites

One hundred years before Martin Luther nailed his 95 theses to the church door in Wittenburg, the Czech preacher Jan Hus (c. 1369–1415) led a proto-Protestant movement agitating for, among other things, church services conducted in Czech rather than Latin, communion in both kinds (i.e., with bread *and* wine) for lay persons, and a cessation of the selling of indulgences. Hus began preaching in the Bethlehem Church in Czech in 1402 and garnered a large following. Naturally, the ruling Catholics voiced their disapproval of Hus, and when Hus refused to obey, he was excommunicated. Hus was then summoned to Constance and promised safe conduct, but upon his arrival, he was remanded into custody. When he refused to recant his teachings, Hus was burned at the stake on July 6, 1415. (For more on Hus, see Chapter 2 in this volume, "Thought and Religion.") Understandably, the Czechs were livid. The Czech nobles proclaimed themselves Hussites, and the university publicly declared itself for communion in both kinds. The chalice became the symbol of the Hussite movement. Between 1416 and 1419 papal loyalists were expelled from churches in Prague and elsewhere and replaced by Hussites, and church lands were seized and monasteries suppressed. This was the beginning of the Hussite revolutions.

In response, the Catholic Hapsburgs attacked in 1420, but the Hussites repulsed attack after attack by their better-armed foes, led by the one-eyed warrior Jan Žižka (c. 1360–1424). Žižka made his army into the most feared in Europe. Simply the sound of his chanting armies was enough to strike terror into the opposing forces. Today, a statue of Jan Žižka on horseback, the largest equestrian statue in the world, sits atop Vítkov hill in the section of Prague named after the famous warrior. Žižka began his military career blind in one eye, and an arrow eventually blinded the other. He fought his final battles totally blind. He died of the plague in 1424 on the eve of a planned conquest of Moravia and Silesia. Procopius took his place and defeated the Germans in two great battles in 1427, and he led the counterattack of the Bohemian armies to Austria, Hungary, Silesia, Saxony, Brandenburg, the Palatine, and Franconia.

George of Poděbrady was the last Czech king, and his line was succeeded by the Polish Jagiellon Dynasty. Then in 1526 the rule of the Czech lands and Slovakia passed to Ferdinand II of Hapsburg, which began nearly four centuries of Hapsburg rule over Bohemia, Moravia, and Slovakia. Ferdinand undertook a process of centralization in his lands and tried to strike a balance between Protestants and Catholics. He also supported the Counter-Reformation, however, which finally led to an open conflict in 1618 when an anti-Hapsburg uprising broke out in Prague, instigating the Thirty Years War.

Finally, on November 8, 1620, the Czechs were defeated at the battle of White Mountain, the most devastating event in modern Czech history. The Hapsburg Emperor Ferdinand quickly took revenge. He entered Prague and publicly executed 27 Czech aristocrats on the Old Town Square. The president of Prague University had his tongue cut out and nailed to the block before he was beheaded. The heads of 12 executed men were mounted on the tower of Charles Bridge for 10 years.

Then the purges began. The indigenous Protestant nobility and intelligentsia were destroyed. Everyone either fled the country or converted to Catholicism. Catholicism became the only religion permitted in the kingdom. Bohemia's population was reduced by half, its economy was in ruins, and German, rather than Czech, was made the official language of state administration, the press, and literature. Czech was reduced to the language of cooks, peasants, and the countryside. The Czech written language died out for 200 years.

The National Revival

After the Battle of White Mountain, Czech literature and language disappeared from society, that is, high society. Peasants, cooks, and villagers continued to speak Czech, but the official language of the Czech and Slovak lands was German—it was the language of government, business, journalism, and literature. This state of affairs lasted for almost two hundred years. Then in the late eighteenth century a nationalistic movement swept across Europe, initiated primarily by a German philosopher, Johann Gottfried von Herder (1744–1803). Herder hypothesized that a nation was not simply a random group of people brought together by chance and ruled over by a leader. A nation was an ethnically distinct group, and each nation possessed its own specific characteristics. Naturally, this idea appealed greatly to the Czechs who were still under Hapsburg rule and compelled to conduct their affairs in German. At the end of the eighteenth century and the beginning of the nineteenth, the Czechs began developing their own form of nationalism. The Czech National Revival continued through the nineteenth century and culminated in the First Czechoslovak Republic, formed in the aftermath of World War I and the disintegration of the Hapsburg Empire.

The first order of business for the Revivalists was the resurrection of the Czech language. Czech scholars, teachers, journalists—all of whom were writing in either German or Latin at the time—joined forces to try to revive Czech as a written language, teach it to their people, and create works of literature equal in value to those of other nations. The two main scholars associated with the National Revival are Josef Dobrovský (1753–1829) and

Josef Jungman (1773–1847). Dobrovský began as a historian, and during the Revival, he began studying Slavic languages. As the first Slavist, he described the most ancient Slavic language, Old Slavic, in a book called *Institutiones linguae Slavicae dialecti veteris* [Study of the old dialect of the Slavic language] in 1822. He also wrote a history of Czech literature, *Geschichte der böhmischen Sprache und Literatur* [History of the Bohemian language and literature] in which he claimed that the peak of Czech literary development came in the sixteenth century. And it is the Czech language of the 1500s upon which he decided to base his new version of Czech. Specifically, he went back to the monument of pre-White Mountain Czech literature, the Kralice Bible, a translation of the bible made in the mid-1500s, and created a revived "contemporary" Czech language, which he described in his *Ausfürliches Lehrgebäude der böhmischen Sprache* [Comprehensive edifice of teachings of the Bohemian language] in 1808.

The difference between Dobrovský's "new" written language and the Czech that was being spoken in his time was, of course, phenomenal. The spoken language had evolved and departed from that of the 1500s tremendously. Furthermore, the language of the Kralice Bible was actually archaic when it was written. Thus, we find an enormous gap between spoken and written Czech around 1800, the beginning of the National Revival, and this difference, although not as large, still exists today. Of course, all languages differ in their spoken and written variants, but in Czech the difference is dramatic. Dobrovský, however, did not give this much thought. He did not believe that written Czech could be revived and used to create works of literature, but other Revivalists did.

Josef Jungmann was among the second generation of Revivalists, and he sought to bring Dobrovský's literary Czech in line with the spoken version. His first action was to invent new words. Two hundred and fifty years is a lengthy span of time in terms of language development, especially if the language is not written down and codified. Furthermore, not only did the new written language possess different grammatical forms and obsolete vocabulary, there was also a lack of words for things and concepts in the eighteenth century that had not existed in the sixteenth. Hence, Jungmann looked to other Slavic languages, and even Old Slavic, to create new Czech words. And to demonstrate the literary capability of this new and improved Czech, Jungmann began translating great works from foreign languages into Czech, such as Milton's *Paradise Lost* and Chateaubriand's *Atala*.[8]

František Palacký (1798–1876) provided the Czechs with a conception of their history. He is known as the "Father of the Nation" *(otec národa)*. Palacký's five-volume magnum opus, *The History of the Czech Nation in Bohemia and Moravia,* was based on primary sources in eleven languages and traced Czech history from the earliest times to the Hussite revolts. Palacký's work was essentially a defense of the Czech nation's right to exist, and he saw Czech history as a never-ending battle between Germans and Slavs. His most memorable line is: "We were here before Austria, and we will be here after it."[9]

The National Revival continued through the nineteenth century, and Czech writers contributed to the movement by creating works of literature based on this new form of Czech. They were essentially trying to teach the Czech language to the Czechs.

The First Czechoslovak Republic

During the National Revival, the Czechs and Slovaks were still under the Austrian Monarchy, and so they began agitating for more autonomy. When World War I erupted in 1914, Czechs and Slovaks were in no way eager to fight for their Austrian overseers. When called up for service, they defected in droves and even formed a coordinated fighting force in Russia comprising several thousand volunteers, which became known as the Czechoslovak Legion. When the empire collapsed at the end of the war, the Czechoslovak Republic was proclaimed in Prague on October 28, 1918, and on November 14, the National Assembly elected Tomáš Garrigue Masaryk the Republic's first president.

Before the war, Masaryk was a famous public intellectual, philosopher, and proto-feminist (he took the last name of his American wife, Charlotte Garrigue, as his middle name). He taught philosophy at Charles University, and during the war fled first to Rome, then Paris, where he, together with Edvard Beneš (who succeeded Masaryk as president), founded the Czechoslovak National Council and then a provisional government in 1918. After prodigious work in Europe and America, Masaryk finally convinced the United States, France, and Britain of the workability of a united Czecho-Slovak state as a counterbalance to German and Austrian hegemony in Central Europe. The Pittsburg Agreement was signed in May of 1918, supporting the foundation of a united Czech and Slovak state, and finally on October 28, the new Czechoslovak Republic was declared with Prague as its capital and Masaryk its first president.

Between the world wars, Czechoslovakia was an island of democracy in Central Europe surrounded by authoritarian and fascist regimes. It was the tenth most industrialized country in the world, comprising more than fourteen million people, with a nationality breakdown (according to the 1930 census) of: 5.5 million Czechs, 3.5 million Slovaks, 3.2 million Germans, 700,000 Hungarians, 549,000 Ukrainians, 80,000 Poles, 186,000 Jews (both

Czech and German), and 50,000 "other."[10] During the early years, the leaders of the republic devoted themselves to harmonizing the demands of these various nationalities and at the same time transforming the country into a European industrialized nation. Between the wars Czechoslovak society was complex, with large landholders, middling farmers, tenants, landless laborers, and a host of specialists in the countryside such as herders, smiths, teachers, clerics, and local officials. The urban scene was equally diverse with hundreds of thousands small-scale manufacturers, shopkeepers, tradesmen, craftsmen, and an articulate intelligentsia. Moreover, the country lacked the extremes in wealth and poverty that marked so much of Central and Eastern Europe during this period.

With the arrival of the Great Depression, however, industrial reform lagged due to lack of money and resources, and ethnic conflicts were exacerbated. The Slovaks and Ukrainians felt they had not been granted the degree of autonomy they had been promised, and by the middle of the 1930s, a large number of Czechoslovakia's German-speakers—who were massed mainly along the German and Austrian borders in the so-called Sudetenlands—were claiming discrimination by the Czechs and agitating for secession from Czechoslovakia to link up with Greater Germany. In the 1935 elections, Konrad Henlein, the leader of the Sudeten German Party (which he founded in 1933), won 67.4 percent of all German votes, and the party thereby became the most powerful group in the Czechoslovak parliament.[11] At the behest of Adolf Hitler, Henlein made increasingly radical demands on the Czechoslovak government; he demanded self-rule for the German minority in Czechoslovakia and rejected concessions from the government guaranteeing equal opportunity in government service and unemployment benefits. Henlein finally demanded complete autonomy for the Sudetenlands and that they be placed under Hitler's direct protection. In May of 1938, his party won 92 percent of all German votes in Czechoslovakia.

The Protectorate of Bohemia and Moravia

Germany annexed Austria in March of 1938, and all the German political parties in Czechoslovakia, except the Social Democrats, refused to participate in the Czechoslovak government. In April of 1938, Henlein repeated and escalated his demands, and the Czechoslovak government offered yet further concessions. Henlein, however, refused to negotiate and fled to Germany. Hitler officially declared his support for a self-determined Sudetenland on September 12, 1938. When Hitler pressed, Britain and France, anxious to avoid war, urged Beneš, the president of Czechoslovakia, to relent and surrender the Sudetenlands. On September 29, 1938, the dictators of Germany and Italy and the Prime Ministers of Britain and France gathered together in Munich to sign the so-called Munich Agreement, according to which Czechoslovakia was to surrender to Germany its borderlands. The Czechs were neither invited nor consulted. The British Prime Minister Neville Chamberlain defended the decision to give the Czechs to Hitler in an infamous radio address: "How horrible, fantastic, incredible it is that we should be digging trenches and trying on gas-masks here because of a quarrel in a faraway country between people of whom we know nothing."[12]

The capitulation precipitated an outburst of national indignation. In demonstrations and rallies, the Czechoslovaks demanded the government stand strong and defend the integrity of the state. A new cabinet, under General Jan Syrový, was installed, and on September 23 a decree of general mobilization was issued. The Czechoslovak army was highly modernized and possessed an excellent system of frontier fortifications. The Soviet Union announced its willingness to come to Czechoslovakia's assistance if the Western powers would join the fray. The West, however, declined, and President Beneš resigned as president of Czechoslovakia, fled to London, and created a Czechoslovak government in exile.

Czechoslovakia lost one-third of its territory along its western and northern borders, which included its best military fortifications, natural defenses, and vast economic resources. At the incitement of Hitler, Poland and Hungary took advantage of the situation to seize long-disputed border territories. Altogether, Czechoslovakia lost 4.8 million people, one-fourth of whom were Czechs and Slovaks.

The Slovaks, too, took advantage of the Czechs' weakness, and ancient and recent grievances against the Czechs came bubbling to the surface. They declared an autonomous government and elected Jozef Tiso as their president. On March 13, Hitler summoned Tiso to Berlin, and the following day the Slovak Diet convened and unanimously declared Slovak independence. Tiso immediately banned all opposition political parties and instituted Nazi-inspired censorship, as well as the deportation of Jews to be exterminated. During the war, over 73,000 Slovak Jews were sent to concentration camps.

Not content with the Czechoslovak borderlands, Hitler marched into Prague on March 15, 1939 and announced from the Prague Castle the creation of the Protectorate of Bohemia and Moravia. Officially, the Protectorate was an independent state within the German Reich, but this was only on paper. The Czech government had no power in matters of defense, foreign affairs, or economics. In reality, the Protectorate was a puppet government under the control of Hitler. Emil Hácha, the nominal Czech president appointed by Hitler, did his best to keep concessions to the Germans to a minimum. He compared the situation of the Czech people in the Protectorate to finding yourself in a locked room with a dangerous madman, advising: all you can do is obsequiously agree and pretend to follow orders, so the madman does not throw himself on you; at the same time keep your eye on the door and wait for it to open to freedom.

The silver lining to occupation rather than military defeat, however, was that the city of Prague, unlike many capitals of Europe during World War II, suffered only minor damage. The Germans needed Czechoslovakia's armaments industry and agriculture for their war. Thus, the widespread terror and destruction we find elsewhere during the period did not exist. Throughout the occupation, Czech books continued to be published, and films continued to be made. As under the Austrians, German was the officially recognized language of the Protectorate, but signs were in both Czech and German. Terror was used mainly against intellectuals, Communists, the resistance, and, of course, Jews. In September 1941, Reinhard Heydrich of the Nazi SS was appointed Deputy Reich Protector of Bohemia and Moravia. He established his headquarters in Prague and soon after created a concentration camp in the town of Terezín, or Theresianstadt, an old Bohemian fortress town 60 kilometers north of Prague. Heydrich expelled the Czech population of the town in November 1941 and transformed it into a camp for Jews from the Protectorate.

Terezín was seen by the world as a "model" concentration camp. In 1944 the Red Cross was invited to inspect it, and the results can be seen in the movie *Theresienstadt*. Actually, Terezín was a way station on the journey to the camp at Auschwitz. Of 139,517 inhabitants of the camp between 1941 and 1945, 87,063 were transported to the east. Also, 33,521 people died there over the same period. In a surreal twist, however, cultural life in the camp flourished. The inmates published newspapers and schooled their children. Classical music concerts took place, and 25 theatrical productions were performed, often with very elaborate set designs. One was Smetana's *The Bartered Bride,* which had its Terezín premier in 1943.[13]

In May of 1942, Czech commandoes who had been trained in London parachuted into Prague and assassinated Heydrich. As a reprisal, the Gestapo and SS hunted down and murdered the Czech agents, resistance members, and anyone suspected of involvement in Heydrich's death—over 1,000 people were executed. In addition, the Nazis deported 3,000 Jews from the ghetto at Terezín for extermination. In Berlin they arrested 500 Jews and executed 152 as a reprisal on the day of Heydrich's death. Finally, Hitler ordered the small Czech mining village of Lidice to be destroyed. All 172 men and boys over age 16 in the village were shot on June 10, 1942. The women were deported to Ravensbrück concentration camp where most died. Ninety young children were sent to the concentration camp at Gneisenau, with some taken later to

Nazi orphanages if they looked German enough. The town itself was then destroyed, building-by-building, with explosives and then completely leveled until not a trace remained. Grain was planted over the flattened soil, and the name was erased from all German maps.

On May 9, 1945, the Soviet army liberated Prague, a few days after Germany's official surrender. The Allies had agreed at the Yalta Conference that the arrangement of political relationships within Czechoslovakia should take place under the aegis of the Soviet Union and that the Red Army would liberate the country. Thus, American troops who had marched into western Bohemia retreated and allowed the Soviets to enter and free Prague.

The Socialist Republic

After the war, the Czechoslovak Republic was revived from the ashes, that is, it became once again a parliamentary system of government. Now, however, its politics were extremely left leaning. The Czechs and Slovaks recalled the betrayal by the West at Munich; they also recalled the problems of capitalism during the Great Depression; finally, the Soviet Union had the psychological advantage because it was the Red Army that had liberated Prague. After World War II, Communism was extremely popular throughout Europe. Right-wing fascism was the great evil of the twentieth century, and many thought capitalism had been instrumental in the rise of fascism.

After the war, the Soviet Union had taken over all of Central and Eastern Europe, except Czechoslovakia. As Winston Churchill put it: "From Stettin in the Baltic to Triest in the Adriatic, an iron curtain has descended across the continent. Behind that line lie all the capitals of the ancient states of Central and Eastern Europe."[14] In Czechoslovakia, the Communists were close to holding a majority in the parliament. Then in the parliamentary elections of 1948, the Czech Communist Party garnered nearly 38 percent of the vote, the largest share obtained by any party. At this point it was simply another political party, but as soon as the Communists seized power, they arranged a putsch in February 1948 with staged demonstrations and strikes. The non-Communist ministers resigned, as did President Beneš; and Jan Masaryk, the son of the founder of Czechoslovakia who was currently Foreign Minister, fell from a window of the Foreign Ministry to his death. It is not clear whether his death was a homicide or a suicide. After February 1948, Czechoslovakia became a Soviet satellite until November 1989. Czechoslovakia, one of the most prominent bastions of democracy in Europe, became a prison. The government staged elaborate mock trials, imprisoning and executing thousands of innocents in an attempt to secure its power through fear, intimidation, and murder. The only woman to be officially executed was Milada

Horáková, a former member of Parliament and one of the most prominent Czech feminists of the interwar period. The most notorious political trial was the Slanský Process, 1951–1952, in which the Jewish deputy premier Rudolf Slanský, who had ordered Horáková's death, was executed on charges of an antigovernment conspiracy. Even after Stalin's death in 1953 and Nikita Khrushchev's historic denunciation of Stalin at the Twentieth Party Congress in 1956, political terror did not abate in Czechoslovakia until the 1960s and the advent of the Prague Spring.

The Prague Spring

The thaw finally came about in the Czech lands partially due to the agricultural disasters of collectivization of the 1950s; workers were unhappy that the enormous constructive activity did not lead to an improvement in their living standards or quality of life. By 1963, the economy was so bad that Czechoslovakia actually had a negative growth rate.[15]

A tendency of social criticism arose in the 1960s among students and the intelligentsia, who called for political and economic changes. A man named

View of Prague Castle and Charles Bridge from the edge of the Vltava River. Charles Bridge (originally called the Stone Bridge) was begun in 1357 during the reign of Charles IV. The bridge is lined by 30 Baroque statues, which were added later between 1683 and 1714. Courtesy of Getty Images/Photodisc.

Alexander Dubček became the head of the Communist Party of Czechoslovakia in March of 1968, and this is technically the beginning of the Prague Spring. Censorship ceased to exist, and there was a great outpouring of public sentiment against the government. Over a few months, Czechs and Slovaks challenged the official policies of the Communist government and made plans for dramatic changes in public life. What they wanted was a form of socialism better suited to what they considered their own democratic traditions and their historic links with the West. Milan Kundera writes of the Prague Spring:

> The Czech nation tried to create at last (and for the first time in its own history as well as in the history of the world) a socialism without the all-powerful secret police, with freedom of the written and spoken word, public opinion that was heeded and served as the basis for politics, a freely developing modern culture, and people without fear; it was an effort in which Czechs and Slovaks stood again for the first time since the end of the Middle Ages in the center of world history and addressed their challenge to the world.[16]

This new brand of socialism became known as "socialism with a human face." It was not capitalism they wanted, but socialism with no censorship and with no limitation of civil liberties. They did not, however, repeal one party rule. Czechs and Slovaks began to air their grievances and come to terms with their Stalinist past, and art flourished like never before.

But this did not last long. Dubček and his supporters found themselves caught between the increasingly radical demands of their people and the increasingly conservative demands of the leader of the Soviet Union, Leonid Brezhnev. Finally on August 21, 1968, more than 200,000 Warsaw Pact troops rolled into Prague to bring the Czechs and Slovaks back into line. Fifty-eight people were killed. The hopes of an entire generation were crushed. Dubček was forced to repeal his reform doctrines in Moscow, and when he returned to Prague, he was replaced by Gustav Husák. Fourteen thousand Communist officials and five hundred thousand party members refused to renounce their beliefs in reform and were summarily expelled from the Communist Party. This was the end of the Prague Spring and the beginning of "Normalization." There was little armed resistance to the invasion and subsequent totalitarian rule, but there was some passive resistance. In January, 1969, a student named Jan Palach set himself on fire to protest the invasion, and his suicide was to be followed by the self-immolation of other students until Soviet forces withdrew. On his deathbed, however, Palach, in extreme agony, urged and finally convinced the students not to carry out the plan.

Normalization

Husák's regime demanded obedience and conformity in all spheres of life. He returned the country to an orthodox command economy, emphasizing industry and central planning, and increased ties with the Soviet Union. In the 1980s, nearly 80 percent of Czechoslovakia's foreign trade was with Communist countries, 50 percent of which was with the Soviet Union. Czech culture was stifled when strict censorship was reinstituted, and intellectual life in general was purged of critical thinking. An estimated half million people were removed from official positions, and thousands emigrated.

The most common attitudes toward public life after the 1968 invasion were apathy and passivity. Most Czechoslovak citizens ignored public political life and retreated during the 1970s into private consumerism, seeking scarce material goods—new automobiles, country houses, household appliances, and access to sporting events and entertainment. Unlike in other Communist countries such as Poland, the Czechoslovak resistance movement was small; but a few organized dissident groups were active. The most famous called itself Charter 77, a "loose, informal and open association of people" committed to human rights. On January 6, 1977, their manifesto appeared in newspapers throughout the West. It was signed by 243 people—among them, artists, former public officials, and other prominent figures, including the country's most famous dissident, Václav Havel. The group became the focus for the regime's reprisals. Signatories were arrested, interrogated, and usually dismissed from their places of employment. Many Czechs and Slovaks emigrated to the West.

The Velvet Revolution and the Velvet Divorce

In 1989 the Communist governments in Central and Eastern Europe collapsed. Following the reforms of Mikhail Gorbachev in the Soviet Union in the mid-1980s—*glasnost* and *perestroika*—Poland and Hungary took advantage of the reformist mood of the region and began a series of protests of their respective governments. In East Germany, the citizens rose up and brought down the Berlin Wall. Czechoslovakia's Communist Party, however, refused to bend. On January 15, 1989, a peaceful demonstration took place on Prague's Wenceslaus Square in memory of Jan Palach. Police and military units brutally suppressed the rally, but further protest demonstrations continued for several days. Then on November 17, a student march in honor of Jan Opletal, who had been shot by the Nazis, became a massive anti-government demonstration. A crowd of 50,000 was cornered by police, over 500 beaten, and more than 100 arrested. Demonstrations spread throughout the country in the subsequent days, culminating in a massive march of 750,000 protesters on Letná Hill in

Prague. Here the leading dissidents and opposition movements, with Havel at their head, formed the opposition group—and future governing party—Civic Forum (*Občanská forum*—OF). They demanded that the Central Committee of the Communist Party resign and that all political prisoners be released. On December 3, they negotiated the government's resignation. At the same time in Bratislava, Slovaks founded the movement Public Against Violence (*Verejnost' proti násiliu*—VPN). The overcoming of Czechoslovak Communism became known as the Velvet Revolution, named both for the nonviolent nature of the transition and for Havel's favorite rock group, the Velvet Underground.

Immediately after the downfall of the government, rumors began to spread that the impetus for the Velvet Revolution had come from a KGB provocateur sent by Gorbachev. The theory goes that Gorbachev wanted reform-minded rather than hard-line Communists in power, but the demonstrations went further than he had intended. The rumors, however, have not been substantiated.

On December 29, a predominantly Communist Parliament met in Prague Castle and elected Václav Havel, a world-renowned playwright and the Eastern Bloc's most famous dissident, as President of Czechoslovakia. A coalition government was created, and the first free elections in Czechoslovakia since 1946 took place in June 1990 without incident. Civic Forum and Public Against Violence won landslide victories in their respective republics and gained a majority in Czechoslovak Parliament.

The leaders of the two parties, however, slowly drifted apart as they set about reforming and modernizing the new republic. The primary question was how to achieve economic reform most effectively. In the early 1990s, the expected foreign investment failed to materialize on the required scale, and the economy fared more poorly than expected. Slovakia suffered disproportionately during the transition to a market economy. The June 1992 elections brought to power the left-leaning nationalist Movement for a Democratic Slovakia *(Hnutie za demokratické Slovensko*—HDZS*)*, led by the fiery and controversial autocrat Vladimír Mečiar, a Soviet-trained lawyer and firm believer in Slovak independence. In July, the Slovak parliament voted to secede from the Republic, and despite numerous efforts, leaders could not agree on a compromise. On January 1, 1993, Czechoslovakia once again ceased to exist, becoming the Czech and Slovak Republics. The divorce, compared to other national separations in the region, was relatively smooth. Václav Havel was elected President of the Czech Republic, and Mečiar became Prime Minister of Slovakia.

The Czech Republic and Slovakia in the Twenty-first Century

After two terms as president, Václav Havel was replaced by former Prime Minister Václav Klaus in March of 2003. It took Parliament three tries to finally elect the abrasive, nearly unconditional fan of the free market. Jiří Paroubek is the current prime minister, elected in April 2005. The Czech Republic joined NATO in 1999 and the European Union in May 2004. Czech currency is expected to become the Euro in 2008. In a national referendum, more than 77 percent supported European Union accession. Turnout for the referendum, however, was only 55.2 percent. The positive vote was somewhat surprising considering the Czech Republic's euroskepticism. An overwhelming 92 percent of Slovaks advocated joining the union, but here again only 52 percent of Slovaks showed up to vote. Many are still skeptical, fearing greater inflation and a skewering of Czech and Slovak national culture. They are also concerned that rich foreigners will invade their land and buy it cheaply.

NOTES

1. Václav Havel, address to a joint meeting of the U.S. Congress, Washington, DC, February 21, 1990. Cited in Václav Havel, *The Art of the Impossible: Politics as Morality in Practice,* trans. Paul Wilson et al. (New York: Fromm International, 1998), 11.

2. Benjamin Kuras, *Is There Life on Marx? Post-communist Central Europe—The Rough with the Smooth* (Prague: Evropský literární klub, 2001), 12.

3. Kuras, 48–49.

4. Figures are cited in the CIA's World Factbook, http://www.cia.gov/cia/publications/factbook/geos/ez.html.

5. CIA World Factbook.

6. Peter Demetz, *Prague in Black and Gold: Scenes from the Life of a European City* (New York: Hill and Wang, 1997), 13.

7. Demetz, *Prague in Black and Gold,* 83.

8. Jungmann translated *Atala* in 1805, *Paradise Lost* in 1811, and Goethe's *Herrmann and Dorothea* in 1841.

9. František, Palacký, *Idea státu rakouského* (1865), section VIII.

10. Joseph Rothschild, *East and Central Europe between the Two World Wars* (Seattle: University of Washington Press, 1974), 89–90.

11. Sayer, 22.

12. Derek Sayer, *The Coasts of Bohemia: A Czech History* (Princeton: Princeton University Press, 1998), 170.

13. Sayer, 228.

14. Winston Churchill, speech at Westminster College, Fulton, Missouri, March 5, 1946.

15. Sharon Wolchik, "Czechoslovakia," in *The Columbia History of Eastern Europe in the Twentieth Century,* ed. Josef Held (New York: Columbia University Press, 1992), 135.

16. "Český úděl," *Tvar* 7–8 (19 Dec. 1968): 5.

Selected Bibliography

Čapek, Karel. *R.U.R. (Rossum's Universal Robots)*. Trans. Claudia Novack-Jones. New York: Penguin, 2004.

Dobrovsky, Josef. *Geschichte der böhmischen sprache und Literatur*. Halle: M. Niemeyer, 1955.

———. *Institutiones linguae Slavicae dialect veteris*. Prague, 1822.

———. *Lehrgebäude des böhmischen sprache*. Prague: G. Haase, 1819.

Demetz, Peter. *Prague in Black and Gold: Scenes from the Life of a European City*. New York: Hill and Wang, 1997.

Sayer, Derek. *The Coasts of Bohemia: A Czech History*. Princeton: Princeton University Press, 1998.

Wolchik, Sharon. "Czechoslovakia." In *The Columbia History of Eastern Europe in the Twentieth Century,* ed. Josef Held. New York: Columbia University Press, 1992, pp. 119–63.

Web Sites

CIA World Factbook: http://www.cia.gov/cia/publications/factbook/geos/ez.html.

Prague's English-language newspaper, the *Prague Post:* http://www.praguepost. com/.

2

Thought and Religion

We have got rid of Vienna. Now we will get rid of Rome!
—Tomáš Masaryk

ALTHOUGH IT IS THE BIRTHPLACE of the religious reformer Jan Hus (c. 1369–1415), the Czech Republic is the second most atheistic country in Europe, just behind Estonia. A 1990 poll conducted by the Holland-based organization European Values Study found that only 33.6 percent of Czechs belong to a religious denomination, and only 11.7 percent attend church services at least once a month.[1] The citizens of Slovakia by comparison are much more devout, similar in their beliefs to the neighboring Poles, and the Catholic and Orthodox Churches were more active in Slovakia under Communism. As in the rest of Central and Eastern Europe, the fortunes of Czech and Slovak Jews were uneven. They were alternately tolerated and suppressed depending on the ruler's whims and on the amount of money he or she thought they could provide. During the First Republic, they thrived under Masaryk's beneficent rule, but the Nazis destroyed nearly the entire Jewish population. This chapter traces the curious history of religion in the Czech and Slovak lands.

EASTERN VERSUS WESTERN CHRISTIANITY

The homeland of the ancient Slavs was present-day Ukraine and Belarus. Between the fourth and the sixth centuries, tribes of nomadic Huns and Avars invaded from the east, pushing the Slavs down into the central and southeastern parts of Europe. By the first decades of the sixth century, the Slavs had reached the banks of the Danube River, arriving on the frontiers of the civilized world at a time when the political and religious center had shifted from the western to the eastern part of the Mediterranean Sea. Rome, although still a religious and political force, had been decimated by invading nomadic tribes, and Constantinople (currently Istanbul) had assumed the seat of Christianity throughout the world. But theological and doctrinal disputes arose between the two churches—Roman Catholicism and Byzantine Christianity (which became known as Eastern Orthodoxy)—one of which concerned language. When Constantine I founded Constantinople in 330, he established Christian churches throughout his realm. The language of worship in these churches was usually the respective local language. Rome, on the other hand, considered only three languages appropriate for worship: Latin, Greek, and Hebrew. Rome, however, did not have much say in the matter because in the mid-sixth century, Europe had been entirely overrun by Germanic tribes. As the two churches gradually Christianized Europe, Rome sought allies against Constantinople and found a powerful one in the Germanic kingdom of the Franks. On Christmas Day, 800 A.D., Pope Leo III crowned King Charlemagne of the Franks the "emperor of the Romans," laying the foundations for the Holy Roman Empire. This was an outright challenge to the Byzantine emperor's authority as the ultimate Christian authority, and it finalized the split between the Roman and Byzantine empires.

Thus the Slavs, spreading south from central Europe into the Balkans and west into Germany, came upon these two adversaries. Toward the end of the sixth century the Slavs had pillaged the entire Balkan peninsula. Early in the ninth century, Mojmir, a Slavic tribal chief, annexed the western part of Slovakia and formed the first Central European dynastic state, the Great Moravian Empire, which was subjected to repeated attacks by the neighboring Franks throughout the ninth century. German missionaries were dispatched to spread the Roman form of Christianity throughout Moravia with some success. Mojmir and his fellow chiefs were baptized at Regensburg Germany. Mojmir's successor Rostislav (846–869), however, feared Germanic political expansion and moreover wanted the Gospel to be preached in Slavic rather than Latin, which was common in the Eastern Church. At this point, all Slavic languages were mutually comprehensible. Hence, Rostislav asked the Byzantine Emperor Michael III (the Drunkard, 836–867) for religious and political aid, writing to him, "Though our people have rejected paganism and observe Christian law, we do not have a teacher who can explain to us in our language."[2] Michael responded by dispatching in 863 the brothers Cyril and Methodius to Moravia, who officially brought Christianity to the Slavs (see Chapter 1 of this volume, "Land, People, and History"). Rostislav's successor Svatopluk (871–894), however, chose to ally himself with the German king, and after the death of Methodius in 885, the Moravian Empire was drawn into the sphere of influence of the Roman Catholic Church.

Around 907 Germans and Hungarians destroyed the Great Moravian Empire. Bohemia became the seat of the Czech lands, and in 950 the Bohemian Kingdom became a fief of the Holy Roman Empire. The influx of German monks and priests into Bohemia proceeded apace. By 1100 the Slavic Church officially ceased to exist in Bohemia, religiously and politically the Czechs allied themselves with Rome, and Latin replaced Slavic as the language of both liturgy and literature.

JAN HUS

In 1198 Bohemia became a powerful kingdom within the Holy Roman Empire, and under Charles IV (reigned, 1346–1378), Prague was the empire's seat. Then at the end of the fourteenth century the proto-Protestant Czech religious reformer Jan Hus began agitating for changes in the Catholic Church. Trained as a Catholic priest, Hus came under the influence of the writings of the English reformer John Wyclif (c. 1828–1324), who championed the people against church excesses, such as the selling of indulgences. Hus began preaching in the Bethlehem Chapel in Czech (rather than Latin) in 1402. He attacked the abuses of the clergy, denied the infallibility of an immoral pope, advocated the administration of the Eucharist in both kinds, that is, bread *and* wine for both clergy and lay persons, and asserted the ultimate authority of Scripture over the church. One hundred years later Martin Luther would adopt many of his ideas for what was to become the Protestant Reformation. The Holy Roman Emperor Wenceslaus supported Hus and appointed him rector of Prague's Charles University in 1409, but Hus incurred the hostility of the archbishop of Prague, who excommunicated him in 1410 and sent him into exile in Tábor, where he composed his chief works. Hus garnered a large following among the Czechs, and the Emperor Sigismund invited Hus to defend his views at the Council of Constance (1414–1418), granting him safe-conduct. When Hus presented himself at the Council in 1414, the Council refused to recognize his safe-conduct, tried him as a heretic, and burned him at the stake when he refused to recant his teachings. An eyewitness, Peter of Mladoňovic (c. 1390–1451), describes Hus' execution:

Then, having tied his hands behind him to a sort of pillar, they stripped off his clothes and bound him to the aforesaid pillar with a rope. Now he was facing the East, and some of those standing around said, "Do not let him point East, for he is a heretic. Turn him toward the West." And that is what happened. Then, when they were attaching his neck [to the pillar] with some smoke-blackened chain, having taken a look at it, he smiled and said, "The Lord Jesus Christ, my Savior and Redeemer, was fettered with a harsher and heavier chain; wretch that I am, I am not ashamed to bear this one for the sake of His Name." The stake resembled a thick plank about half a yard in breadth. Having sharpened it at one end, they knocked it into the earth of the aforesaid meadow. Then two faggots mixed with straw were placed around his body right up to his chin ... one could see him moving before he breathed his last for as long as it would take to say quickly two or, at most, three Lord's Prayers ... the henchmen knocked the corpse together with the stake onto the ground and, having fed the fire with a third barrow-load of wood, burnt it and crushed the bones with cudgels to accelerate its turning into ashes. And, having found the head, they smashed it into little pieces and threw it into the fire. Then, when they found the heart among the innards, they sharpened a staff and stuck it through the heart and roasted it.[3]

Hus' ashes were scraped from the ground and tossed into the Rhine River so that nothing of him should get back to Bohemia.

Hus' martyrdom galvanized the preacher's followers in the Czech lands. Hussites invaded and conquered Prague, tossed Catholic clergy from the town hall windows, and assumed control of the country for the next fifteen years. Czech nobles publicly proclaimed themselves Hussites, and the university declared itself for communion in both kinds. The chalice became the symbol of the Hussite movement. Between 1416 and 1419, papal loyalists were expelled from churches in Prague and elsewhere and replaced by Hussites, and church lands were seized and monasteries suppressed. This was the beginning of the Hussite revolutions.

Crusade after crusade was launched against the Hussites under the banner of the Cross and were defeated one after another by the Hussite "warriors of God." King Sigismund and representatives of the Catholic Church were compelled to open negotiations with the Hussites at the Council of Basle in 1420, where the Hussites laid down their demands, which were considered heretical: "1) Communion of the body and blood of the Lord under both kinds for all lay people. 2) Proper and free preaching of the word of God. 3) Priests should be such living examples to us as the Lord Christ commanded and his Apostles and after them the holy fathers instituted. 4) The common weal of the kingdom and our Czech language and the cleansing of the kingdom and the Czech language from evil and false rumor."[4] The first three demands plus another, that clergy be responsible and punishable for mortal sins, came to be known as the Four Articles of Prague.

Hussite demands were not immediately met, and Sigismund attacked Hussite-held Prague in 1420, but the Hussites repulsed attack after attack, led by Jan Žižka (c. 1360–1424), who hailed from southern Bohemia. Žižka introduced modern methods of drilled combat, and his troops were the first to use artillery systematically as a major tactical arm. Revolutionary Bohemia threatened to control all of Middle Europe. Pope Martin V called a general council at Basel in 1431 to launch yet another Crusade, which again went down in overwhelming defeat. Negotiations were finally begun with more moderate Hussites called Utraquists (from the Latin *utraque,* "each of two," referring to bread and wine). Finally at the Council of Basel in 1433, the Hussites received some form of religious recognition from the Catholic Church. A year later, however, the Utraquists allied themselves with the Catholics and defeated the radical Hussites at the Battle of Lipany in 1434. For a century thereafter, a modified form of Catholicism formed the basis of Czech religion until the Reformation and Martin Luther's teachings penetrated the region in the 1520s. Protestantism subsumed Hussitism and became the dominant Czech religious ideology for the next two hundred years.

The Union of Brethren *(Jednota bratrská)* was a sect inspired by the teachings of Jan Hus founded by Petr Chelčický in 1457. The Brethren emphasized intelligence and hard work and rejected violence and material gain. Although small, the Brethren attracted the main intellectuals of the time. It was they who first translated the bible into Czech (Kralická bible). The most famous follower Jan Amos Komenský (1592–1670) became a well known reformer of education and went into exile after the Battle of White Mountain (see section below). The teachings of the Brethren survived the Thirty Years War and spread to other countries. Legend has it that Komenský was offered the first presidency of Harvard University.

WHITE MOUNTAIN

On November 8, 1620, invading Catholic armies defeated Czech Protestant forces at the Battle of White Mountain, putting an end to the sovereignty of the Czech state. The Czech lands were reduced to the status of imperial crown lands of the Hapsburg Empire, and Catholicism became the only religion permitted until 1781, when Emperor Josef II issued a Tolerance Patent guaranteeing freedom of religion. During this period, the Czechs looked upon Catholicism as the religion of the empire, of subjugation, and they never forgot their reformist hero Jan Hus, whom they would invoke in times of nationalistic fervor. Thus, nominally the Czechs were Catholic, but they would express their nationalism through Protestant religious symbols, Jan Hus, and the Hussite symbol of the chalice.

At the end of the eighteenth century, Czechs began making their national aspirations known, and Hussite symbols came to signify Czech independence.[5] The National Revival was a product of the Enlightenment, and Enlightenment values of reason and clarity in political and social issues came to characterize the movement, which also carried over into linguistic and literary matters. In Josef Jungmann's translation of Chateaubriand's *Atala,* for example, (see Chapter 1 of this volume, "Land, People, and History"), a tragic and poetic love story about American Indians, the Czech scholar modified the text, purging it of most of its mystical and dreamy Christian imagery. While not outright atheistic, the National Revival was anti-Hapsburg and concomitantly largely anti-Catholic. Josef II's Toleration Patent of 1781 guaranteed freedom of religion, and Jan Hus assumed almost cult-like status. In 1868, 400 Czechs made a pilgrimage to Constance, the site of Hus' immolation, and a commemoration for the Czech martyr took place the following year in Prague on July 5, the eve of his death.[6] A monument to Jan Hus was begun in July of 1903 on the Old Town Square, and it was unveiled on July 6, 1915, the 500th anniversary of Hus' immolation. The Austrian government outlawed any ceremonies during the event.

JEWS

The history of Czech and Slovak Jews is similar to the histories of Jews in other Central European countries. Until the end of the nineteenth century, they were allowed to live only in certain designated areas and were often subject to expulsion, restrictions, and even mass-murder. The Jews came to the Czech lands at the very beginning of the tenth century, migrating from Germany, Hungary, and the Byzantine Empire.[7] The primary Jewish community eventually developed on the right bank of the Vltava River near Prague's Old Town. Times of royal toleration of the Jews in Prague and throughout the Czech lands alternated with times of persecution. In 1262, King Premysl Otakar II instituted the *Statuta Judaeorum,* establishing legal rights for the Jews in the empire and respecting their own religious and civil self-administration. One of the most important aspects of the statutes was the prohibition against accusations of blood libel because, as it was said, Jews have no use for blood.[8] When the Church challenged Otakar to justify his favorable treatment of the Jews, he responded that because Jews were *servi camerae,* that is, under the authority of the imperial treasury, the Crown had the right to collect Jewish taxes and regulate Jewish affairs.[9]

This symbiotic relationship between the Crown and the Jews continued throughout the Middle Ages with some ups and downs. Under Charles IV, tensions heightened between Jews and Christians as competition from

Christian capitalists increased. Although Charles protected his Jews, he was not above standing aside and cashing in on the results of unexpected pogroms that took place in his realm. In the Easter pogrom of 1389, which occurred eleven years after Charles' death, over three thousand Jews were killed by swords, clubs, and fire. All abandoned Jewish property was then brought to the town hall for the king, but the people who had broken the laws went unpunished.[10]

During the Hussite revolutions of the 1420s, Jewish fortunes were uneven. As the authority of Vienna weakened, so too did the legal protections of the Jews, who were often accused of aiding the Hussites in their struggle against the Catholic Church. Many Hussites, on the other hand, respected the nation of the Old Testament and their stalwart morality; and although Czech and Moravian Jews did suffer, their lot was far better than the Jews in Vienna, for example, who were entirely wiped out in retaliation for allegedly selling weapons to the Hussites.[11]

Under Maximilian II (reigned 1564–76) and Rudolf II (reigned 1576–1612) Prague Jews experienced what has been called their Golden Age. Upon his ascension to the throne, Maximilian granted permission for Jews to remain in Prague indefinitely, and on a summer day in 1571, he honored Prague's Jewish Town with a ceremonial visit to demonstrate his royal favor. Rudolf, in a charter of 1577, provided the Jews with new privileges and promised they would never be expelled from Prague again. Under Rudolf, Prague became the cultural, artistic, and scientific center of the empire, and the Jewish community grew from a few dozen to perhaps ten thousand as Jews fled to Prague from pogroms in Poland and Vienna.[12]

Upon Rudolf's demise and over the course of the Thirty Years War (1618–1648), Prague was ravaged and its population decimated. The fortunes of Czech and Moravian Jews, however, were surprisingly good. Emperor Ferdinand II mobilized all of his forces and utilized all of his assets, including money raised from the Jews, to put down the Protestant rebellions. As soldiers pillaged Prague, they were under orders not to touch the Jewish section, and after the rebellions were suppressed, Ferdinand reaffirmed all previous rights of the Jews and guaranteed them freedom of residence and protection from expulsion.[13] By 1705, Jews constituted almost one-quarter of Prague's inhabitants.[14]

After the civil wars, a backlash occurred against the close Jewish ties to the Crown, and frequent complaints reached Vienna concerning the uncontrolled growth of the Prague Jewish communities. Prague burghers urged the emperor to reduce the number of Jews in the Bohemian capital. Naturally, the royal treasury balked at such proposals, fearing a reduction in Jewish tax revenues. Emperor Charles VI decided that rather than expel a number of Jews from Prague, he would cap the current population. Thus, in 1726 and

Old Jewish cemetery in Josefov, the former Jewish ghetto. It was used from 1439 to 1787 and is the oldest existing Jewish cemetery in Europe. Over 100,000 Jews are buried here with graves layered 12 deep in some places. Hitler ordered that the cemetery be left intact and was planning to build a Jewish museum in Prague after the war. Courtesy of Getty Images/Photodisc.

1727, he passed the Familiants Laws *(Familiantengesetze)*, which limited the number of Jews that would reside in Bohemia and Moravia. The laws permitted only one son of each Jewish family to marry and resulted in large-scale emigration to Slovakia, Poland, and Hungary. From 1700 to 1800, more than 30,000 Moravian Jews emigrated to and settled in Hungary.[15]

Maria Theresa (reigned 1740–1780) continued to persecute her Jewish subjects, and on December 18, 1744, in a fit of anti-Semitic rage, she proclaimed that the entire Jewish community must abandon Prague forth-with. However, vocal opposition from the army, Vienna, the Bohemian Estates, England, and even the pope to this extremely harsh edict convinced Maria Theresa to change her mind; and she allowed the Jews to return at a price of 300,000 gold pieces.[16] Maria Theresa's son, Josef II (reigned 1780–1790) attempted to centralize, streamline, and integrate his realm. Thus, beginning in 1781, he passed a series of Toleration Edicts *(Toleranzpatent),* which granted Jews, Protestants, Greek-Orthodox, and other non-Catholic minority religions official recognition. Roman Catholicism was still the official state religion, but if at least one hundred families of another faith lived in close proximity, they were allowed to build their own house of worship.[17] Josef also began closing certain cloisters and monasteries, the so-called meditative orders, which did not serve the sick and the poor or contribute to the education of the people. He thought that too many religious holidays and too many Catholic institutions were receiving government support and closed 400 monasteries and cloisters throughout the empire.[18]

Josef's goal was to break down restrictions to economic growth, and he opened all avenues of trade and commerce to the Jews, encouraging them to erect factories and take part in agriculture. The Moravian Toleration Edict reads in part:

> Thus the preferential treatment accorded to the Jewish nation through the present amendment is due to the following: Our aim is to make them more useful and of greater service to the state, in particular through better education, instruction of their young people, and through the use of the sciences, arts, and crafts.[19]

The changes that had the most long-term and far-reaching consequences for the Jews, however, were Josef's new language laws. Josef abolished the use of any language other than German in official documents, and he established elementary schools throughout the land in which the language of instruction was German.

> With the opening of so many opportunities to earn a living, and the consequent diverse relations with Christians, the maintenance of mutual trust demands the abolition of the Hebrew language as well as the mixture of Hebrew and German, the so-called Jewish language and script. We therefore expressly forbid the use of this in all public proceedings, judicial and non-judicial, and ordain that they should instead use the language of the country from now on.[20]

Thus, German became the sole linguistic medium by which a citizen of the empire could advance and succeed in society. Previously the Jews spoke Czech or a local Yiddish dialect called "Jewish-German." Hebrew was the language of scholarship and religious services. Josef's reforms dictated that Jews become proficient in the standardized German of the empire. All legal and commercial documents and correspondence of the Jewish community were to be written in German, and all Jews had to accept German surnames. After the revolutions of 1848, when the various peoples within the Hapsburg Empire began to emphasize their national heritage (which ultimately led to the collapse of the Empire after World War I), Czech patriots assumed that their erstwhile Czech-speaking Jewish neighbors had switched sides. The Jews had assumed the German language because it appeared as the best, most pragmatic choice at the time; but in their struggle for freedom, Czech nationalists saw the Jews as apostates in the struggle to create an independent, Czech-speaking nation. In a review printed in the Prague newspaper, *The Czech Bee,* the Czech patriot Karel Havlíček wrote in 1846: "There is surely no need to prove that one cannot have two homelands, two nationalities, or serve two masters. Therefore, anyone who wishes to be a Czech must cease to be a Jew." And further: "It is not our concern … to attend to the affairs of the Israelites. But should they be inclined to heed our humble opinion, we would exhort the Jews, if they wish to abandon their natural language and literature, to join the Germans and their literature, since German has, over the years, become a second mother tongue to the Jews." [21] Between the 1850s and 70s, the majority of Prague and urban Bohemian Jews adopted the culture and language of Austria's German middle class. Culturally it was more prestigious than Czech and offered a window upon a wider, European civilization. Thus anti-German (pro-Czech) sentiment often became anti-Semitic, even though Czech and Moravian non-Jewish Germans were in no way more hospitable to the Jews. Then, however, the 1867 constitution was passed in which all national languages in Austria were considered equal. Here Prague German-speaking Jews apparently began switching their allegiance to Czech. According to an Austro-Hungarian census from 1890, 73.8 percent of Prague's Jews gave their language of everyday intercourse as German. By 1900 the number dropped to 45.3 percent. More than 4,000 of the 18,000 Jews in Prague had switched loyalties from German to Czech. [22]

Furthermore, before 1900, it seems, the Prague and Bohemian Jews had no desire to be considered a separate people or culture equal to that of the Czechs and Germans. Around the turn of the century, Czech Jews did begin to manifest a longing to be seen as a separate people, but it was not a widespread movement. Only after 1907 did a Zionist group form in Prague, committed

Tomáš Garrigue Masaryk (1850–1937) was the first president of Czechoslovakia and served four terms as president from 1918 to 1935. A "cult of Masaryk" develped around him, and he was referred to, apparenly unironically, as "little father." © Corbis.

to the idea of the Jews as a separate people, but before World War I, the group attracted an extremely small following.[23]

THE FIRST REPUBLIC

Upon the conclusion of World War I and the collapse of the ruling Austro-Hungarian Empire, Tomáš Masaryk founded the First Czechoslovak Republic. In the new state, the fortunes of the Jews became similar to that of the other peoples and religions suddenly enfranchised. This was the beginning of Jewish assimilation in the Czech lands. Whereas previously the Jews struggled for religious liberty and freedom in general, now they sought to live side by side with the Czechs as fully equal Czechoslovak citizens. Catholicism, on the other hand, was soon to come under attack.

Masaryk had converted to Protestantism earlier in life and was quick to separate the new state from the Catholic Church. For most Czechs, the Catholic Church stood as a bitter reminder of White Mountain and three hundred years of Austrian oppression. In early November 1918, for example, a mob of Czechs celebrating their freedom tore down a statue of the Virgin Mary in Prague's Old Town Square. Upon his ascension to the presidency, Masaryk proclaimed: "We have got rid of Vienna. Now we will get rid of Rome!" The two major Protestant Churches, the Reformed and the Lutheran, passed a resolution in 1918 uniting the two churches into the Evangelical Church of the Czech Brethren, thereby resurrecting the fifteenth-century Union of Brethren *(Jednota bratrská)*, a church organization based on the teachings of Jan Hus. The Brethren's rolls surged. Between 1921 and 1922, 55,769 joined the church, and by 1927 membership had reached 255,758.[24]

Some Catholic priests as well were so exhilarated by the novelty of liberation that they began agitating for church reforms. One group of Catholic clergy approached Rome and demanded, among other things, that they be allowed to marry and to use Czech as the language of liturgy. Rome curtly rejected the petition, whereupon the reformists established, on January 8, 1920, the Czechoslovak Church. Two days later it issued its manifesto:

> The Czechoslovak Church, founded … on the basis of Christ's gospel, provisionally takes over, until such a time when its own order is established, the present religious order of the Roman Catholic Church, adjusted to the spirit of democracy.[25]

The new church expanded rapidly. It was by no means Protestant, but rather anti-Roman. As a Catholic body, however, the church required a system of government. At the end of 1920, the Czechoslovak Church approached the Serbian Orthodox Church with a readiness to submit to its regulations and accept its dogma with, however, several exceptions, including the use of the Czech language in liturgy and permission for clergy to marry. The Serbian Church responded favorably overall but rejected the marriage provision—whereupon the Czechoslovak Church split into two factions, one accepting the Serbian response, which became the Czech Orthodox Church, and a more modernist faction that continued as the Czechoslovak Church, renouncing its former pro-Orthodox orientation. In the end, the Czechoslovak Church became both anti-Roman as well as anti-Orthodox.

In another fit of anticlerical verve, the new government passed a law stating that if more than half the population of a village was in favor of the

Czechoslovak Church, the property of the Catholic Church would pass to the Czechoslovak. By the end of 1925, the new church had 200,000 members and 150 parishes.[26] Taxes were applied to lands belonging to the Catholic Church in the amount of 140 million crowns annually, and the Church was forced to sell works of art to pay for them. Rome was not pleased. But this was only the beginning of Masaryk's anticlerical choler. The president had the old Hussite motto *Pravda Vítězí* [Truth Prevails] incorporated into the emblem of the republic, and the government proposed to make the day of Hus' immolation a national holiday. In a further insult to the Vatican, the Hussite national flag, with the symbol of the chalice of the Czech National Church, was hoisted above Hradčany, the Czech castle, directly opposite the Papal Nuncio. When the Nuncio formally issued a protest about the presence of the Czechoslovak president at this anti-Catholic ceremony to Edvard Beneš, the foreign minister, Beneš responded that the president had been present in a private, rather than official, capacity.[27] The Vatican, understandably unsatisfied, broke off all relations with Prague.

The government's bias and policies soon, however, met an impasse. Despite the support of the president and high government ministers, by 1926 the Catholic-dominated Christian Social Party outnumbered Protestant and Czechoslovak Church representation in parliament. If Masaryk and his prime minister Edvard Beneš wanted to remain in power, they had to seek the support of either the Sudeten German Party, who were vociferously advocating a return to Germany, or the Christian Social Party, strongly Catholic but good Czechoslovak patriots. Masaryk and Beneš naturally chose the lesser of two evils, allied themselves with the Christian Socialists, and sought reconciliation with Rome. A *modus vivendi* was signed in 1928, in which the Czechoslovak state conceded, among other things, to return to the Catholic Church lands confiscated in the land reforms.[28] Table 2.1 presents the 1930 census information on religious affiliation in Czechoslovakia.[29]

Table 2.1 Religious Affiliation in Czechoslovakia in 1930

Roman Catholic	73.5%
All Protestants	7.67%
Czechoslovak Church	5.39%
Greek Catholic and Armenian Catholic	3.97%
Jews	2.42%
Orthodox Church	.99%
No affiliation	5.8%

During World War II, nearly 600,000 Germans left Czechoslovakia, and two and a half million were expelled immediately thereafter. Nearly all were Roman Catholic. In addition, the Jewish population of Czechoslovakia was nearly wiped out. Of a population of 350,000 in 1930, the Nazis murdered approximately 250,000, and many others fled the country.[30]

RELIGION UNDER COMMUNISM

The common image of religion in Central and Eastern Europe under Communism is that of an underground church of Christian martyrs faithfully carrying out their traditional rites beyond the public eye. This is a distortion of the actual situation but an understandable one. Marxist society is an atheistic one, and Marxism is a programmatic ideology dedicated to the reconstruction of all aspects of life. From a Marxist point of view, religion is a sign of the imperfection of the social order. Yet religious life in the countries of the former Eastern Bloc did persist and was not entirely hidden from public view. By the twentieth century, because of the lingering shadow of Catholic Hapsburg oppression, Czechoslovakia had become fairly secularized, and the strength and vigor of its various churches cannot be compared to that of religious life in other Eastern Bloc countries, such as Poland, for example, which had great and sometimes overwhelming influence on the Communist regime. Public religious life in Czechoslovakia did, however, persist. When the Communists took power in 1948, rather than ban organized religion altogether, they tried to curb its influence in various ways. The 1960 constitution reads:

> Freedom of confession shall be guaranteed. Everyone shall have the right to profess any religious faith or to be without religious conviction, and to practice his religious beliefs insofar as this does not contravene the law. (Article 32/1)
> Religious faith or conviction shall not constitute grounds for anyone to refuse to fulfill the civic duties laid upon him by law. (Article 32/2)[31]

In practice, however, the government imposed many restrictions upon churches and worshippers. It announced it would not interfere in the activities of the church as long as the churches confine themselves solely to religious matters and refrain from commenting on public life. In practice, this meant that if a preacher analyzed a biblical passage and tried to apply it to one's everyday situation, he could be imprisoned. Under Communism, believers and clergy were subject to persecution and harassment.

The Catholic Church bore the brunt of the Communist assault on religion. The new government saw the church as historically reactionary and loyal to an outside entity, that is, Rome. In 1948, the government passed two laws detrimental to the Catholic Church, one on agrarian reform and one on education. The agrarian reform law led to the confiscation of almost all church lands, a total of 320,000 hectares. The law on education suppressed all Catholic schools and abolished religious instruction in school. The Communists banned religious orders, closed eleven of thirteen seminaries, seized monasteries and convents, and sent 3,000 monks and 10,000 nuns to "concentration monasteries."[32] The average time of imprisonment was five years, and death from overwork and exhaustion was high. The Greek-Catholic Church was banned, and its priests and worshipers were compelled to join the Orthodox Church. In response, Pope Pius XII issued the Excommunication Decree in July 1949, whereby Communists were expelled from the Church.

Protestants fared less poorly. Their numbers were much smaller than the Catholic Church, and the various denominations were somewhat fragmentary, answering to no single higher religious body. To the Communists, Protestants were less of a threat. Moreover, as heirs to the fiery preacher Jan Hus, some Protestants welcomed revolutionary political change along with the curtailing of the enormous power of the Catholic Church. Nevertheless, a considerable number of Protestant clergy and church members were imprisoned and perished under Communist persecution.

The fate of the Czechoslovak Church was somewhat different. In the immediate aftermath of the Communist takeover, a group of pro-Communist clergy supportive of the new government assumed the leadership of the church. Most worshipers, however, did not back the regime, especially after 1968.[33]

Throughout the 1950s and 1960s, church membership decreased dramatically. Of course, church membership does not necessarily correspond to religiosity. One may be religious without attending church service, especially in a country where a visit to a church results in reprisals in one's professional and personal life. And visa-versa, someone who has lost his faith may belong to a church. Table 2.2 illustrates the decline of religiosity in the Czech lands. The numbers refer to percentages.[34]

The general trends are clear. Between 1946 and 1963, there was a sharp drop in religiosity by one half with respect to belief in God and one quarter with regard to belief in Christ. Moreover, it seems there was a significant rise in atheism, that is, active disbelief.

The relaxed political atmosphere of the Prague Spring in 1968 led to a surge in religious interest and activity. Imprisoned clergy and church members were released, the Catholic Church was allowed to form its own clerical organization, and the Greek Catholic Church was once again

Table 2.2 Religious Belief and Practice (%)

Question	Yes	Doubtful	Never think about it	No
Do you believe in God?				
1946	64	16	8	12
1963	34	11	17	38
Do you believe Christ was the embodiment of God?				
1946	33	18	11	37
1963	25	10	23	41
Do you believe in post-mortal life?				
1946	38	21	13	28
1963	24	9	18	49
Do you go to church?	Regularly	Occasionally	On Special Occasions	
1946	20	43	14	24
1963	13	21	15	51
Do you pray in private?				
1946	28	28	14	29
1963	16	17	11	56

legalized. In eastern Slovakia, 83 churches and 47 parish houses were built in 1968.[35] Christian speakers spoke on broadcast radio programs, and the first Christian-Marxist dialogue was held in April 1968 in Prague, attended by over three thousand people. On August 21, 1968, however, Warsaw Pact troops invaded the country and cut short the brief period of "socialism with a human face." The government purged the Communist Party of about a half million reformist members and re-imposed hard-line totalitarian rule. Nearly 180,000 people left Czechoslovakia. Artists, writers, and the church were hardest hit. Government officials, unnerved by the surge of religious inter- est during the Prague Spring, launched an all-out attack on religion through radio, television, newspapers, film, and theater. Government pressure on the church was unrelenting until 1989.

In 1977, 243 Czechoslovak intellectuals joined together to create the most prominent expression to opposition during the Normalization period, Charter 77, a manifesto critical of the government's failure to guarantee and protect human rights as set down in the Czechoslovak Constitution. Among the freedoms violated were freedom of expression, freedom of equal access to education, the right to freely assemble, and freedom of religion:

> Freedom of religious confession, emphatically guaranteed by article 18 of the first Covenant, is continually curtailed by arbitrary official action; by interference with the activity of churchmen, who are constantly threatened by the refusal of the state to permit them the exercise of their functions, or by the withdrawal of such permission; by financial or other transactions against those who express their religious faith in word or action; by constraints on religious training, and so forth.[36]

The Charter appeared in the European press January 7, 1977 and received widespread attention. The manuscript circulated in samizdat form in Czechoslovakia, and its signatories, more than one thousand, were subject to harsh reprisals: more than 160 were dismissed from their jobs, 30 were sent in exile, and 20 were tried and sentenced for alleged offences. The churches were urged to condemn the document but refused.

This official harassment gave rise to the Hidden Church (Skrytá církev), an underground organization, particularly strong in Slovakia, that came into existence in 1977 alongside Charter 77. The Hidden Church operated parallel to official religious bodies but was beyond the reach of the State and in contact with other underground activists. It ordained its own priests, celebrated Mass in private homes, the woods, or on mountain hikes, and distributed its own illegal publications. The Vatican described the Hidden Church as "not only the secretly ordained priests and bishops, secret convents and secret printing establishments in the country, but also the existing Catholic organizations and spiritual underground movements, as well as all priests and believers who are working illegally in the sphere of the church." Its number were said to be between 10,000 to 25,000 priests and believers.[37]

POST-REVOLUTION

With the end of Communism in November 1989, true freedom of religion was reinstituted. But the upshot of this distressed religious history is that today the Czechs are phenomenally uninterested in religion, with nearly as many people professing atheism as Roman Catholicism, the largest religious denomination by far. If asked, Czechs are likely to answer without hesitation that there is no God, and they are for the most part free of such romantic notions as life after death. In Slovakia, by comparison, religion and the Catholic Church are still strong and, especially in nonurban areas, play a large role in everyday life. Both republics, however, are fairly intolerant of new religions, which they consider "sects." The governments favor what they call "traditional" religions, and the smaller religions are regarded as foreign or strange. One method of sidelining these smaller religions is to institute registration policies, which are often discriminatory. The governments take it upon themselves to assess the goals of the group and their statements of faith. The process itself is arbitrary and not subject to control. In both the Czech and the Slovak republics, the governments require a minimum membership for registration, 10,000 and 20,000 respectively. Registration does not necessarily infringe on religious freedom but is necessary to obtain state funding and other privileges. In Slovakia new religious movements must register as civic-interest associations with the Ministry of the Interior.

NOTES

1. ESDS International, www.esds.ac.uk/International/access/evs.asp.

2. Marvin Kantor, *The Origins of Christianity in Bohemia: Sources and Commentary* (Evanston: Northwestern University Press, 1990), 5.

3. Petr z Maldoňovic, *Zpráva o mistru Janu Husovi v Kostnici,* ed. Zdeněk Fiala, trans. František Heřmanský (Prague, 1965), 73. Cited in Robert B. Pynsent, *Questions of Identity: Czech and Slovak Ideas of Nationality and Personality* (London: Central European Press, 1994), 200.

4. Derek Sayer, *The Coasts of Bohemia: A Czech History* (Princeton: Princeton University Press, 1998), 38. See also Jan Milič Lochman, "The Contribution of the Czech Reformation to Western Christianity," in *The Common Christian Roots of the European Nations: An International Colloquium in the Vatican,* 2 vols. (Florence: Le Monnier, 1982), 192–98.

5. Ladislav Holy, *The Little Czech and the Great Czech Nation: National Identity and the Post-Communist Transformation of Society* (Cambridge, UK: Cambridge University Press, 1996), 41.

6. Sayer, *The Coasts of Bohemia,* 138.

7. Hillel Kieval, *Languages of Community: The Jewish Experience in the Czech Lands* (Berkeley: University of California Press, 2000), 11.

8. Peter Demetz, *Prague in Black and Gold: Scenes from the Life of a European City* (New York: Hill and Wang, 1997), 44–45.

9. Kieval, *Languages of Community,* 12.

10. Demetz, *Prague in Black and Gold,* 116.

11. Demetz, 167–68.

12. Demetz, 201; Kieval, 15.

13. Kieval, 18–19.

14. Demetz, 241.

15. Kieval, 22.

16. Demetz, 246.

17. Demetz, 248.

18. Demetz, 249.

19. Willibald Müller, ed., *Urkundliche Beiträge zur Geschichte der mährischen Judenschaft im 17. und 18. Jahrhundert* (Olomouc 1903). Cited in Wilma Abeles Iggers, ed., *The Jews of Bohemia and Moravia: A Historical Reader* (Detroit: Wayne State University Press, 1992), 50.

20. Iggers, *The Jews of Bohemia and Moravia,* 51.

21. *Česká včela,* November, 1846. Cited in Iggers, 135.

22. Gary B. Cohen, *The Politics of Ethnic Society: Germans in Prague, 1861–1914* (Princeton: Princeton University Press, 1981), 101.

23. Gary B. Cohen, "Jews in German Society: Prague, 1860–1914," *Central European History* 10 (1977): 28–54.

24. *Deset let Českobratrské evangelické církve, 1918–1928* (Prague, 1928), 13 ff., cited in Matthew Spinka, "The Religious Situation in Czechslovakia," in *Czechoslovakia,* ed. Robert J. Kerner (Berkeley: University of California Press, 1940), 298–99.

25. Spinka, "The Religious Situation in Czechoslovakia," 294.

26. Anthony Rhodes, *The Vatican in the Age of Dictators, 1922–1945* (London: Hodder and Stoughton, 1973), 90.

27. Rhodes, *The Vatican in the Age of Dictators,* 91.

28. Rhodes, 93.

29. Peter A. Toma and Tilan J. Raban, "Church-State Schism in Czechoslovakia," in *Religion and Atheism in the U.S.S.R. and Eastern Europe,* ed. Bohdan R. Bociurkiw and John W. Strong (Toronto: University of Toronto Press, 1975), 274–75.

30. Trevor Beeson, *Discretion and Valour: Religious Conditions in Russia and Eastern Europe* (Philadelphia: Fortress Press, 1982), 227.

31. Beeson, *Discretion and Valour,* 230–231.

32. Pedro Ramet, *Cross and Commissar: The Politics of Religion in Eastern Europe and the USSR* (Bloomington: Indiana University Press, 1987), 77.

33. Beeson, 239–40.

34. This table must be taken with a few reservations. The 1946 survey was performed by the Research Institute for Public Opinion in Prague and investigated only the Czech lands. The only other investigation was conducted in 1963, which covered only the religiosity of the North Moravian region. At the time, the region had a population of 1,631,579, it was the most industrialized region in Czechoslovakia, and is second only to Southern Moravia in the religiosity of its people in the Czech lands. Thus, it may be presumed that the actual drop in religiosity is larger than the table suggests. From Erika Kadlecová, "Czechoslovakia," in *Western Religion: A Country by Country Sociological Inquiry* (The Hague, Paris: Mouton, 1972), 123. Kadlecová, a prominent sociologist, headed the secretariat for religious affairs under Dubček. She was condemned for "misguided humanist views" after the Russian invasion in August 1968.

35. Toma and Raban, "Church-State Schism in Czechoslovakia," 283.

36. "Charter 77 Declaration," in Václav Havel et al., *The Power of the Powerless: Citizens against the State in Central-Eastern Europe,* ed. John Keane (Armonk, NY: M. E. Sharpe 1985), 218.

37. *Daily Telegraph,* March 6, 1981. Cited in Ramet, *Cross and Commissar,* 136.

SELECTED BIBLIOGRAPHY

Beeson, Trevor. *Discretion and Valour: Religious Conditions in Russia and Eastern Europe.* Philadelphia: Fortress Press, 1982.

Cohen, Gary B. *The Politics of Ethnic Society: Germans in Prague, 1861–1914.* Princeton: Princeton University Press, 1981.

Demetz, Peter. *Prague in Black and Gold: Scenes from the Life of a European City.* New York: Hill and Wang, 1997.

Holy, Ladislav. *The Little Czech and the Great Czech Nation: National Identity and the Post-Communist Transformation of Society.* Cambridge, UK: Cambridge University Press, 1996.

Hromadka, Josef. *Thoughts of a Czech Pastor,* trans. Monika and Benjamin Page. London: SMC Press, 1970.

Kantor, Marvin. *The Origins of Christianity in Bohemia: Sources and Commentary.* Evanston: Northwestern University Press 1990.

Kieval, Hillel. *Languages of Community: The Jewish Experience in the Czech Lands.* Berkeley: University of California Press, 2000.

Pynsent, Robert P. *Questions of Identity: Czech and Slovak Ideas of Nationality and Personality.* London: Central European Press, 1994.

Rhodes, Anthony. *The Vatican in the Age of Dictators 1922–45.* London: Hodder and Stoughton, 1973.

Sayer, Derek. *The Coasts of Bohemia: A Czech History.* Princeton: Princeton University Press,1998.

Schenker, Alexander M. *The Dawn of Slavic.* New Haven: Yale University Press, 1995.

Šmahel, František. "The Hussite Movement: An Anomaly of European History?" in *Bohemia in History,* ed. Mikuláš Teich. Cambridge, UK: Cambridge University Press, 1998, 79–97.

3

Marriage, Women, Gender, and Education

A society that underestimates women is a polygamous society.
—Tomáš Masaryk[1]

CZECH AND SLOVAK WOMEN are beautiful, educated, and unspoiled by Western feminism—at least that's the common stereotype in the West and a chief reason young American men flock to Prague and Bratislava looking for love.[2] This chapter will consider the vicissitudes of a woman's place in Czech and Slovak life over the years, including issues of marriage, feminism, and even Harlequin romances and *Cosmopolitan* magazine. The Central European experience of women differs enormously from that in the West, where equality in the public sphere is the primary measure of emancipation. For Czech and Slovak women, who have legally been compelled to work since 1948, emancipation might just as often mean the right *not* to work and stay at home, care for children, and watch soap operas. A further topic of this chapter is education, a feature of Czech life of which the Czechs are understandably proud. Moravia was the birthplace of Jan Amos Komenský (1592–1670), the first modern educator and scientist of education, and Charles University is the oldest university in Central Europe, founded in 1348 by the Holy Roman Emperor Charles IV. Under Communism, however, education was considered less important than personal connections for life success. We will also look at the role of the *intelligentsia* in Czech life, a class not quite comparable to our own concept of "intellectuals."

WOMEN

Due to centuries of oppression by foreign rulers, a certain solidarity has formed between Czech men and women against the "common enemy," whether it be Austrians, Germans, or Russians. In the nineteenth century during the National Revival, Czech men encouraged the education of women and participated in the struggle for their right to vote. Women's emancipation was seen as contributing to the strengthening of Czech national aspirations against the ruling Hapsburg Empire. Thus, the women's rights movement gained strength from its identification with Czech nationalism. Women were allies of the men in their struggle for independence. The Czechs even elected a woman to the Austrian legislature in 1912, an event unprecedented in Europe.[3] Women were given the right to vote in Masaryk's First Czechoslovak Republic (1918–1938), and women actually exercised that right in greater numbers than men. President Masaryk was a fiery proponent of women's emancipation. He has written, "This modern effort of men and women is a necessary continuation in the work of national revival…. The modern Czech woman signifies for our small nation a doubling of our strength."[4] One scholar has even argued that Masaryk was the most influential male intellectual involved in the worldwide women's movement.[5] Then in 1948 the Communist government made work compulsory for both men and women. By 1989, women composed 45 percent of all university students and 56 percent of all specialists with a secondary school education.[6] Employment and education were not absent from Czech and Slovak women's lives.

Feminism

After the fall of Communism in 1989, Western feminists headed to Central and Eastern Europe in droves, a region they saw as virgin territory for the propagation of feminist values of emancipation and equality. When they arrived, however, they were met with near wholesale scorn by both men and women. The Communist government had endorsed and propagated full female emancipation during its 40-year rule. The entire Eastern Bloc had sought to break with the capitalist system and equalize the role of men and women in the labor force; thus, the government established the obligation for both sexes to work. The number of employed women was high, yet it was also the woman of the family who, in addition to her professional duties, maintained the upkeep of the household—shopping, cooking, cleaning, and child rearing. The system created the impression that women were emancipated, but, in fact, they were overworked and highly stressed.

When feminists turned up in Prague and Bratislava seeking to propagate their ideas of equality, which had been developed in the West, Czechs and Slovaks questioned the relevance of this system of ideas for their situation. They saw Western feminists on a crusade bearing an ideology that would rescue their "backward" Eastern sisters from patriarchal oppression. It was not only this condescension that offended, but also this new way of thought. After 40 years of Marxist–Leninist rhetoric, Czechs and Slovaks were suspicious of anyone claiming to bear a new worldview, another "scientific" ideology to improve their lives. Much of the language of feminism—emancipation, equality, oppression—resembled that of the defunct Communist regime. In the early 1990s, anything with an "-ism" was suspect.

In Czechoslovakia, women were never under the illusion that gainful employment was tantamount to liberation and "self-actualization." In Central and Eastern Europe in general, men were not seen as rivals but, rather, as exploited and downtrodden by the Communist government. Because men were usually the main breadwinners in the family, they were forced to conform more closely to the strictures of the Communist government in the workplace. It was the men who were compelled to attend the party meetings and participate in political life. Women did not allow themselves to be pressured and manipulated as much as men, and membership in the Communist Party was predominantly male. Paradoxically, because of their duties at home, women often viewed home life as a refuge from an oppressive public life. Furthermore, Communism tended to erase gender distinctions. Class was the only permitted means of differentiation. After 1989, for many the idea of *not* working became the ideal of emancipation. Thus, it is not surprising that today Czech and Slovak women tend to emphasize their femininity not through work, but through consumerism, something the Communist government fostered throughout the 1970s and 1980s after the failure of the Prague Spring.

Women's Books and Magazines

In general, Czech and Slovak women have resisted organizing themselves into groups recognized as overtly or primarily feminist. Feminism and its concomitant ideology of political correctness are often subject to ridicule in the media and seen as something that has gone beyond all reasonable control in the West. Several well-known Czech intellectuals such as Josef Škvorecký, Iva Pekárková, and Milan Machovec have contributed to the dissemination of this view.[7] The general thinking is that this ideology is being sown by frustrated women simply lacking a fulfilling sex life.

Yet while many reject overtly feminist writings, the discussion of women's issues does occur—in women's magazines, for example. Journals such as

Tina, Katka, Mladý svět, which advertise themselves as geared toward the "intelligent modern woman," in addition to articles on how to be a good mother and housewife include advice on self-assertiveness, independence, and even women's rights. But the language of these articles is in no way informed by rebarbative feminist terminology of repression and patriarchy. The language employed is, rather, what appears to be innocuous psychobable, something that on the surface could never incite women to militant feminism and tossing men from town hall windows.

Take Harlequin Romances, for example. While disdained in the West as unromantic, anti-intellectual drivel that extends patriarchal imperialism, the novels have a positive image in the Czech Republic. Romance novels were banned after the 1968 revolution and thus by their very nature are already imbued with an image of liberation for many in the Eastern Bloc. Romance novels represent an escape from the drudgery of working full time and managing a household; they are nothing of which to be ashamed. The editors of Harlequin have taken this image of liberation and transformed the books into a women's discussion forum. Harlequin began publishing in the Czech Republic in 1992 and was ranked the fourth largest publisher in 1996 despite the fact that the books are two to three times more expensive than other novels.[8] Czech Harlequin romances are published a month apart (28 days, actually, to match the menstrual cycle), and each novel is accompanied by a newsletter offering advice columns, discussion forums, and coupons. In addition, each novel concludes with an interactive section, providing readers with the opportunity to discuss issues from the novel.

The content of the novels themselves differs from their Western counterparts. Czech translators not only translate, but also adapt the novels to suit the Czech context. Czech Harlequin readers are more likely to be adolescents or young women, and the translators often transform the heroines of the novels, making them more attractive to the younger audience. They are more complex, and the storylines themselves are often given absurd twists, more in keeping with the bizarre mentality of the Czechs. The heroines are certainly looking for their man, but they are also independent and career-oriented. Perhaps they run their own company, coach a women's soccer team, or take an active part in politics. Czech Harlequin readers decidedly do not sit at home awaiting their Prince Charming.[9] According to Czech Harlequin's own reader's survey, the most popular Harlequin endings are those in which a successful career woman falls in love with and marries an American Indian or Cowboy, or those in which a single mother manages to marry a single father.[10] In the end, however, the feminist potential of Harlequin romances is limited by the demands of the genre. It is highly unlikely that a

Harlequin heroine would ever come out of the closet, for example, and seek self-fulfillment through a same-sex relationship.

The Czech version of *Cosmopolitan* magazine is likewise seen as a serious women's publication. Here a reader will not find articles on how to care for the home and family, subjects covered in a score of other women's journals. Czech *Cosmopolitan* targets the modern independent woman interested in exotic travel, the latest fashions, and even automobiles. While the American version of the magazine is seen as a woman's alternative to *Maxim,* the Czech edition is associated with more sober women's issues, such as harassment in the workplace, salary inequalities, and so on. Still, however, the language of these articles is far from the rhetoric of American feminism. To a westerner it may seem to be mere psychobabble, but those interested in women's issues, see *Cosmopolitan* and Harlequin romances as a way to reach women and address their concerns.

Work and Family

In the 1930s during the First Republic, women made up more than 30 percent of the workforce; in 1948, 36 percent; 1968, 46 percent; and in 1989, 48 percent. That is, by the end of Communism, 94 percent of all Czech and Slovak women were working.[11] Under socialism, all were required to work, and all guaranteed employment. The regime needed the labor of both men and women, and the government fostered the image of the working woman, disseminating and advertising images of women laboring in traditionally male occupations—driving trucks and tractors, for example, or working in factories and breweries. A quota system was instituted, 30 percent, and May 8 became International Women's Day. Nearly all women entered the labor force, and the government constructed hundreds of daycare centers and kindergartens to enable both parents to work. Thus, "emancipation" simply meant "non-differentiation"—women could be utilized as cheap sources of labor. Individuality and uniqueness were lost, along with dignity and identity. On the other hand, women as well as men were provided the opportunity for higher education. In 1948, women composed only 23 percent of the total number of university students. In 1989, they composed 45 percent of all university students and 56 percent of all specialists with a secondary school education.[12] In the latter years of Communism, Czechoslovak women were more likely than their Western counterparts to be professional and technical workers.[13]

An unintended effect of full female employment and increased educational opportunities, however, was a decrease in fertility rates. To stem the decline, the Czechoslovak government in the 1960s instituted new reproductive policies, such as generous maternity allowances and maternity leaves, as well as higher costs for abortion. In 1975, Czechoslovakia had one of the highest birthrates in Europe.[14] By 1980, nearly everyone was married (only 2.8% of women between the ages of 50 and 54 had never been married), the average age of first marriage had dropped dramatically (23 for men, 20 for women), and half the brides were pregnant at the time of marriage.[15] Also, voluntary childlessness had practically vanished. Only 5.5 percent of women were without children, an artificially low number considering an estimated 4 percent of the population is infertile. In the West, one-fifth of couples are without children.[16]

By the mid-1970s, everyone got married and had children as soon as possible. The government offered lengthy maternity leave, tax incentives for married couples, and deductions for childbirth, as well as the near impossibility for childless couples and single persons to secure an apartment. Vladimír Páral's novel *Lovers & Murderers* (1969) offers a dark portrait of one such housing situation under Communism. Life under Communism also offered little in the way of social opportunities for single men and women. Travel was severely restricted, political activism was naturally discouraged, and private enterprise was illegal. Public life was a hypocrisy, and the family was one of the few means to achieve self-fulfillment. The Communist government actually strengthened family ties and intergenerational bonds. People found refuge in the family from a hypocritical and oppressive public life.

One of the few attractive features of life under Czechoslovak Communism, and one that fostered intergenerational dependency, was an early retirement age—60 for men and 57 for women, and two years earlier for each child she had. Consequently, most women concluded their professional careers at the youthful age of 53. Early retirement, on the other hand, led to a permanent labor shortage, and retirees were allowed to continue working at full pay in addition to receiving their retirement benefits. Most men, and just under half of women, continued to work after retirement.[17] In retirement, most Czech men and women were making the most money in their lives, and this money they invested in their children. Because of the frequent currency devaluations under Communism, depositing money in the bank was foolhardy. Thus, to ensure they were cared for in old age, retirees turned their attention to their own children and grandchildren, presenting them with monetary gifts, helping to build or purchase a dwelling—a country house or an apartment—and so on. Moreover, by having a child in her early twenties, a woman could rely on the assistance of two generations—her own mother who was in her forties could offer infant care, and her grandmother, in her sixties, could offer financial help. But this window of opportunity was narrow; five to seven years later the mother would turn her attention and resources to her own mother (the grandmother) who had reached her seventies.[18]

This system of mutual assistance strengthened family ties, and after 1989 with divorce rates rising and mobility increasing, the family is now experiencing a profound and, for most, disturbing transitional period. Women are opting more than ever to forego motherhood and concentrate on their careers, and more people are deferring marriage for higher education. In 1996, 79 percent more students went to the university than in 1989.[19] According to the 2001 census, the marriage age has risen to 29 for men and 27 for women. Birth rates are plummeting. In 1990, 130,564 births were registered, but only 93,957 in 2003.[20] Divorce rates, moreover, are skyrocketing—in 2003, 67 percent of marriages ended in divorce.[21]

To stem the decline in the birthrate, in 1995 the Czech government extended parental leave to men as well as women and increased unpaid childcare leave from three to four years. Parents in the Czech Republic now have the longest time off to care for their children than any parents in the world.[22]

Abortion

Czechoslovakia fully legalized abortion in 1957 following the lead of the Soviet Union, which had done so two years earlier. Before 1957 an estimated 100,000 illegal abortions were performed annually. And until 1986 a woman seeking abortion had to appear before a moralistic abortion committee who decided the woman's eligibility for an abortion, the "acceptability" of her reasons for seeking abortion, and the amount she would pay according to her socio-economic status. Milan Kundera offers a debased fictional account of such an abortion board in his novel *The Farewell Waltz* (1979). The Czechoslovak government abolished these boards in 1986, and abortions were performed free of charge. This became the most common method of family planning. This abortion liberalization combined with the limited availability of birth control gave Czechoslovakia the sixth highest abortion rate in the world in 1991.[23] In 1993, only 6 percent of sexually active women used oral contraceptives, five times lower than in the West.

In 1992, the Czechoslovak government ended its free abortion policy, and costs for an abortion were raised to 2,831 Kč (US$166) up to the

eighth week of pregnancy and 3,460 Kč (US$203) between the eighth
and twelfth weeks.[24]. This made abortion prohibitively expensive, where
the average monthly salary was 4500 Kč (US$265). One of the reasons
advanced for raising abortion prices and putting the procedure in the same
category as cosmetic surgery was to discourage women from Poland seeking abortions in Czechoslovakia. In March 1993, Poland adopted one
of Europe's strictest abortion laws. Only if the pregnancy threatened the
mother's life, was the result of rape or incest, or the fetus was shown to
be seriously and irreversibly deformed could a pregnancy be terminated.
Doctors performing abortions for other reasons could be imprisoned for
two years.

HOMOSEXUALITY

The overall attitude toward homosexual behavior in the Czech Republic
and Slovakia is indifferent or even hostile, but this position is perhaps best
explained by both a lack of direct contact with gays and lesbians, as well as
a general reluctance to discuss questions of sexuality. A recent study by the
Sexological Institute of the Czech Republic has shown that more than one-
half of all Czechs claim to have never met a gay or lesbian personally,[25] and a
1994 survey found that 33 percent of Czech men and 41 percent of women
consider homosexuality a disease.

In some respects, the Czech attitude toward sexual relations is quite liberal.
Premarital and extramarital sex is common. Ninety-eight percent of women
have sexual intercourse before marriage, and several studies have shown extra-
marital sex to hover between 25 percent and 30 percent. Only 18 percent
of men and 31 percent of women say extramarital sex is "ethically unac-
ceptable behavior."[26] As a world famous dissident, Václav Havel was well
known for his penchant for philandering, which his wife looked upon as
adolescent behavior rather than moral malefaction. He was elected president
three times by an overwhelming majority. Czechs and Slovaks followed the
Monica Lewinsky trial with rapt but somewhat amused attention, wondering
about our American sexual conservatism.

On the other hand, the widespread attitude of the majority of Czech
and Slovak people toward non-heterosexuality—whether homosexuality,
bisexuality, or transsexuality—is not altogether favorable. The primary reason is perhaps the enforced cultural orthodoxy of 40 years of Communism.
Czechoslovak society was not allowed to develop naturally; the government
suppressed public debate in almost all areas of life. Western countries have
been discussing more or less openly questions of sexuality for the past 50

years, but under Communism there was only one model of acceptable sexual behavior, and that was within a 2.5-child marriage along with the odd extra-marital adventure. The Czechs and Slovaks are only now emerging from their 50-year cultural hibernation.

From 1948 to 1961, homosexual behavior was illegal in Czechoslovakia. It was a crime against society, an act "incompatible with the morality of a social-ist society."[27] In 1961, the government decriminalized consensual homosex-ual behavior, but under the law some acts were illegal, for example, having sex with a person under 18 or if a dependent person was exploited, as in a student–teacher relationship. Furthermore, penalties for criminal sexual acts were greater for homosexuals than heterosexuals. In the 1970s and 1980s, the Czech gay club scene grew with the importation of disco and transvestite shows, but despite the decriminalization of homosexuality, gays and lesbians were still subject to police persecution. In 1990, the government passed a law equalizing homosexual and heterosexual behavior. In March 2006, the Czech Republic adopted a same-sex partnership law, becoming the second post-Communist country in Europe (after Slovenia) to legally recognize lesbian and gay families.

EDUCATION

Czechs have a long history of higher education. In 1348, Holy Roman Emperor and King of Bohemia Charles IV established Charles University in Prague. It was the first university in Central Europe, based on the ancient universities of Paris and Bologna. From its foundation Charles University was devoted to general studies, and in accordance with medieval conceptions of the academic range of a complete university, the newly established institution had four faculties—theology, law, medicine, and arts. The university soon developed links with medieval intellectual movements, especially through the activities of Jan Hus, who was agitating for church and societal reform. After the Czech defeat at the Battle of White Mountain in 1620, foreigners ruled over the Czechs until 1918, and it was the intellectual class, the so-called intelligentsia, who became the bearers of Czech national identity and kept Czech national aspirations alive.

From the seventeenth through the nineteenth centuries the Czechs had no native aristocracy. Their rulers were Austrian. In other European countries, the aristocracy was the center of education and culture. Czech intellectuals assumed the role of the aristocracy in these areas. Thus, intellectuals and education are highly respected among the Czechs, and one always includes one's degree title (of which there are an astounding number), both in professional life and in polite conversation (see Chapter 4 of this volume, "Holidays, Customs, and Leisure Activities").

Under the dictatorship of the proletariat, however, a university education lost some of its cachet, since Marxist–Leninist ideology dictated that a blue-collar worker should be held in higher esteem than the university educated. In reality, personal connections were the most important factor in the work-place, and participation in higher education, even today, is quite low. After 1989, the importance of a university education increased significantly for social status and living standard. The Czechs realized that a well-educated and highly skilled workforce was one of the only ways to compete in the global market. In 1992, one-third of all Czechs (33%) believed education to be important for success. This percentage was more than double in the West (80%). By 1997, the Czech's positive attitude toward education had increased to 61 percent.[28] Between 1989 and 1996, the total number of students in post-secondary institutions rose by 48 percent, yet demand for higher education exceeds the number of available spaces. In 1997, only 40 percent of applicants were admitted.[29]

Before 1990 the content of education—what was taught in schools—was strictly controlled by a central authority, which emphasized math and sci-ence over the humanities. Learning was authoritarian, with students learn-ing reams of facts with very little room for interpretation or even dialogue between students and teachers. Curricula are now being reformed and diver-sified. Naturally, Russian is no longer obligatory, and foreign language study is westward oriented. Religion, a major taboo under Communism, has been instituted as an area of study as well.

Educational System

Nursery school *(mateřská škola)*, ages 3 to 6, is not compulsory, but 86 percent of children attend. Most schools are free, but parents may be asked to pay for up to 30 percent of the school's operating costs. From ages 6 to 15, school attendance is mandatory—it has been since 1774. It lasts for 9 years, most of which is spent at the basic school *(základní škola)*. At the end of their fifth year, students can leave the basic school and attend an eight-year general secondary school, the *gymnázium;* or students can leave the basic school at the end of the seventh year and attend a six-year *gym-názium.*

There are three types of secondary schools in the Czech Republic: general secondary school *(gymnázium)*, secondary technical school *(střední odborná škola—SOŠ)*, and secondary vocational school *(střední odborné učiliště—*

SOU). To enter any of these institutions, pupils must pass an entrance examination.

Gymnáziums are four-to-five-year general secondary schools, which prepare students for university studies. They conclude with a general final exam, the *maturita*. The main part of the *maturita* is the oral exam. The week before the exam, students are given approximately 50 questions and a week to prepare answers. This is the so-called Holy Week, *Svatý týden,* during which students get together to pool their knowledge. On the day of the exam, students don in their best clothing, enter the exam room, and select a single question at random, which they must proceed to answer. Present are the student's homeroom teacher, the school inspector, and a specialist on the subject in question. Should the student fail, he or she must attend summer school and then retake the exam or repeat the entire year. Passing grades are often obtained by bribes. During Holy Week, students dress up in costumes in the evening and go around begging for donations for the graduation party, which is an all-night drinking bout for both students and teachers. Several books and films have been made based on the *maturita* experience.

Approximately 17 percent of all students entering secondary education enroll in a *gymnázium,* but this number has been rising dramatically. Secondary technical schools provide four years of secondary vocational education and likewise end with a *maturita* exam. Around 40 percent of school time is devoted to general education and 60 percent to vocational technical education. The practical courses are taught in school laboratories and workshops. Around 37 percent of students enter this type of secondary school. Secondary vocational schools offer apprenticeship training for two to three years. The time spent on practical training and on general education is roughly even, and the practical training focuses on acquiring manual labor skills. The percentage of students attending this type of institution is around 45 percent, but this number is dropping at an alarming rate due to a decreasing Czech birth rate and the growing importance of expertise in technical fields. The director of Charles University's Education Policy Center believes that within five years the number will reach 15–20 percent, and half the vocational schools will shut down.[30] The Communist government set quotas for how many students could enter *gymnáziums* and how many vocational schools. With that system gone, students are opting for technical or university degrees, which will better help them in their professional careers.

Post-secondary school can be of the university type or the non-university type—both are defined as *vysoká škola,* literally "high school," but they are, in fact, post-secondary institutions. Graduates of a technical secondary school may enter a "higher professional school" *(vyšší odborná škola)* for two to three-and-a-half years of study to receive the title DiS., specialist with diploma. Post-secondary schools of the university type offer bachelor, master, and doctoral study programs and are much more specialized than in the United States. Students study a single subject in depth over the course of their university stay rather than take a variety of courses.

Currently the Czech higher educational system is in the midst of a financial crisis, and poorer students are finding it difficult to enroll in post-secondary schools. Since 1994, the budgets of public universities have declined, and the government has not taken any measures to stem the drop in revenue. The Czech Republic ranks 28th out of 30 OECD countries in percentage of GDP devoted to post-secondary education. Schools in other countries with low GDP spending on education make up the difference by charging tuition and other fees, but Czech law does not permit charging tuition.

Entrance to higher education is becoming more difficult as well, due to the financial situation and widespread corruption within the system. Competition to be admitted is tremendous, and the spots tend to be given to students from the higher social strata.

The primary problem in the Czech educational system overall, however, seems to be the attitudes of many teachers. More than 15 years after the fall of Communism, the Czech educational system remains tremendously inflexible. Instructors still teach enormous amounts of encyclopedic data, which they think they must cram into the heads of their unfortunate students. Such a teaching method puts Czech primary and secondary students well above the OECD average in math, science, and geography, but Czech schools do not cultivate independent critical thinking. Perhaps the educational system will change in another 15 years.

NOTES

1. Karel Čapek, *Talks with T.G. Masaryk,* trans. Michael Henry Heim (North Haven, CT: Catbird Press, 1995), 129.

2. The recent horror film *Hostel* (2005), directed by Eli Roth, exploits this stereotype. Three unsuspecting backpackers head to Bratislava with erotic expectations but are met with bludgeoning and death instead.

3. Katherine David, "Czech Feminists and Nationalism in the Late Hapsburg Monarchy," *Journal of Women's History* 3, no. 2 (Fall 1991): 27.

4. *Masaryk a ženy,* cited in H. Gordon Skilling, *T. G. Masaryk: Against the Current, 1882–1914* (University Park: Pennsylvania State University Press, 1994), 117.

5. Marie Neudorfl, "Masaryk and the Women's Question," cited in Skilling, *T. G. Masaryk,* 127.

6. Jiřina Šiklová, "Are Women in Central and Eastern Europe Conservative?" in *Gender Politics and Post-Communism: Reflections from Eastern Europe and the*

Former Soviet Union, ed. Nanette Funk and Magda Mueller (New York: Routledge, 1993), 81.

7. See, for example, Josef Škvorecký, "Je možný sex bez znásilnění?" *Respekt,* August 10–16, 1992, 10; Iva Pekárková, "Americké lesbičky si pěstují bradku," *Rudé pravo,* January 15, 1998; and Milan Machovec, "Nezhloupnout psedoaktivitou," *Feminismus devadesátých let českěma očima,* ed. Maria Chříbková et al. (Prague: One Woman Press, 1999), 234–41.

8. Jacqui True, *Gender, Globalization, and Postsocialism: The Czech Republic After Communism* (New York: Columbia University Press, 2003), 119.

9. Eva Houserová, "Cosmopolitan a harlequinky: plíživá emancipace ze Západu," *Jedním okem* 5 (1997): 10.

10. True, *Gender, Globalization, and Postsocialism,* 122.

11. Šiklová, "Are Women in Central and Eastern Europe Conservative?" 75.

12. Šiklová, 81.

13. True, 31.

14. True, 37.

15. Ivo Možný, "The Czech Family in Transition: From Social to Economic Capital," in *Social Reform in the Czech Republic,* ed. Stein Ringen and Claire Wallace (Prague: Prague Digital Arts, 1994), 59.

16. Jiří Večerník and Petr Matějů, *Ten Years of Rebuilding Capitalism: Czech Society after 1989* (Prague: Academia, 1999), 110.

17. M. Bartošová, *Analýza ekonomické aktivity důchodců* (Prague: UUNV, 1991). Cited in Možný, "The Czech Family in Transition, 61.

18. Možný, 64.

19. Večerník and Matějů, *Ten Years of Rebuilding Capitalism,* 101.

20. Český statistický úřad (Czech Statistical Bureau), www.czso.cz.

21. Český statistický úřad.

22. True, 59.

23. Tanya Cook, "Remember, Nothing's Impossible: An Outside Look at Access to Abortion in the Czech Republic," *One Eye Open/Jedním okem* 1, no. 2 (Summer 1993): 67.

24. Alexandra Buresova, "The Change in Reproductive Behavior in the Czech Republic," in *Ana's Land: Sisterhood in Eastern Europe,* ed. Tanya Renne (Boulder, CO: Westview Press, 1997), 88.

25. Věra Sokolová, "Representations of Homosexuality and the Separation of Gender and Sexuality in the Czech Republic Before and After 1989," in *Political Systems and Definitions of Gender Roles,* ed. Ann Katherine Isaacs (Pisa: Edizioni Plus, 2001), 276.

26. The Humboldt University of Berlin Magnus Hirschfeld Archive for Sexology, http://www2.hu-berlin.de/sexology/.

27. Karel Matys et al., *Trestní zákon-komentář* (Prague, 1980).

28. Večerník and Matějů, 47.

29. Večerník and Matějů, 51.

30. Katya Zapletnyuk, "Job Trend Puts a Squeeze on Vocational Schools," *Prague Post,* February 10, 2005, praguepost.com/po3/2005/spsect/0210/sp3.php.

SELECTED BIBLIOGRAPHY

Kundera, Milan. *The Farewell Waltz.* Trans. Aaron Asher. New York: Harper-Flamingo, 1998.

Možný, Ivo. "The Czech Family in Transition: From Social to Economic Capital." in *Social Reform in the Czech Republic,* ed. Stein Ringen and Claire Wallace. Prague: Prague Digital Arts, 1994.

Páral, Vladimír. *Lovers & Murderers.* Trans. Craig Cravens. North Haven, CT: Catbird Press, 2001.

Šiklová, Jiřina. "Are Women in Central and Eastern Europe Conservative?" in *Gender Politics and Post-Communism: Reflections from Eastern Europe and the Former Soviet Union,* ed. Nanette Funk and Magda Mueller eds. New York: Routledge, 1993.

True, Jacqui. *Gender, Globalization, and Postsocialism: The Czech Republic after Communism.* New York: Columbia University Press, 2003.

Večerník, Jiří, and Petr Matějů. *Ten Years of Rebuilding Capitalism: Czech Society after 1989.* Prague: Academia, 1999.

WEB SITE

The Humboldt University of Berlin Magnus Hirschfeld Archive for Sexology: http://www2.hu-berlin.de/sexology/.

4

Holidays, Customs, and Leisure Activities

Athletes do not drink or smoke or indulge in debauchery.

Tomáš Masaryk[1]

NATURALLY THE AMOUNT of beer and wine drunk in the Czech Republic and Slovakia frequently puts the inhabitants into a celebratory spirit, but surprisingly the number of beer and wine festivals does not match that of neighboring Germany, which boasts hundreds of inebriating festivals throughout the year. During the summer, however, breweries will organize small beer festivals in all parts of the two countries. In general Czechs and Slovaks take a festive and relaxed attitude toward life. Work is less important than family and relaxation, and traditional cultural events form an important part of social life. Czech and Slovak holidays and customs are for the most part celebrated as elsewhere in Europe and America, but with some slight variations. Few other cultures, for example, celebrate Easter and Christmas with birch-rod whipping and carp-bashing, respectively.

HOLIDAYS

Many Czech and Slovak holidays are a synthesis of pagan and Christian religious traditions, for example, Christmas *(Vánoce)* and Easter (*Velikonoce*—literally "Great Nights"), which are the two most widely celebrated holidays.

Christmas

Christmas begins on December 24th, Christmas Eve or *Štědrý večer,* which translates as Generous Evening, probably for the sizable amount of food served at the evening meal. Christmas preparations, however, begin several weeks earlier with the baking of Christmas cookies and the purchasing of the Christmas tree and Christmas carp. Carp is sold in large tubs on the street. Customers pick which one they would like and have it killed on the spot or take it home and let it swim around in their bathtub. The Christmas tree remains undecorated until Christmas Eve, and the carp is clubbed over the head by Father in preparation for Christmas dinner. In the past, carp was the only meat the poor could afford at Christmas, and it eventually became a rather lucrative tradition for carp farmers. In the fifteenth century, the number of carp ponds in Bohemia numbered around 78,000.

On Christmas Eve, the family fasts for the entire day, which is supposed to bring on a vision of the golden piglet, *zlaté prasátko,* a harbinger of good luck for the coming year. When the first star of the evening appears, dinner is served, customarily consisting of mushroom or fish soup, potato salad, and carp, followed by a dessert of cookies and cake. Czech and Slovak carp is not the tasteless bottom-feeding fish we know in the United States. It is meatier and tastier, but like the American version it is chock full of bones. Every Christmas Eve dozens of Czechs and Slovaks end up in the emergency room to have bones extracted from their windpipes. After dinner, the family may sing Christmas carols at the table, and then everyone goes to the Christmas tree, which is now decorated and lit, with presents placed beneath it not by Santa Clause, but by the Baby Jesus, *Ježíšek,* who is a rather shadowy and indistinct figure to Czech and Slovak children. Some imagine him as a wrinkled old man, and some as a little baby. Before Christmas, Czechs and Slovaks wish each other a *bohatého Ježíška* or rich little Jesus.

Some families build elaborate nativity scenes, a tradition brought to the Czech lands by the Jesuits in the sixteenth century. By the eighteenth century, the tradition had become entrenched in villages and towns. The scenes feature elaborate background sets, hosts of characters, and moving mechanical parts. Many of these nativity scenes now reside in museums. The largest is in Jindřichův Hradec measuring 60 square meters and containing 1,400 figures.

Under Communism the Russian version of Santa Clause, *Děda Mraz* (Grandfather Frost), sporting a white beard and red suit, was imported from the Soviet Union. In 1952, the president of Czechoslovakia, Antonín Zapotocký, publicly announced that *Ježíšek* had grown up and become *Děda Mraz.* Despite a heavy advertising campaign, the tradition never really caught on and remains today in the Czechoslovak cultural consciousness only because of the Czech version of "Jingle Bells" and the cult Russian film *Mrazík.*[2]

Easter

The second most popular holiday is Easter *(Velikonoce)*, celebrated in April on Easter Monday rather than Sunday. Remember the Czechs are an atheistic nation, and Easter Sunday is simply the middle of a three-day weekend, and it is celebrated with a tremendous amount of alcohol. Traditionally, Easter was a pagan springtime ritual called *pomlázka* (which means "braided birch branches"), during which boys whipped girls' legs with birch branches and were then rewarded with colored eggs or a shot of alcohol. Czech and Slovak boys eagerly continue the tradition today, and sometimes adults gleefully join in. Whipping is supposed to confer youth and fertility for the coming year and is often accompanied by drenching with water.

St. Nicholas Day

St. Nicholas Day *(Mikuláš)*, a traditional Catholic holiday celebrating Pope Nicholas I, falls on December 5. Parents array themselves to look like either St. Nicholas, who oddly enough somewhat resembles Santa Clause and represents good, or the devil, who has horns and a tail and symbolizes evil. Nicholas and the devil saunter through town visiting houses where children live and inquire whether they have been good or bad. Naturally, most children maintain they have behaved without reproach throughout the year and then sing a song or recite a poem, whereupon Nicholas rewards them with candy or fruit. If a child admits less than exemplary behavior, he or she is presented with a sack of coal or potatoes instead and is whisked off forthwith to hell, symbolically, of course.

New Year's Eve, the Burning of Witches, and Three Kings

New Year's Eve is called *Silvestr,* named after the saint whose name day it is (see below). It is celebrated by the Czechs and Slovaks as it is everywhere else—with a lot of drinking and singing with friends. At midnight Czechs and Slovaks sing their respective national anthems rather than "Auld Lang Syne." Also Czechs and Slovaks are more likely to send out greeting cards for New Year's rather than Christmas. The cards are called PF cards and are decorated with beautiful pen and ink drawings. PF comes from the French *pour félicité.* The most anticipated television show of the season is broadcast on New Year's Eve, an extravaganza featuring all the major celebrities chatting and making jokes. New Year's Day is spent recovering and eating a traditional bean soup, which is supposed to bring luck and cure hangovers. A more recent tradition has been taken up by those Czechs and Slovaks who wish that the split between their two countries had never happened. Beginning December 29,

Czechs and Slovaks come together for four days in a mountain resort near the Czech/Slovak border. The celebrants go hiking, mountain climbing, and skiing during the day and sing, dance, and drink the nights away in the hope of generating good relations between the two countries.

On April 30, Czechs and Slovaks celebrate the Burning of Witches *(Pálení čarodějnic)*. Most European countries have something like this Night on Bald Mountain, a time of supernatural occurrences, cauldron-stirring, spell-chanting, skeleton-dancing, and howling at the moon. In most Germanic countries, it is referred to as *Walpurgisnacht*. Anglicized countries know it as May Day.

The Czechs and Slovaks celebrate the event on the evening of April 30, and continue into the early hours of May 1. Originally, the celebrations were held on a grave mound or mountain top; pagan elements included the chanting of magical spells to protect animals, the banning of all trolls from houses, processions around the village with decorated birch trees or conifers (the "May Tree"), and of course the lighting of bonfires, which lightened the gloom and dispelled the memory of long, hard, dark winters. It was also a time for peasants to clean up their properties and retire to the highest mountain top to ward off witches by burning old brooms—literally a spring cleaning.

Nowadays young people all over the country build witches they then burn in bonfires to exorcise the evil spirits that are supposed to arise on the eve of May Day. Celebrants stay out all night, and as the fires die down toward morning, young couples leap over the dying embers hand-in-hand.

Under Communism, May 1 was the largest annual celebration, and as everywhere else in Europe it was commemorated as International Workers' Day. All workers were compelled to gather at parades and march en masse through cities and towns toting red banners or portraits of Marx, Engles, and Lenin. Each factory demonstrated its production techniques on floats, and everyone shouted out repeated slogans of "Long live the Soviet Union!" or "Long live the First of May!" Television stations would broadcast concurrent parades in the Soviet Union. Today, May Day is celebrated with less nationalistic vigor, but as in times past, the day ends with heavy drinking.

Three Kings Day *(Tři králové)* celebrates the arrival of the three biblical kings and their presentation of gold, frankincense, and myrrh to the newborn Christ. It takes place on January 6 and designates the formal end of the Christmas season. Children walk around in groups of three, and they dress in white robes and wear crosses around their necks. They knock on doors, sing a song, and then receive donations for charity. Today, Gypsy children are the ones who walk around asking for alms, which they most likely do not donate to charity. The Slovaks celebrate Shrovetide or *(Fašiangy)*—marking the transition from winter to spring—from the Three Kings to Ash Wednesday, the final few days of which are called Crazy Days *(bláznivé dní)*, a period of dancing and entertainment.

Other Events

The Prague Music Festival began in 1946 and quickly became a major event showcasing local and international classical and chamber music. It runs for three weeks from May 12 to June 2. The celebration begins on the birthday of the Czech National Composer Bedřich Smetana and opens with a performance of his symphonic poem "My Homeland" *(Má vlast)*. Performances of orchestras, chamber music, soloists, and ancient and contemporary music take place throughout the period, ending with a performance of Beethoven's 9th Symphony.

The *Porta* folk music festival was an important venue for emerging Czech and Slovak folk and country musicians who were influenced by music seeping in from the United States. It was first held in 1967 as *Porta Bohemica* and referred to as the Czech Woodstock. Upon the arrival of Normalization, bands were compelled to change their names from Western- to Slavic-sounding names, as well as to refrain from performing protest songs. In the1970s and 1980s, folk music was an alternative to the officially sanctioned pop music, and the authorities tried to keep it from becoming popular.

Karlovy Vary hosts an international film festival beginning the final weekend in June and running for eight days. The festival began in 1946 in neighboring Mariánské Lázně and today attracts filmmakers and film buffs from all over the world. At first there was no competitive element to the film screenings, but in 1948 a jury was chosen to judge the films. Prague began its own film festival in 1995, the Golden Golem Festival, focusing on domestic films, thereby underscoring the increasing number of domestic films after levels dropped in the early 1990s.

Every day in the Czech and Slovak Republics is somebody's Name Day *(jmeniny)*, the feast of a saint whose name one bears. Usually Czechs and Slovaks refer to it as someone's "holiday," *svátek,* rather than name day, as in "it's your holiday today." The day is celebrated similar to a birthday, with the giving of presents and wishes of health and happiness. Women usually receive flowers from co-workers, and men receive a flask of rum. Odd as it may sound, a government office in charge of names exists, which must be consulted if parents want to give their baby a name other than one of those on the calendar.

The Communist government encouraged folk festivals and celebrations in an attempt to foster patriotic traditions. Thus, these celebrations continue throughout both countries, especially in eastern Moravia and Slovakia.

The two-day festival Ride of the Kings *(Jízda králů)* takes place on the last weekend in May in Vlčnov, in the southeastern part of the Czech Republic, to celebrate the new crops and a young man's coming of age. The festival features singing and dancing as well as the Ride itself. A 10- to 12-year-old boy, the king, rides blindfolded with a rose between his teeth. He and his two assistants, who may be up to 18 years of age, don women's clothing and ride through the village on festively decorated horses. The assistants call out verses and request gifts in the king's honor, whereupon they receive money, food, and glasses of plum brandy or *slivovice*. The Ride supposedly symbolizes King Wenceslaus' escape from captivity wearing a disguise. Milan Kundera in his novel *The Joke* (1967) gives a good, if somewhat wistful, description of the celebration.

The village fair, or *pout'*, is held annually in towns and villages. The word literally means "pilgrimage" and began as a pilgrimage to the village church where the entire village would head for a special thanksgiving mass. Nowadays few people go to church but instead eat, drink, and make merry. Preparations for the *pout'* begin several weeks in advance with housewives stocking up their larders and baking enormous quantities of kolačes and cookies. On the day of the *pout'* merry-go-rounds and other rides are set up on the town square, and merchants sell sweets, beer, wine, and rum from small wooden stalls. The *pout'* ends with an evening of music and dancing.

The most famous folk festival in Slovakia takes place in the small village of Východná at the end of June or beginning of July. Celebrants come from all over Central and Eastern Europe to attend this showcase of folk music and dance.

Since the fall of Communism in 1989, new traditions have been seeping into the country from the West. Santa Clause is now frequently seen idling about department stores at Christmastime, and befuddled adults now stock up on candy on October 31 in anticipation of Halloween trick-or-treaters.

Social Customs

Time and again throughout their history, the Czechs and Slovaks have been overrun and dominated by foreign powers; Austria, Hungary, Germany, and most recently the Soviet Union have all taken their turns ruling over the Czechs and Slovaks. And during those periods when they acquired or lost their freedom—1918, 1938, 1948, and 1968—in no instance did the Czechoslovaks fire a shot; the citizens and government consistently avoided armed resistance and bloodshed. Rather than revolution, Czechs and Slovaks have repeatedly expressed their patriotism and opposition to foreign domination and rule through passive, small-scale resistance. Jaroslav Hašek demonstrated this typically Czech characteristic in his novel *The Fortunes of the Good Soldier Švejk in the Great War* (1921–23). The protagonist Josef Švejk is a malingering, good-natured Czech residing in Bohemia under the Austro-Hungarian Monarchy at the outbreak of World War I. When he is called up to fight for the Austrians against the Russians, Švejk feigns stupidity, hoodwinks nearly all of his superiors, and ends by undermining the army and the monarchy.

This apparently inherent pessimistic pacifism can be seen as a, perhaps unconscious, small-nation survival strategy: when overwhelmingly outnumbered, outright rebellion is most likely one's worst choice. Yet this survival strategy has endowed the Czechs and Slovaks with somewhat of an inferiority complex. They are a peaceful folk, fonder of cooling their heels in pubs instead of manning the barricades. A common complaint heard throughout Czech and Slovak history is that this is a land where activity is hopelessly dissipated in beer.

Czechs and Slovaks will sit in a pub for hours on end, drinking beer and playing cards; they are not a jolly folk, however, and dark, cynical humor is one of their salient national characteristics. Unlike Americans, Czechs and Slovaks do not smile as a social signal of greeting, but only when they are genuinely pleased. This characteristic may make the people seem unfriendly or standoffish, but to a Czech or Slovak, a serious demeanor is a sign of respect. Forty years of totalitarian rule, during which it was often difficult to know whom to trust, might also have something to do with their reserved nature. Along the same lines, Czechs and Slovaks do not ordinarily appear at someone's house unannounced. But for that, when invited, the guest is considered royalty. Traditionally, the guest is sacred and is offered the best of what the household has to offer, even if it means the family will have to do without. When coming for a visit, it is polite to bring flowers for the hostess and a bottle of wine or liquor for the host, and one *always* removes one's shoes when entering the house, whereupon one may be provided with a pair of house slippers, *pantofle,* or remain in one's stockings for the duration of the stay. This is similar to the custom of changing into "home clothes" after work, a habit meant to preserve the quality of one's good clothes as well as the cleanliness of the household. It is impolite for men to cross an ankle over the knee or for anyone to place feet on furniture. Pointing with the index finger is likewise rude.

Also, one notices an astounding number of titles, which are often used in polite conversation. A medical doctor has MUDr. before his name, a lawyer is a JUDr., and a pharmacist a Pharm.Dr.; a college graduate with a master's degree is a Mgr., and a graduate with a bachelor's is a Bc. Furthermore, one does not address others by the first name unless invited to do so. A foreign visitor may offend his host by addressing him by his given name.

Czechs and Slovaks are fond of their free time, and even though the two countries are moving toward an American work ethic, especially in the capitals Prague and Bratislava, relaxation and family still take precedence over the office. They do get up astoundingly early for work, though. The Czech workday typically begins at 7:00 A.M. (seven is a lucky number). The leisurely lunch break, however, is standard, and Czechs and Slovaks tend to knock off early, especially on Friday when they rush off to their country houses for the weekend. Most Czechs are supportive of the welfare state. Health care and primary and secondary education are free, and four weeks of paid vacation annually is the legal minimum. Relaxation is more important than career success.

One disturbing aspect of Czech and Slovak culture is their xenophobia: both nations are quite suspicious of anyone even slightly different from themselves, such as Roma (or Gypsies), foreigners, gays, or even those who merely think differently from themselves. This xenophobia, however, is restricted to the personal sphere. The two governments are highly supportive of minority rights. Homosexuality is legal, and in 2006 parliament passed a law legalizing same-sex partnership.

LEISURE ACTIVITIES

On the whole, the Czechs and Slovaks are very bookish and sedentary. Recently, the Public Opinion Research Center at the Sociological Institute of the Czech Academy of Sciences published a study of how Czechs spend their leisure. Reading, it turns out, is the most popular way to spend one's free time. While 70 percent of respondents read a magazine at least once a week, only 34 percent participate in a sport.[3] Due to the geography of their country, Slovaks spend more of their leisure in the great outdoors than the Czechs. Slovakia is second to none in its wealth of natural sights, unspoiled natural woodlands, mountain peaks, glacial lakes, national parks, castles, and waterfalls. It is perhaps Central Europe's most popular outdoor destination.

On the other hand, Czechs are great fans of professional sports and have traditionally done very well in the international arena. Soccer, ice hockey, and tennis are their favorite spectator sports. Perhaps the abundance of lakes and ponds throughout the two republics has contributed to the popularity of ice hockey. The 1940s was the golden age of Czech and Slovak hockey, during which they won several international medals. Then in 1950 disaster struck: just before setting off for the World Cup, most of the Czechoslovak national team was arrested out of fear they would defect. Most suspected that the Soviet Union orchestrated the arrests, and from then on, ice hockey

Slovak shepherd Daniel Bartko enjoys a cigarette while tending his 28 sheep in the High Tatra mountain range in northern Slovakia. Slovakia is unparalleled in its wealth of natural beauty. © Corbis.

competition between the two countries was fierce, especially after the Soviet invasion of 1968. The following year at the world championships in Sweden, the Czechoslovak team beat the Soviets twice with fans chanting, "*Vy nám tanky, my vám branky*" [you send us tanks, we send you goals]. Celebratory rioters in Prague shattered the windows of the Soviet airline company Aeroflot, leading to the government's hard-line political and cultural crackdown known as Normalization.

The Czechoslovak national ice hockey team has won the European championship 17 times, the world title 10 times, and the Olympic gold medal once. Dominik Hašek—the "Dominator"—was considered the world's best goaltender after he helped the Red Wings win the Stanley Cup in 2001. Jaromír Jágr is even more famous. He had the good fortune of coming of age just after the Velvet Revolution and could sign freely with foreign teams. He is one of the leading scorers in the NHL and won Stanley Cups with Pittsburg in 1991 and 1992 and now plays for Washington. He wears number 68 in memory of the 1968 Soviet invasion and sports a mullet, the standard haircut of all Czech and Slovak athletes. He is an idol among Czech boys.

In tennis, the Czechs have always had a disproportionate number of stars on the world stage, including Ivan Lendl, Jana Novotná, and Martina Navrátilová, who made an impressive comeback at Wimbleton in 2004 at the age of 47. The Slovaks do not do as well in international tennis, but they do have their occasional star, such as Miroslav Mečír and Daniela Hantuchová, who currently resides at number 19 in the world standings.

Soccer *(fotbal)* is the real game of the Czechs and Slovaks even though they do not tend to do well in the international arena. Games are preceded and followed by beer drinking, and the crowd is composed almost exclusively of young men shouting obscenities. The few times the Czecho-Slovaks have done well are part of the national consciousness: two second-place finishes at the World Cup (1934 and 1962) and one European Championship (1976) won by Tonda Panenka's weak penalty shot lofted over the head of a surprised goalkeeper. HC Sparta Praha and HC Slavia Praha are Prague's two favorite teams, both founded in 1893. The two clubs dominated the league between the wars, and nearly all Czechs could be divided into those who rooted for Sparta and those who rooted for Slavia. Under Communism both were forced to change their names, and the newly created army team Dukla Praha rose to the top. Today, Sparta leads the league and buys up all the top players.

Emil Zátopek (1922–2000) was voted Czech Athlete of the Century just after his death. At the 1952 Olympic games in Helsinki, he won three gold medals in the 5K, 10K, and the marathon, a feat never to be equaled. On the track, Zátopek was known for his odd running style; known as the "Bouncing Czech," he seemed always on the verge of collapse. His face was contorted, his head would often roll, his torso swung from side to side, and he often wheezed and panted loudly. When asked about his odd facial expressions, Zátopek replied "It isn't gymnastics or ice-skating, you know." From 1948 to 1954, he dominated long-distance running, winning 38 consecutive 10K races. He set 18 world records at distances from the 5K to 30K. Zátopek revolutionized racing by incorporating intense interval training, which is standard today. He once remarked about interval training: "Everyone said, 'Emil, you are a fool!' But when I first won the European Championship, they said: 'Emil, you are a genius!'" The Communists celebrated Zátopek as a national hero, but when he expressed publicly his support for the Prague Spring, he and his wife became *persona non grata.*

Those who participate in recreational sports choose mainly soccer and ice hockey. Despite the international repute of Czech and Slovak tennis players, tennis is oddly not popular. Prague has recently become a hot spot for alternative sports competitions, such as skateboarding and hacky sack (or footbag). A sport little known internationally but enormously popular among Czechs is *nohejbal,* which literally translates as "football" but

Known as the "locomotive" or the "bouncing Czech" because
of his odd and ungainly running style, Emil Zátopek (1922–
2000) is considered one of the greatest distance runners in the
history of the sport. He won three gold medals at the Olympic
Games in Helsinki in 1948: in the 5,000- and 10,000-meter
races and in the marathon. © Corbis.

is acoustically similar to the Czech word for volleyball, *volejbal*. *Nohejbal*
is played in two-man teams on a volleyball or tennis court with the net at
tennis height. The rules are an eclectic mix of soccer, volleyball, and tennis.
You can strike the ball with any part of your body, and the ball can bounce
once between each hit. Although it is nowhere written down in the official rulebook, a common requirement holds that participants must compete
with a beer in one hand and sip between volleys. Onlookers, likewise, imbibe
while they observe, thus acquiring a sense of active (though nonaerobic) participation. In the summer, you can find *nohejbal* tournaments all across the

two republics. A new health-conscious generation is going to fitness centers, which are springing up everywhere providing aerobics classes, swimming pools, and so on. Even squash is catching on.

During the summer, people set off on weekend hiking and camping trips called the *čundr*. The Czech Hiking Club, founded in 1888, has developed an extensive network of hiking trails that have been marked out by hundreds of club members covering 23,870 miles of hiking trails. They are maintained on a purely voluntary basis. The marking system is easy to follow, and hikers will see painted signs on posts, rocks, and trees along the way and sign posts at main hiking route junctions detailing kilometers to the nearest towns. During the *čundr*, people hike all day and end up in a tavern or *hospoda*, or they gather around a campfire to sing songs accompanied by a guitar—someone on the *čundr* always has a guitar—and roast *špekáček*, a short, thick sausage essential to any hiking trip. In the evening people spread out and sleep under the stars *(pod širákem)*. Canoe trips down the various rivers throughout the two republics are also a popular summer pastime. It's a great excuse to take a few days off to float down the river with a bottle of rum and pitch a tent.

Besides sports, Czechs and Slovaks are quite fond of theatre and film, or just sitting around with friends in a pub drinking beer or wine and playing *Mariáš*, or Marriage, a Czech card game. Also, unlike Americans and many Western Europeans, Czechs and Slovaks spend a lot of their time with their family and friends. Work hours are typically shorter than ours, and Czechs and Slovaks do not spend much time shopping for clothes or going to restaurants. Both countries average a couple of holidays a month, and in the summer, shops typically close down for extended periods of time as their owners depart for three-week vacations in August. This is what the Czechs refer to as the *okurková sezóna*, or the Cucumber Season, the time of year when cucumbers are harvested, and the joke is that many people disappear off into the country to harvest cucumbers. Of course, this is not true, but Czechs in fact take three to four weeks of vacation in August and decamp to their country houses. A country house is less of a luxury than it sounds. Most Czech and Slovak families own one, and they often remain in various states of disrepair. In fact, one of the chief activities during the Cucumber Season is fixing up the cottage or working in the garden.

Another popular summer activity is mushroom hunting, *houbařství/hubárenie*. All varieties of mushrooms grow wild in the Czech Republic and Slovakia during the summer, from city parks to remote mountain peaks. Most Czechs and Slovaks are experts at telling the difference between edible and poisonous mushrooms, but dozens of people do die every year from mushroom poisoning. The gathered mushrooms are usually dipped in batter and fried or made into mushroom soup. According to a recent survey, up to 80 percent of Czechs and Slovaks spend at least one day a year searching for mushrooms. Historically, the activity began during times of famine, especially during the devastating Thirty Years War and the two World Wars. Families foraged the fungi as an emergency food supply. Now, however, it has become a national hobby, and every year the Czechs and Slovaks hold a contest for the best pickled mushrooms.

Another revered gastronomic pastime is the *zabíjačka* or pig slaughter, an ancient tradition during which families gather for a day of pig roasting and beer drinking. Celebrants come together in the morning to slaughter and roast the pig, during which enormous quantities of beer and plum brandy are served. For many village families faced with rising prices, the butchering of a pig provides the only meat for the entire year. The pig is shot in the head and then has its throat slit. When the pig's final convulsions have ceased, it is hung by its rear legs, shaved, cleaned, and cut up. Virtually every piece of the pig is used. Intestines become sausage receptacles, blood-rich organs become blood sausage, and the blood itself is collected and whipped into a froth to be spread on bread. The fat is boiled and stored as lard or used to make soap. The afternoon and evening of the *zabíjačka* are devoted to a dinner featuring various versions of pork and dancing. In January of 2001, Miloš Zeman, the former Czech prime minister invited his former political rival Václav Klaus, the president, to his country house for a *zabíjačka,* during which the two buried the hatchet.

Notes

1. Karel Čapek, *Talks with T.G. Masaryk,* trans. Michael Henry Heim (North Haven: Catbird Press, 1995), 91.

2. *Mrazík* [Old Father Frost] (1967) has been shown annually since its release. Czechs know it by heart. It is the only foreign fairy tale to be shown regularly in the Czech Republic.

3. "Co doláme ve svém volném čase?" www.cvvm.cas.cz/index.php?lang-O&disp=zpravy&r=1&shw=100351.

Selected Bibliography

Hašek, Jaroslav. *The Good Soldier Švejk and His Fortunes in the World War.* Trans. Cecil Panott. New York: TY Crowell Co., 1973.
Hord, Alfred. Ed. *Czech & Slovak Republics.* Boston: Houghton Mifflin, 1994.

5

Cuisine and Fashion

A nation of peasants, tradesmen, and petty officials is not going to cook
à la Versailles and Brillat-Savarin.

—Pavel Eisner, Czech writer, translator and philologist[1]

I suppose that drinking beer in pubs has had a beneficial influence on
the behavior of Czech society because beer contains less alcohol than for
example wine, vodka or whisky and therefore people's political chat in
pubs is less crazy.

—Václav Havel[2]

Take a gander at any fashion show's lineup of living mannequins and
you might think it was the Warsaw Pact countries that won the Cold
War.

—Michael Y. Park, Fox News[3]

CZECH AND SLOVAK CUISINE is among the least healthful in the world. The
Czecho-Slovak diet revolves around large portions of pork or beef smothered
in meat-based sauces and accompanied by large portions of bread dumplings
or potatoes. Moreover, due to Communist homogenizing tendencies, whereby
cooks were compelled to attend rigorously standardized cooking schools, there
are almost no variations in the typical fare regardless of where you go in the
two republics. Many say that the purpose of Czech and Slovak food is, in fact,
to line the stomach and prepare one for an evening of beer drinking, for the
Czechs are far and away the highest per capita beer drinking nation in the
world. The typical Czech adult male will drink five half-liter (16 oz.) mugs of
beer at one sitting, and drinking ten to fifteen mugs is far from uncommon.

Tastes are changing rapidly, however. With the demise of Communism and the onslaught of tourists demanding lighter and spicier fare, the number of ethnic restaurants has grown throughout the two republics, and the Czechs and Slovaks themselves are experimenting with nontraditional spices. Beer, on the other hand, is not likely to change. Even though almost all Czech and Slovak breweries have been purchased by foreign companies (Budějovický Budvar is a proud exception), traditional brewing methods and ingredients remain obstinately, tenaciously, and intractably the same.

Perhaps Czech and Slovak fashion models subsist on different food and drink, for the models of these two nations have stunned the world with their incomparable beauty, and according to a recent calculation by the German advertising and marketing service BBDO Consulting, the 5'11" blonde Czech supermodel Karolína Kurková can expect to earn more money during her career than any other world supermodel—an astonishing $53.7 million.[4] Although Czech and Slovak fashion models have conquered the fashion world, Czech and Slovak fashion has not. Clothing under Communism was unremittingly dour, unexpressive, and standardized. But things are looking up.

Food, drink, and fashion are three of the clearest and most readily accessible manifestations of a nation's culture. In this chapter we will look at Czech and Slovak dining, drinking, and clothing habits. Note that the names of dishes are given first in Czech and then in Slovak separated by a slash (/); if the terms are the same in both languages, there is no slash.

Food

Czech and Slovak dietary habits are shocking. The cuisine has been influenced by a long history of peasant culture—piles of meat, loads of potatoes and dumplings, and occasionally something resembling a fresh vegetable, but which has been pickled, mercilessly boiled, or doused with mayonnaise. Czech writer Pavel Eisner writes:

> Czech cuisine is heavy, unimaginative, bloating, and in general quite deleterious to the soul. It involves a lot of coarse and rather barbaric spices. It manages to thoroughly ruin all vegetables with detestable sauces and gravies and to destroy all salads with acidic vinegar.... A certain European gastronomic guide says cruelly but justifiably that baked goose is one of the very few dishes that a Czech cook cannot spoil despite the enormous dose of caraway seeds added.[5]

The Czech and Slovak aversion to fresh vegetables is probably due to the cool climate in the two republics where in the past vegetables were available only seasonally. Czech and Slovak dishes have been handed down for generations, and the natives are particularly proud of them; they are especially pleased when foreigners throw caution to the wind and indulge in their literally heart-stopping specialties.

Meat is the centerpiece of the Czech and Slovak meal—primarily pork and beef. Chicken is considered "lighter" fare. To add to the nutritional nightmare, slabs of meat are often topped with ham, cheese, or a fried egg. Not only is meat the centerpiece of the meal, it is also featured in all types of soups and salads as well. Vegetarians beware: even if the dish comes under the menu heading "*Bezmasá jídla/bezmäsité jedlá*" [Meat Free Dishes], always ask if it contains meat, "*Je to bez masa?*" If that were not enough, most meat, potatoes, and dumplings are smothered in thick, meat-based sauces, but it is precisely these flavorful sauces—made with dill, paprika, garlic, and butter—that provide a tantalizing twist to what might otherwise be an ordinary meal.

Needless to say, vegetarians have a tough time in the two republics. If present at all, vegetables are usually pickled, fried, boiled, or wallowing in a thick coagulation of mayonnaise. On the other hand, ethnic restaurants are springing up throughout the larger cities offering "non-standard" fresh vegetables and fruits, and one can always find an outdoor stand selling fruits and vegetables if one wants to do one's own cooking.

The main meal of the day, as in most European countries, is the midday meal, *oběd*, which may soon, however, be a thing of the past, especially in Prague and Bratislava, where the hour-long sit-down lunch is being replaced by a quick sandwich or often nothing at all. Breakfast, *snídaně/raňajky*, is likewise a European affair. At home Czechs and Slovaks begin their day with bread, cold cuts, cheese, boiled eggs, or yogurt. Commuters are likely to grab a sausage from an outdoor stand as they rush through the metro station or hop aboard the streetcar. The modest evening meal, *večeře*, consists of, perhaps, a sandwich or even fruit-filled dumplings with whipped cream.

Soup and a main dish compose the typical Czech/Slovak main meal. Appetizers, *předkrm/predjedlo*, are quite heavy in themselves and are usually ordered as something to go along with your beer rather than as a prelude to your meal. Cheese platters, pieces of Edam along with a glob of butter and perhaps a pickle, are popular and come with a basket of rolls. The little pink pickled sausage called *utopenec*, literally "drowned man" sounds macabre but is actually quite tasty. *Tlačenka*, on the other hand, head cheese or pig offal suspended in aspic, is recommended only for those who relish unidentified animal parts in gelled form.

Soup is the true prelude to the Czech and Slovak meal and is sometimes the highlight. Potato soup, *bramborová polévka/zemiaková polievka*, contains potatoes, mushrooms, onions, and garlic floating in a thick base of flour and cream. Cabbage soup, *zelná polévka/kapustnica*, is especially popular in Slovakia—sauerkraut and pieces of sausage in milk or cream. Chicken and beef broths, *slepičí* and *hovězí vývar,* respectively, are clear soups swimming with bits of chicken, beef, and noodles. Garlic soup, *česneková polívka/cesnaková polievka,* is a marvelous hangover cure enjoyed by teetotalers and indulgers alike.

Salads, *salát,* are somewhat sketchier. They may contain fresh ingredients, but these have usually been soaked in sweet vinegar or coated in mayonnaise. Fresh, untainted vegetables can usually be found, however, in the *šopský salát,* a combination of tomatoes, cucumbers, onions, and peppers topped with feta cheese. The tossed salad, *míchaný salát/miešaný šalát,* is also fresh—lettuce, cucumbers, and a tomato slice or two—but it may be topped with a glob of sour cream to offset any potential health benefits.

The main course is a monster of meat and potatoes or dumplings smothered in a rich meat-based sauce. Menus are divided by types of meat so you can better choose the type of pork, beef, or chicken with which you would like to obstruct your arteries. Pork is the most traditional dish by far with beef a close second, but duck, goose, pheasant, and wild game are also popular, especially on festive occasions. Next to your serving of pork, you will most likely find a bread dumpling—a fluffy piece of boiled dough of which the Czechs and Slovaks are inordinately proud—along with a small serving of crunchy boiled cabbage. This is the traditional meal—pork, dumplings, and cabbage, *vepřo-knedlo-zelo,* which you'll also find in Germany and Austria. Gastronomically, it is not that inspiring, but to Czechs and Slovaks, it is the ultimate comfort food. According to popular mythology, the health hazards of the heavy pork and dumplings are offset by some heart-friendly element in the cabbage and beer. The high rate of heart disease in the two countries— one and a half times higher than Western Europe—would seem to belie this myth. Potato dumplings *(bramborové knedlíky/zemiakové knedlíky)* are also fairly common as a side dish, made from potatoes, egg yolks, and flour. Another traditional dish, and one distinctive to the Czechs and Slovaks, is beef in sour cream, *svíčková na smetaně.* Beef is marinated in red wine vinegar and water for several hours, then roasted and served in a sour cream sauce. Mildly spicy goulash, *guláš,* is standard in every restaurant. Pieces of pork or beef are mixed with onions, tomatoes, onions, salt, pepper, and paprika and served on a plate. According to the traditional recipe, it should be allowed to sit around at least a day unrefrigerated to improve the flavor. New hygiene rules, however, have made this a thing of the past.

Roast chicken, *kuˇr e/kura,* is popular served with potatoes or dumplings and topped with garlic sauce. Fish can be found everywhere as well. Because of the abundance of freshwater streams, trout *(pstruh)* and carp *(kapr/kapor)* are the most common, roasted or fried, with a side, again, of potatoes or dumplings.

Slovak cuisine differs only slightly from Czech, primarily in its heightened spiciness—a remnant no doubt of Hungary's hundred-year domination of the region. In addition to the aforementioned dishes, Slovaks are quite proud of their *bryndzové halušky*, which has no equivalent in English. Small potato dumplings, akin to the Italian gnocchi, are mounted with sheep's cheese and fried cubes of bacon. Slovaks often wash down their *halušky* with *žinčice*, a buttermilk-like beverage made from sheep's whey. Czechs often refer to Slovaks as *halušky*.

There are two vegetarian options in Czech and Slovak restaurants—red cabbage and green cabbage—or so goes the local expatriate joke. In fact, life is not easy for vegetarians in the Czech and Slovak Republics, but this is rapidly changing. Fried cheese, no matter how strange or unhealthy this may sound, is an old Czech favorite among vegetarians and carnivores alike. Edam or Gouda cheese is sliced in quarter-inch thick slabs, dipped in flour and egg and then rolled in breadcrumbs before it is quickly fried and served typically with tartar sauce and fries. Vegetarians may also opt for side dishes as their main course, such as potato salad *(brambový salát/zemiakový šalát)*, potato pancakes *(bramboráky/zemiakové placky)*, or even fruit dumplings *(ovocné knedlíky)*.

Desert after the meal is not common, for the rich cakes and torts are almost as heavy as the main course. Desserts are usually consumed as an afternoon snack along with a cup of coffee, but ordering dessert after a meal is fine as well. Due to the country's proximity to Austria, cakes and strudel are as ubiquitous in Prague, Brno, and Bratislava as they are in Vienna. Czechs and Slovaks are also fond of sweet boiled dumplings filled with poppy seed, plum, apricot, or cherry filling. The most traditional dessert is *pala' c inky*, a version of the crepe, smothered in chocolate sauce and whipped cream or jam.

Coffee *(káva* or *kafe)* is more common than tea *(čaj)*, which tends to be weak and tasteless. Coffee is served Turkish style—hot water poured over coffee grounds in the cup. Be sure to let it settle and don't take the last sip unless you relish the taste of wet coffee grounds. Espresso *(presso)* is becoming more common, but you have to ask for it. The teahouse *(čajovna)* has been making inroads as well and serves a wide variety of imported teas. It tends to be frequented, however, by the more bohemian crowd.

Naturally, no Czech or Slovak meal is complete without a half-liter of pilsner beer.

BEER

Beer is not alcohol. This is the creed to which most Czechs and Slovak adhere. "It's just beer." Beer is a sign of national identity, a medium of camaraderie, "a gift from heaven," according to the composer Bedřich Smetana,[6] and a character from a story by Bohumil Hrabal exclaims:

Waiter, what beauty you've brought us in this pint of beer! What splendid foam! This isn't foam, it's whipped cream. It's not whipped cream, it's chilled pudding. It's not pudding, it's the winning goal! Waiter, this pub of yours, it's not a dive, it's the Bethlehem Chapel, in which every guest becomes, in the course of conversation, what he used to be, or what he would like to be. Waiter, this pub of yours is a loud and deafening solitude, in which one dreams best of all.[7]

Even though Czechs did not discover beer, it was fittingly a Czech who discovered who did. In 1913, a Czech archeologist named Bedřich Hrozný deciphered five-thousand-year-old Mesopotamian tablets and learned that this ancient culture, ancestors of Saddam Hussein, brewed nineteen different types of beer. In the Czech lands hops were already being cultivated in 859 and were being exported by 1088. Czech beer was such a prized commodity that King Wenceslaus (907–935) declared the death penalty for anyone caught smuggling hop plants from Bohemia. Pope Pius II (1405–1464), who composed a history of Bohemia, wrote in a letter to the young Bohemian king Ladislav Pohrobek (1440–1457) shortly after his coronation that the Czechs would not let their new boy-king go "until he masters Czech and—beer drinking."[8]

Rudolf II's personal physician Tadeáš Hájek (1525–1600) was an expert on beer and composed a treatise called *On beer and methods of its preparation, its essence, strengths and virtues* published in Latin in 1585 in which he wrote, "When properly prepared, this beverage is extremely healthful and nutritious; it strengthens our spirits and improves and exhilarates our minds." Hájek also commented on the different types of beer, noting their various beneficial effects. "Keep in mind that beer can be made from oats, barley, and wheat, each of which creates beer of a different quality and character. Beer made of oats is colder because oats are cold. Beer made from barley and oats constipates one less, causes less wind, and does one less good. Beer made from wheat is hotter, is more necessary, and constipates one more."[9]

Rudolf passed several laws regulating the sale of beer: beer could not be thinned with water, it had to be served in containers clearly marking the volume, such as half-liter mugs, and these containers often bore such humorous inscriptions as *nehněvej se, ženo má—kde je pivo tam jsem já* ["oh wife of mine, don't worry about me—wherever there's beer, that's where I'll be"]; *kdo pivo pít přestane, do pekla se dostane*" ["whoever stops drinking beer, goes straight to hell, don't you fear"]; and *do půlnoci u pěny, od půlnoci u ženy* ["till midnight with foam, from midnight with wife at home"]. In Rudolf's time competition began among the various pubs in town, so pub owners began placing signs outside their shops enticing thirsty customers. Signs were

Czech streetcars, made by the Škoda car company, are phenomenally reliable, so much so that the city of Portland, Oregon purched seven of them in 2001. In the industry they are known as the "Portland Car." Courtesy of Getty Images/Photodisc.

displayed with such sayings as *Sladování, chmelení, života jsou koření* ["Malting and hopping, these are the spices of life"] or *Dobré pivo, děvče hezké, to jsou dary země české* ["Good beer and beautiful chicks, these are the gifts of the land of the Czechs"]. Often one heard the popular contemporary song emanating from a pub window: *Můj táta byl šenkýř, šenkýřem jsem já; táta sudy narážel, holky zase já* ["My father was an innkeeper, an innkeeper am I; he tapped barrels, whereas I tap girls"].

In the eighteenth century, František Ondřej Poupě of Bohemia wrote the world's first beer brewing textbook, and during the nineteenth century, the pub was a fundamental institution in the development of a Czech national culture. Czech writer and journalist Jan Neruda (1834–1891) noted famously: "If the ceiling caved in at the White Lion Pub, it would be all over for the Czech people."[10] During the nineteenth century and earlier, the language of the Czech intelligentsia and the upper classes was German, and addressing someone in Czech in a public place could be considered an insult or a sign of the social inferiority of the speaker. In the pub, however, people could freely establish the language of communication. The pub was the meeting place primarily for Czechs, whereas cafes and wine bars were mostly frequented by Germans and Austrians. Thus, certain Czech pubs became enclaves of Czech nationalism.

Also in the nineteenth century a Bohemian brewer invented pilsner beer, and in the twentieth century, under Communism, beer drinking was one of the few sanctioned leisure activities. The Communists subsidized beer heavily, thus keeping prices artificially low and Czechoslovak citizens relatively sedate. From the mid-1950s to the mid-1980s, the price of beer in the Czech and Slovak lands remained virtually unchanged. Then in 1984 the government nearly doubled the price of a half liter from one crown seventy ($.30) to two crowns fifty ($.50), which led ineluctably to the Velvet Revolution five years later. Because the Slovaks tend to drink more wine than beer, after the Velvet Divorce in 1993, the Czechs became the highest per capita beer drinkers in the world. The Czechs drink an astounding 163 liters (287 pints) per person per year. This includes men, women, and infants, and because women and infants tend to drink less beer (preferring wine and milk, respectively) Czech men consume a lot of beer. The average Czech man drinks five half-liter (16 oz.) mugs at one sitting. A 1985 study found that drinking five beers at one sitting was acceptable behavior to most Czechs, and 41 percent said it was normal to drink from six to eight beers in an evening.[11]

What Is Czech Beer?

Compared to Czech beer, the beer in the United States is frighteningly bad. In the past decade or so, quality microbreweries have arisen throughout the United States, but Czechs would not consider the bulk of the brew (which is injected with chemicals meant to improve the head and increase shelf life) produced and consumed in the United States fit for scrubbing floors. Czech purity laws are similar to the renowned German *Reinheitsgetbot:* only hops, yeast, malt, and water are permitted. The most common type of beer is a lager we refer to as a "pilsner," named for the Bohemian town of

Plzeň. To a Czech, the city of Plzeň is associated with beer the way Cologne is associated with perfume, Hamburg with Hamburgers, and Germany with shepherds. In 1842 a Plzeň brewer from Bavaria was experimenting with a cold-fermented lager and hit upon what we know as pilsner-style beer: a light, highly hopped, and therefore bitter, lager with a clear golden color. This last characteristic added to the beer's repute. Traditionally, beer had been drunk in opaque clay or wooden mugs, and the beer itself was a muddy brown. In the mid-nineteenth century, however, clay was giving way to clear glass, and the new golden translucent beer served in a transparent glass was a novelty. This style soon spread throughout Bohemia and Bavaria marketed under the type "pilsner." The company then added the qualifier *Urquell* in German and *Prazdroj* in Czech, both of which mean "original source," to identify it as the original. The beer was so popular that by 1865, three-quarters of the brewery's production was exported, and beginning in 1900, a "beer train" left Plzeň daily bound for Vienna. Today, most beers in the world call themselves pilsners, but Czechs know there is only one, even though most Czech beers are brewed in the same manner. Pilsner's distinctive flavor comes from the area's extremely soft water, which has a low saline content, and barley with a low protein content, but mostly the flavor comes from the abundant use of the world famous Žatec hops (also known as Saaz hops), which are exported around the world. Most Czechs remember joining the annual hop-picking brigades under Communism. Students were released from school in September to go out and help hop farmers harvest their crop. A beloved film from the 1960s *Starci na chmelu* [The Hop Pickers], relates the story of a teenage rebel who does not want to participate in the collective effort.

The world's first Budweiser comes from the south Bohemian town of České Budějovice (Budweiss to the Germans). Beer brewing in this town goes back to at least 1265, and by the mid-nineteenth century several local breweries had settled on a particular type of slightly sweeter "pilsner style" beer, selling it as Budvar to the Czechs and Budweiser to the Germans and the rest of Europe. In the United States a wine and liquor importer by the name of Carl Conrad, however, registered the name Budweiser as a brand in the nineteenth century, and in 1875 Adolphus Busch purchased from Conrad the rights to the name and began selling his own "Budweiser" beer. Anheuser-Busch encountered obstacles when they tried to trademark the name in the United States. A German brewer claimed it was a geographical name like Burgundy and Bordeaux. Anheuser-Busch, the German Brewer, and Budějovický Budvar reached a settlement in 1911 according to which Anheuser-Busch would not market its product in Europe, and Czech Budvar would sell its product in North America under the name "imported Budweiser." The agreement was later modified, and Czech Budvar was disallowed from selling its product in North America. Now the Czech beer is sold in the United States as Czechvar, and American Budweiser can be found throughout Europe as Bud. The lawsuits, however, continue.

There are basically two types of beer in the Czech and Slovak lands— light beer or *světlé pivo,* not to be confused with low-calorie American light beer, and dark beer, *černé pivo,* literally "black" beer. In the United States and Britain, dark beers are usually heavier, higher in alcohol content, and perceived as typically men's drinks. The reverse is true in the Czech Republic and Slovakia. The dark beers have more calories, but they are much sweeter and are looked upon as women's drinks. Other styles of beer such as ambers, ales, bitters, or fruity beers are simply not considered beer.

The strength of Czech and Slovak beer is measured by degrees, which does not directly correlate to the percentage of alcohol and is often a source of confusion to foreigners. The degree system was developed by Carl Balling in the seventeenth century and indicates the amount of malt extract used in brewing. The more malt extract used, the greater the alcohol content. Most beer is either 12 or 10 degree, and 12 degree is considered "premium." It commands a higher price and has more alcohol—between 4 and 5 percent. One also finds 7 and 8 degree beer, which under Communism was a popular mid-morning refreshment for blue-collar workers. If you plan an all night drinking session, you may want to stick to the 10-degree variety.

Beer is usually consumed in a tavern, or *hospoda/krčma,* in half-liter mugs, never in pitchers. On the other hand, patrons often appear bearing their own two- or three-liter ceramic pitchers, which the bartender gladly fills with beer to take home. The name of a *hospoda* is typically preceded by the preposition "U," which translates to something along the lines of "At the Sign of." Bohumil Hrabal's favorite haunt, for example, was *U zlatého tygra,* meaning "At the Sign of the Golden Tiger," and Jaroslav Hašek immortalized *U kalicha,* or "At the Sign of the Chalice." Prague's oldest *hospoda* is *U fleku,* which is now a popular tourist site. The *hospoda* is a casual place to gather primarily to drink beer and talk. Wine and perhaps liquor is served as well, but beer is by far the beverage of choice. Each *hospoda* is associated almost exclusively with a single brand of beer and serves only that brand—usually both the light and dark variety as well as the 10 and 12 degree strengths. The tavern itself is a well-lit single-story ground floor or basement establishment usually with long wooden tables at which new arrivals seat themselves alongside perfect strangers. One simply asks if a seat is free: *Je tady volno.* Waiters assume that men will be drinking half-liter beers, and the only question may be whether one prefers 10 or 12 degree beer: *desítku nebo dvanáctku/desiatku alebo dvanástku?* But you shouldn't be surprised if a beer appears on the table in front of you even if no communication has passed between yourself and the waiter. Also, holding up an index finger will get you two beers; a raised thumb, one. Women, by contrast, are more unpredictable, and the waiter may inquire if they would like a small beer, *malé pivo,* or a dark beer. Finally, although Czechs claim to be connoisseurs, they drink their beer in mighty gulps rather than graceful sips.

After the waiter delivers the beer, he scribbles a hatch mark at the bottom of a slip of paper—the bill—and leaves it at the table next to you. At the end of the night, the headwaiter will come by to add up the amount. As a rule, customers pay separately. Unlike in the United States, patrons do not usually stand each other drinks or buy rounds for the table. This is sometimes a source of frustration for Slovaks, who often buy each other drinks and share their beer snacks with the table. According to Slovaks, this reflects their more generous "Slavic" nature. Tipping is not common practice; one simply rounds up the bill. If the amount is 95 crowns, for instance, simply hand the waiter 100 crowns and wave your hands in a manner meant to convey the message that he or she can keep the change. Never leave money on the table because it will be snatched up by the next patron. And because the person taking your money is rarely the person who served you, there is really no reason to reward him or her with a particular tip.

There are a few unspoken rules Czechs and Slovaks observe while consuming beer. First of all, beer is never wasted nor is it ever mixed—either with other alcohol or with other beer. One always finishes one's half-liter. Not doing so is a sign that the beer is bad, has gotten warm, or perhaps that the glass was not properly rinsed, and some leftover soap has affected the taste of the beer. Mixing beers is also an unexpectedly egregious faux pas. Beer should not be diluted with anything else (as is the case with the German concoction, the *Radler,* beer mixed with Sprite), nor under any circumstances should the remnants of one beer be poured into another. An exception to the no-mix rule is the *rezané pivo,* literally "cut" beer, a 50/50 mixture of light and dark beer. This is not the same as the black and tan where one type of beer floats atop the other. Rather, the beers are blended together to produce a slightly sweeter drink.

Although the Czechs are the leaders in beer production and consumption, Slovaks produce several quality beers as well, all in the pilsner style. Slovaks were home brewing as early as the eleventh century, but the government soon saw the profit to be made in beer and banned home brewing altogether, replacing it with officially licensed breweries that soon turned into monopolies. Forbidden from brewing their own beer, the peasantry took to distilling plum brandy—slivovice/slivovica—which is now the national drink (see section on Wine and Liquor below). Beer production remained strong, however, and the product was primarily intended for city dwellers. In 1842

Pilsner Urquell developed its signature beer, and the style spread throughout the Slovak lands.

WINE AND LIQUOR

Whereas the Czechs are a nation of beer drinkers, Slovaks are more partial to wine. Both republics produce some decent varieties, but 40 years of Communism did much to hinder the development of world-class wine. Only in the last decade or so has there been a resurgence of interest in quality wine. Until recently, it was assumed that the Romans introduced wine to the Czech and Slovak lands, but in the 1950s archeologists uncovered evidence that the Celts—who settled the region several hundred years before the Romans— grew vines and produced wine. In general, Czech and Slovak wines are sharp and strong. Only now are more delicate, less acidic wines being produced. The whites are the best since climactic conditions are much more suited for white varieties, which take up around 70 percent of all vineyards. Because Bohemia is the coldest region, it has the fewest vineyards, about 400 ha. (988 acres) north of Prague; Moravia is second, but most grapes are grown in Slovakia, about 26,000 ha. (64,247 acres)—two-thirds of former Czechoslovakia's vineyards. Grape varieties are similar to those in neighboring Austria, Germany, and Hungary. The most common are Silvánské zelené, Veltlínské zelené, Rizlink Rýnský, and Rizlink Vlašský. The most commonly produced wine in the Czech Republic is Müller-Thurgau. The most common red varieties are Frankovka and Vavřinecké or Stavovavřineecké.

Unlike beer, there is no social ban on diluting your wine. The wine spritzer, *střík*, a 50/50 mix of soda and white wine, is a popular summertime drink, as is the *houba*, literally "mushroom," a peculiar potion composed of red wine and cola. During the winter, Czechs and Slovaks drink a lot of mulled wine *(svařené víno/ varené víno)*, and fall brings out *burčák*, the fermented juice of the first grapes, which is sold on every street corner. It is sweeter and lower in alcohol than most wine, but the taste can be deceptive: it is still wine, and the morning after will prove it.

Besides beer and wine, Czechs and Slovaks enjoy stronger alcoholic beverages as well. The Czechs are proud of their Becherovka, an herbal liqueur in the same family as Jägermeister but much smoother and heavier on the cloves. It was invented by a visiting Englishman in the spa town of Karlovy Vary, and the recipe was entrusted to Jan Becher. It has always been kept a secret. At one point the only two people who knew it had to travel in separate cars lest they both perish in an accident and the recipe be lost forever. Cloves, chamomile, and cinnamon can be detected by most people, and more spices by the discerning drinker. Becherovka was originally intended as a theraputant, and indeed Czechs employ it liberally to thwart looming colds and impending ailments. They also like a dram in the morning to face the day. Fernet is a bitter herbal spirit introduced by the Italians in 1927 (in Italy it is known as Fernet Branca). It too is said to possess therapeutic qualities such as purifying the blood and improving the nervous system. It is often mixed with tonic to create a drink called a *bavorák* or Bavarian.

Slivovica is the Slovak national firewater and home remedy, a fiery plum brandy well suited to the Slovaks' more fiery temperament. The slivovica served in bars is more fiery than fruity, however, and the home-distilled, fruitier libation (which is very common) is well worth the accompanying burning throat and watery eyes. Plums (or other fruit) are gathered, stored, and left to rot for a few weeks; then the mush is boiled and distilled. Some like to bury the result for several years and thereby strengthen the taste. Slivovica is drunk in a single shot *(na ex)* and is a common libation employed when welcoming friends or on any celebratory occasion.

Absinthe is another popular spirit among the more stouthearted drinkers. Traditionally it is made from wormwood and hence hallucinogenic (it still is in some western European countries). Czech and Slovak absinthe, however, is merely flavored with wormwood oil and is simply tremendously alcoholic (75%), strong enough to make you hallucinate. Original non-Czech absinthe had a chemical structure similar to cannabis, which resulted in its hallucinatory properties. The Greeks and Romans had a version of absinthe, but it wasn't until 1792, when a Swiss doctor began to market the beverage, that it became popular in Europe. The proper way to drink absinthe is to soak a cube of sugar in it and then light it on fire. After the sugar has melted, stir it in the glass and drink the absinthe in one gulp.

Although landlocked, the Czechs and Slovaks also consume a good amount of rum, which is distilled from sugar beets rather than cane and thus has a much different, sweeter flavor. The European Union, however, has declared that Czech and Slovak rum is not, according to their rules, genuine rum and cannot be sold as such. In response, the Czechs have simply dropped the "r" from the label and now sell their product as "Um." Josef Švejk would be proud (see the chapter on literature in the volume).

FASHION

Traditional Costume

For much of their history, the majority of Czechs and Slovaks were peasants who wore clothing made in their own villages out of homemade woven cloth. Traditional dress was influenced to a great extent by geography, climate, and economic status. In lowland areas, clothing was loose-fitting and made of flax or hempen linen. In the mountainous regions, clothing fit more snugly around the body, and wool and fur were used along with linen. With the rise of textile mills in the nineteenth century, cotton, wool, and even silk began to be used along with brighter colors. Several dozen different styles of national costume existed up until the middle of the nineteenth century in Bohemia, and over twenty-eight in Moravia and Slovakia. The traditional Chodsko costume in western Bohemia consisted of a long, colored skirt and a white bonnet embroidered with black for women and a long white coat for men. The women of Plzeň, also in western Bohemia, added a white bonnet with big wings.

The women of Haná in Moravia wore a broad white skirt, a white collar, and a white scarf on their heads. Men wore a white coat with collar. In Moravian Slovakia, women wore short skirts with wide, ample sleeves, and the men sported narrow blue or red trousers and white shirts with embroidered sleeves. Those of the White Carpathian mountains on the border between today's Czech and Slovak Republics added woolen stockings and felt slippers. All these folk costumes and more can be seen in various ethnographic museums throughout both countries.

In the twentieth century during the First Czechoslovak Republic, folk dress vanished from the cities but was still common in outlying villages. Under Communism, however, the government encouraged folk celebrations, and folk costumes assumed a new social function, that of fostering national and community identity. Czech and Slovak singers donned their national costumes proudly in manifold celebrations throughout Czechoslovakia.

Modern Clothing

During the First Republic (1918–1938), there was an efflorescence of Czechoslovak fashion and tailoring. Fashion houses were set up with clientele both at home and abroad. Fashion in the capitals resembled that of Western Europe, especially nearby Germany and Austria. One Czech specificity, however, was Bat'a shoes. Tomáš Bat'a established the Bat'a Shoe Organization on August 24, 1894 in Zlín, Czechoslovakia: it was one of the first modern-day shoe manufacturers. Bat'a shoes were of excellent quality, and by the 1920s, the company had branches in Poland, Yugoslavia, Holland, Denmark, Great Britain, and the United States. By the early 1930s, they were the world's leading footwear exporters.

After World War II and establishment of the Communist regime, the government sought a distinctive type of socialist fashion that would set the Czechoslovaks apart from the bourgeois capitalist world, and fashion came under strict ideological control. Fashion advertising promoted Communist work ideals. In fact, Klement Gottwald, the first Communist president, attended fashion shows to ensure fashion adhered to party guidelines. Those who wished for a different type of fashion had to make their own clothing themselves or purchase items on the rare trip to the West. Young people went to great lengths to buy western name brands such as Levi-Strauss, and the Czechoslovak government mass produced generic versions of Western fashion goods, but they were of much lower quality. In 1950, the Italian brothers Fratini decided to challenge Levi-Strauss' monopoly on jeans, and they began exporting their own brand, Rifle. Rifle conquered the East Bloc market, and even today Czechs and Slovaks often refer to any type of jeans as *rifle*, pronounced "ree-fleh." Young women interested in fashion would stand in line all night to get their hands on a fashion magazine, which were sold once a month, and then would make their own clothing.

Today, Czechs and Slovaks dress much like Americans and Western Europeans. At work, Czechs and Slovaks dress more formally than Americans, although the American casual look is gradually making inroads, especially among the younger set. The Czechs currently have the highest GDP in Central and Eastern Europe, and a young, upwardly mobile middle class is emerging with a large disposable income and a partiality to foreign-made clothing. High-end foreign clothing shops are well represented in Prague: Hugo Boss, Versace, Dolce & Gabbana, Emanuel Ungaro, Calvin Klein, Kenzo, and others have branches there. Some local manufacturers of Czech clothing exist, but they are not up to the design standards of Western products. TESCO, a British company, is the largest clothing retailer in the Czech Republic and Slovakia. It is a typical Western-style department store, but the company plans to take its clothing more up-market.

Bratislava, the capital of Slovakia, is not the clothing Mecca that Prague is, and fashion-conscious Slovaks often journey to the Czech capital or to Vienna for their high-end clothing needs.

Several local fashion designers work in Prague but are not known abroad. They are establishing a fashion center just off the town square. Upon the narrow, cobblestone streets of Dlouhá and Dušní Streets, young designers such as Tatiana Kovařiková, Klára Nademlýnská, and Timour et group have set up several fashion boutiques among the upscale cafes and restaurants, creating a small trendsetting oasis of fashion away from the beer-swilling tourist bustle of the city center.

The first Prague Fashion Week took place in March of 2004, showcasing work of both Czech and foreign designers. The overwhelming attendance demonstrated the avid interest in fashion, but—although dozens of Czech and Slovak fashion models are working abroad—Czech and Slovak fashion designers have not yet succeeded in making it big outside of their respective countries.

Notes

1. Pavel Eisner, *Chram i tvrz: Kniha o češtině,* 2 vols. (Zurich: Konfrontation Velag, 1974), vol. I, 289.
2. Václav Havel, October, 1995.
3. Michael Y. Park, http://www.foxnews.com/story/0,2933,155403,00.html.
4. Radio Praha, July 28, 2005, http://www.radio.cz/en/article/69013.
5. Eisner, *Chram i tvrz,* vol. I, 289–90.
6. *The Bartered Bride,* Act II, Scene I.
7. Bohumil Hrabal, "Morytát o prasecích hodech," in *Morytáty a legendy* (Prague: Mladá fronta, 2000), 32. Orginally published in 1968.
8. Derek Sayer, *The Coasts of Bohemia* (Princeton: Princeton University Press, 1998), 42.
9. Radko Pytlík, *Ve stínu pípy* (Prague: Emporius, 1996), 26.
10. Jan Neruda "Rudolf Pokorný," *Podobizny III,* Vol. 31 of *Spisy Jana Nerudy,* ed. Miloslav Novotný (Prague: SNKLHU, 1954), 238.
11. Timothy M. Hall, "*Pivo* and *Pohoda:* The Social Conditions and Symbolism of Czech Beer-Drinking," *Anthropology of East Europe Review* 21, no. 1, http://condor.depaul.edu/~rrotenbe/aeer/V21n1/Hall.pdf.

Selected Bibliography

Hall, Timothy M. "*Pivo* and *Pohoda:* The Social Conditions and Symbolism of Czech Beer-Drinking." *Anthropology of East Europe Review* 21, no. 1, http://condor.depaul.edu/~rrotenbe/aeer/V21n1/Hall.pdf.

Foulkes, Christopher, ed. *Larouse Encyclopedia of Wine,* trans. Alison Hughes. New York: Larousse, 2001.

Jackson, Michael. *Michael Jackson's Beer Companion.* Philadelphia: Running Press, 1993.

Muir, Angelina. "The Czech Republic and Slovakia." In *Oxford Companion to Wine,* ed. Jancis Robinson. New York: Oxford University Press, 1999.

Starci na chmelu. Directed by Ladislav Rychman. 1964.

Uchvalová, Eva. *Czech Fashion for Salon and Promenade.* Prague: Olympia, 1999.

Weiner, Michael A. *The Taster's Guide to Beer: Brews and Breweries of the World.* New York: Macmillan Publishing, 1977.

Web Sites

Fox News: http://www.foxnews.com.
Radio Praha: http://www.radio.cz.

6

Literature

Poets and artists in general meditate on life and its problems no less than philosophers, and they are more concrete.

—Tomáš Masaryk[1]

IF THERE IS ONE THING that characterizes Czech literature, it is humor. But this is not to be confused with optimism or cheerfulness. Because of their geographical position at the crossroads of Europe beneath the successive empires of Hapsburgs, Nazis, and Soviets, the Czechs have developed an oddly unsentimental, dark, yet humorous view of the world, which is reflected in their literature of the twentieth century. The stories of Jaroslav Hašek, Bohumil Hrabal, and even Milan Kundera, to take three of the most renowned Czech authors, abound with characters and situations, which walk the line between the realistic and the grotesque. Furthermore, the Czechs have not developed much of an epic tradition or cultivated epic heroes. The smaller forms, such as the short story and the novella, dominate Czech literature, and Czech heroes—with several exceptions and qualifications—can be characterized as heroes of the everyday and the ordinary. Slovak literature has an independent history and will be considered separately. It is not as well known in the United States, nor as widely translated as Czech literature, perhaps because the most significant works of Slovak letters are in poetry rather than prose, which always has a more difficult time finding an audience in translation. This survey of Czech and Slovak literature begins in the distant past but will concentrate on the most recent works in the twentieth and twenty-first centuries.

THE PAST

Czech literature commences in the ninth century when Prince Rostislav of Great Moravia invites the brothers Cyril and Methodius from Byzantium to introduce Christianity to his kingdom. Before the journey, Cyril invented an alphabet called Glagolitic to be used for the Slavic language. At the time, all Slavic languages were mutually comprehensible, and we now refer to the language of this period as Old Slavic or Old Slavonic. Consequently, the first written work of Old Slavic was probably a translation of the Bible. Other works such as legends and saints' lives soon followed, but these were composed using the Cyrillic alphabet, created by Cyril's followers. Finally, Latin was introduced in the Czech lands as the language of the church at the end of the eleventh century, and Cyrillic fell out of use.

Until the end of the thirteenth century, most writing in Bohemia and Moravia was in Latin or German. King Charles IV (reigned 1346–1378) encouraged writing in both languages, and Czech and German literatures flourished in the fourteenth century. Jan Hus set about reforming Czech orthography in the fifteenth century and introduced diacritical marks above certain letters. Hus' church reformation activity also initiated a great deal of religious writing in the Czech vernacular. By the seventeenth century, Czech literature could boast of a host of prose and poetic works from the religious to the burlesque. In 1620, however, with the Czech defeat by the Hapsburgs at the Battle of White Mountain, Czech literature entered a period of decline. Bohemia was ravaged and its population decimated by executions and emigration. Culture naturally deteriorated as well. The nobility were Germanized, and the destitute bourgeoisie showed little interest in literary culture or intellectual life in general. The German language replaced Czech in all official capacities including almost all genres of literature. Czech literary production became nearly the exclusive concern of the clergy, and the greatest literary creation of the Czech Baroque period was the hymn.

The official Hapsburg policy of Germanization and the Counter-Reformation avalanche of Latin and German literature obliterated any sense of cultural continuity with pre-1620 Czech literature. By the end of the eighteenth century, there was little hope that the Czech literary language and literary culture would recover from this Teutonic onslaught. The Czech language had not died out, but it had retreated to the countryside and the kitchen to become the patios of peasants, cooks, and servants.

THE NATIONAL REVIVAL

As discussed in Chapter 1 of this volume ("Land, People, History"), toward the end of the eighteenth century in Bohemia, a group of Czech intellectuals (who wrote and spoke in German) seized upon ideas of German nationalism and initiated the so-called National Revival. Only a part of the nobility lent its support to this movement. The revivalists joined forces to recreate the Czech literary language and combine it with the current Czech spoken by servants and peasants. The goal was to undo the consequences of the defeat at White Mountain, so they studied ancient Czech literature and history in an attempt to gain greater literary and patriotic awareness. The Revival continued throughout the nineteenth century, and over this period Czech writers attempted to put this newly created Czech language into poetic use, that is, employing it to create literary works that could stand side by side with other national literatures, and which would literally instruct the population of Bohemia and Moravia in this new Czech language.

One of the earliest literary genres cultivated during this period was the folktale. Czech intellectuals went out to the countryside and collected, transcribed, and reworked folktales and folksongs, which had remained beyond the reach of the official Austrian policy of Germanization. Karel Jaromír Erben (1811–1870) and Božena Němcová (c. 1820–1862) were two of the great folktale collectors of the nineteenth century. Although they worked independently, Erben and Němcová hold a comparable significance for Czech literature as the brothers Grimm do for German. They collected thousands of folktales and songs, which they published either without modifications or stylized significantly. In general, what distinguishes Czech, and even Slovak, folklore from that of other national traditions is the amount of trickery and roguery involved. Historically, both peoples have been repeatedly dominated by foreign rulers, and their folklore is replete with ordinary Czechs and Slovaks outsmarting kings, giants, and wizards.

The great figure of nineteenth-century Czech poetry was Karel Hynek Mácha (1810–1836), the first (and only) Czech Romantic poet. His masterpiece, the lyrical epic poem *May* (1836), broke away from the folk poetry of Mácha's contemporaries who were preoccupied with celebrating the glories, genuine or invented, of the Czech nation. He was ignored in his time. *May* is a Byronic existential poem of parricide and romantic betrayal, in which Mácha demonstrates the iambic potential of Czech verse. Mácha's poetry had scant influence until the twentieth century when his legacy comes alive, most notably in the work of Vítěslav Nezval (1900–1958) and Jaroslav Seifert (1901–1986). The latter won the Nobel Prize for Literature in 1984.

Poetry made great strides in the course of the nineteenth century, but prose lagged somewhat behind. The Realistic novels of Russia and the West—Tolstoy, Flaubert, Balzac—had little effect on the Czechs until the turn of the century. Czech prose writers were mired in Biedermeyer idylls of noble peasant life. The most acclaimed Czech novel of the nineteenth century is Božena Němcová's uneventful *The Grandmother* (1855), which covers a year in the life of the eponymous heroine. The novel is a near catalogue of folk customs and traditions, and the title character herself is folk wisdom incarnate. Many of her phrases have become Czech proverbs.

The other great nineteenth-century prose writer is the Prague native Jan Neruda (1834–1891). As a lifetime journalist, Neruda worked within the genre of the feuilleton, and his most recognized work, *Tales from the Little Quarter* (1878), is an outgrowth of his reportage. Neruda populates his stories with typical Prague denizens going about their workaday life, and illuminates them with gentle sympathetic humor and irony. His characters come alive for the reader, and the author is able to elicit sympathy for all his characters no matter how foolish or petty. The Chilean Nobel Prize winning poet Pablo Neruda took his pen name from the Czech author.

Alois Jirásek (1851–1930) is the Czechs' most renowned nationalistic novelist. His dozens of historical novels created one version of the Czechs' cultural image of themselves. Jirásek's *Old Czech Legends* (1894) introduced the nation to legendary figures of Czech mythology such as Libuše, Přemysl, and Šárka, which had been described in Kosmas' twelfth-century chronicle. He romanticized and popularized the Hussite warriors Jan Žižka and Prokop Holý in *Against All* (1893), and spread the notion of a time of *Darkness* (1913) after the defeat at White Mountain.

LITERATURE OF THE FIRST REPUBLIC

From 1918 to 1938 is considered one of the peaks of Czech literature, often referred to as its Golden Age. To a great extent, the literature of the nineteenth century was a literature of translation, both literal and figurative. Not only did Czechs translate foreign works into Czech, they also imitated and borrowed foreign literary models (and they were usually 50 years behind the times). The period of the First Republic is the climax of the National Revival attempts to revive the Czech language, literature, and culture. Now literature no longer had to educate the people, nor did it act as a replacement for an undeveloped cultural life. The Czechs now had their own state, and literature did not have any patriotic service to perform. In the nineteenth century, the Czechs employed Czech literature as a substitute or replacement for politics and public life. They were still under the Hapsburgs, and Czech literature was often used as a tool to encourage Czech nationalism. But after 1918, Czech literature comes into its own.

Jaroslav Hašek (1883–1923)

Until Milan Kundera, Jaroslav Hašek was the most recognized and widely translated Czech author in the world. He wrote over 1,200 comical short stories and sketches, and his masterpiece, *The Good Soldier Švejk and His*

Fortunes in the World War (1921–1923) has been translated into dozens of languages and been the subject of several theater and film adaptations. The character of the good soldier himself, to the dismay of many Czech intellectuals, has come to represent the modest revolt of the ordinary Czech against external foreign domination.

Hašek was a drinker, vagrant, alcoholic, and anarchist, and his creative works batter and belittle the Austrian monarchy, religion, patriotism, small-minded bourgeois attitudes, and just about everything and everybody but the downtrodden. Yet unlike other Czech authors who similarly lambasted the Austro-Hungarian Empire, Hašek was no champion of "Czechness" or "Slavdom" either. As an Austrian soldier, Hašek defected to Russia during the war and became a Communist for a significant time, but he ultimately had no patience with ideologies of any kind. In Prague Hašek was known as a writer, but he was more famous as a figure in pubs where he drank beer (35 pints of pilsner a day, by his own admission), performed in cabarets or dinner theater, or simply regaled the clientele with his celebrated improvisations. It was also in a pub where he founded a political party, The Party of Moderate Progress Within the Bounds of the Law, which parodied the rhetorical bombast of Austro-Hungarian political life.

Hašek's most important work is *The Good Soldier Švejk,* a sprawling novel of a soldier's experiences in the Austro-Hungarian army, which begins with the assassination of Archduke Franz Ferdinand, the immediate cause of World War I. The title character "volunteers," in the way only a Czech army reservist could volunteer under the monarchy, for military service, and the novel follows him and his exploits through the war. Švejk, like most Czechs, and like Hašek himself, had no desire to fight for his Austro-Hungarian overlords, and he makes his way through the war with cleverly feigned stupidity and mock displays of inappropriately timed patriotic outbursts, all of which drive his superiors insane and lay bare the absurdities of war, patriotism, religion, and the monarchy. The novel itself is a picaresque conglomeration of tales unified by the title character and his endless stream of anecdotes, which often shock due to their combination of absurdity and earthy humor. For example, one passage reads:

> I remember once a woman was sentenced for strangling her newly-born twins. Although she swore on oath that she couldn't have strangled twins, when she'd given birth to only one little girl, which she had succeeded in strangling quite painlessly, she was sentenced for double murder all the same.[2]

Švejk has an inexhaustible number of these stories, which he employs to befuddle and benumb his superiors. The author and his friends first published and sold the novel themselves in cheap notebook editions since booksellers refused to carry it. One publisher called the book "literature for communists, not Czechs!" The first to appreciate its literary merits was the Czech writer Ivan Olbracht (1882–1952) and Kafka's friend, the Prague German writer Max Brod (1884–1968). Olbracht suggested that the character of Josef Švejk represented a new literary type, comparable to Don Quixote, Hamlet, and Faust. According to Max Brod, Švejk was a character that "emerged from the darkest depths of the soul of the people … it not only expresses something ineffable in the Czech people, but corresponds to something in the most secret depths of mankind."[3] It was due to the efforts of Brod that *The Good Soldier Švejk* became known in the German speaking lands and thereafter the rest of the world.

Today, *The Good Soldier Švejk*, beside the works of Karel Čapek and Milan Kundera, belongs to those few Czech works that have entered world literature, and the characters of the undercover police officer Brettschneider, the innkeeper Palivec, the drunken Catholic priest Otto Katz, and Švejk's superior Lietenant Lukáš have entered Czech cultural tradition. Furthermore, Hašek's way of writing began a style called the Pub Story, which was continued by Karel Čapek and Bohumil Hrabal. Finally, and to the dismay of many Czech intellectuals, the term *švejkism,* which designates a combination of feigned idiocy and artful cunning, is often applied wholesale to the Czechs as a nation.

Franz Kafka (1883–1924)

Franz Kafka was almost an exact contemporary of Hašek and likewise a Prague native, but he wrote in German rather than Czech. As the famous, though surely apocryphal, story has it, Kafka and Hašek drank at the same Prague pub, Kafka his coffee upstairs and Hašek his beer downstairs, one writing in German, the other in Czech, both knowing both languages and greeting one another on the stairs. But does Kafka's work belong to Czech or German literature? Ask a Czech and a German, and you're certain to get two different answers.

Kafka spoke both Czech and German from birth, but because his father Hermann thought it best that his offspring (Franz had three sisters, who all later perished in Nazi concentration camps) be raised to speak the language of the monarchy, he took care that his children received an exclusively German education. Prague's Charles University was at the time divided into Czech and German halves. Prague itself at the turn of the century was known as the City of Three Peoples—Czechs, Germans, and Jews. Ninety-five percent of the inhabitants were Czech speakers, but the center, where Kafka worked and lived, was nearly entirely German. Thus, Kafka's German milieu was literally surrounded by a sea of Czechs, and unlike many German speakers in Prague, Kafka sought contact with the Czech population. Of the Czech language, he once told his friend Milena Jesenská that he felt the Czech language was "warmer" *(herzlicher)* than German and that from the beginning it seemed to strengthen the barrier between himself and his mother.[4]

Certainly we can say without hesitation that Kafka was a *Prague* writer. He noted famously to a friend, "Prague doesn't let go. This little mother has claws…. One has to give in or else." Even though Kafka doesn't mention the city in his fiction, his stories and novels are permeated with the Baroque atmosphere of Prague.

During his lifetime, Kafka's writings were known only to a small circle of his friends. He published a mere handful of short stories, among them "The Judgment" (1913), "The Metamorphosis" (1915), and "In the Penal Colony" (1919), which today stand as classics. These along with his posthumously published novels, *The Trial* (1914–1915), *The Castle* (1926), and *America* (1927), have solidified Kafka's reputation as the first twentieth-century Existentialist and the most prescient portrayer of the state that has come to be called "the alienation of modern man." Kafka's writings combine absurd dream-like situations, detailed psychological exploration, and a very powerful sense of unexplained guilt. Gregor Samsa of "The Metamorphosis" awakes one morning to find himself transformed into a bug; Josef K. of *The Trial* is suddenly arrested "without having done anything truly wrong" and is executed without ever discovering his crime or his accusers; and the land surveyor K. spends over 400 pages unsuccessfully seeking entrance to the eponymous *Castle*. All of Kafka's works are pervaded with a sense of impotence and bootless struggle against a faceless higher power.

Karel Čapek (1890–1938)

Karel Čapek is the writer most associated with the First Republic and is best known in the West for his Robots and Newts. In 1921 his scientific drama *R.U.R.* introduced the word "robot" to the world, actually coined by his brother Josef. Then, 15 years later, on the brink of World War II, his dystopian novelistic satire *War with the Newts* (1936) warned of runaway technology and militarism. Besides these two works, however, few Westerners are aware that Čapek was a prolific and versatile novelist, short story writer, dramatist, travel writer, poet, and even the biographer of Czechoslovakia's first president Tomáš Masaryk.

Čapek studied philosophy at Charles University as well as attended lectures on art and aesthetics. In 1915, he defended his doctoral dissertation entitled *Objective Methods in Aesthetics*. It was a long article he composed on American Pragmatism, however, that seems to have most influenced his later writing and thinking. After a brief stint as a tutor, Čapek assumed the post on the editorial board of the Prague daily *Národní listy* and remained a journalist for the rest of his life. Čapek began writing short fiction with his brother Josef. His first independent work is a collection of short stories, *Wayside Crosses* (1917), which consider epistemological and metaphysical questions and usually hinge on an inexplicable mystery such as a solitary footprint. As he was working on these stories, Čapek published his own translations of French avant-garde poetry including poems by Apollinaire and Baudelaire. The impact on post-war avant-garde Czech poets such as Jaroslav Seifert and Víteslav Nezval was immense.

In 1921 Čapek achieved worldwide fame with his drama *R.U.R.* (written in 1920). The play presents artificial beings used as slaves, who ultimately revolt against their masters. The play was immediately translated and performed in dozens of languages throughout the world, and it introduced the world not only to Čapek but to Czech literature as well. Other dystopian works soon followed, such as the scientific fantasy novels *Factory for the Absolute* (1922) and *Krakatit* (1924). Čapek's drama *The Makropulos Affair* (1922) considers the effect of an elixir of life and inspired Leoš Janáček's opera of the same name in 1926.

In the 1920s Čapek also published several lighter works more in line with his journalistic vocation, volumes on gardening, everyday objects around us, and even words. Each of his trips abroad resulted in a book—*Letters from Italy* (1923), *Letters from England* (1924), *Letters from Spain* (1930). All were well received. Čapek also delved into the detective genre with *Tales from One Pocket* and *Tales from the Other Pocket,* both published in 1929 and then collected in *Tales from Two Pockets* (1932).

When Czechoslovakia achieved its independence following World War I, Čapek was heavily involved in its cultural and public life, and his career is intimately linked to the First Czechoslovak Republic. Čapek's friendship with President Masaryk was close, and from 1928 to 1935, he published three biographical volumes of the president. Also in the 1930s, during Hitler's rise to power, Čapek wrote a series of essays critical of fascism and communism, and expounded the public duty of intellectuals to resist these extreme ideological positions. It was at this time that Čapek's creative work reached its zenith with his trilogy of novels *Hordubal* (1933), *Meteor* (1934), and *An Ordinary Life* (1934), investigations into epistemology and identity. As Hitler's power grew next door in Germany, Čapek's warnings against war and the nature of totalitarian power continued with his novel *War with the Newts* (1936) and the dramas *The White Plague* (1937) and *The Mother* (1938). A group of French writers repeatedly asked the Nobel committee to award the prize for literature to Čapek, but the Swedes refused for fear of offending neighboring Nazi Germany. When the committee asked Čapek to write something that would offend no one, he replied, "I've already written my doctoral dissertation." Čapek died on Christmas Day, 1938, shortly after the Western powers' appeasement of Hitler with the Munich Agreement, which ceded the Czechoslovak border regions to Germany, and shortly before Hitler's invasion and dismemberment of the country.

The literature of the first part of the twentieth century is not limited to these three giants, but they tend to overshadow the numerous other writers, especially in the Anglophone world. There were many others, for example Vladislav Vančura (1891–1942), who introduced a peculiar archaic language and style into modern Czech literature, which tended in the opposite direction of Čapek's. Whereas Čapek's writing gravitated toward the spoken idiom and concrete expression, Vančura's was complex and stylized; it abounded in metaphor and figurative language, recalling the language of a sixteenth-century Czech translation of the Bible called the Kralice Bible. Ivan Olbracht (1882–1952)—mentioned above with regard to Kafka—was a journalist and novelist who put his robust narrative abilities in the service of the proletariat. Despite Olbracht's left leaning, collectivist political orientation, his narrative talents tended toward the Romantic, isolated individual—the outcast as hero. And in his Ruthenian stories, Olbracht shows a particular affinity for those small peasant communities walled off from the rest of the world. The stories lament a lost time and a primeval natural landscape and people untouched by civilization. His masterpiece *Nikola Šuhaj the Robber* (1933) is a lyrical prose ballad singing the exploits of a sub-Capathian Robin Hood character who represents Natural Man.

THE GERMAN OCCUPATION (1938–1945)

During World War II, cultural life for the most part went on relatively undisturbed, but little of note was created in the realm of literature. The Nazis forbade experimental prose, and many writers, such as Vančura, focused on historical subjects, which were intended to address contemporary issues. Václav Řezáč broke new ground in the psychological novel. Works such as *Dark Corner* (1940) and *When the Mirror Breaks* (1944) penetrate and examine the psyche of nearly psychotic characters against the background of a morally bereft society.

THE PRAGUE SPRING AND BEYOND

After the war and upon the 1948 Communist takeover, many authors expressed their support for the regime and its concomitant aesthetic program of Socialist Realism, which prescribed the "optimistic depiction of socialist society in conventionally realistic terms." Socialist Realism glorified the political and social ideals of Communism. Modernism and experimentation were forbidden. Art had to be simply understood by everyone, and it had to demonstrate the victory of the working class over the evils of capitalism. This artistic ideology had been proclaimed compulsory in the Soviet Union in 1932 and in the Czech lands in 1948. Socialist Realism gave rise to little that was artistically valuable, and writers who did not conform were at best not published or at worst imprisoned. Many writers found safety in children's writing or even science fiction, a much more respected genre in the Eastern Bloc than the West.

Nikita Khrushchev's 1956 denunciation of Stalinism at the Twentieth Party Congress of the Soviet Union initiated a cultural thaw throughout the Soviet Bloc—but not in Czechoslovakia, where show trials were still in full swing. Finally, toward the end of the 1950s and the beginning of the 1960s, the tough ideological character of the regime relaxed, censorship was eased, and a great cultural awakening began, culminating in the 1968 Prague Spring. Censorship was abolished, and art flourished as never before. The literary production of the early 1960s is notable for its spirit of critical self-reflection, a coming to terms with the past, and a renewal of ties with the artistic production of the West. For the generation that came of age in the 1960s, the question was not simply whether to be for socialism or against it. The issues were larger and involved problems of political, ideological, and individual freedom. This creative effervescence, unfortunately and sadly, however, was cut short by the Soviet clampdown in August of that year. Many artists went underground, fled abroad, or adapted their writing to the renewed artistic restrictions.

Josef Škvorecký (b. 1924)

Josef Škvorecký was one of the first authors to cast a critical and reevaluative eye on the immediate Czech past. His first novel *The Cowards* (written just after the war but not published until 1958) signaled the beginning of the Thaw in Czechoslovakia. The protagonist and narrator of *The Cowards* is the twenty-year-old sex and jazz obsessed Danny Smiřický. He provides an account of the May 1945 uprising against the Germans far different from the official hagiographic version. The cowards of the title are all Czechs who are more interested in jazz and girls than rising up against their occupiers, who are in retreat anyway. Danny himself is downright cynical in his disregard for heroism, Communism, religion, or ideology of any kind. The novel was wildly popular, not least of all because of the author's slangy and scatological Hemingway influenced dialogue (Škvorecký had translated *A Farewell to Arms*). The novel was critically controversial, however, and was shortly pulled from bookstores. The time was not yet ripe for openness.

Škvorecký emigrated to Canada upon the renewal of hard-line Communism at the end of 1968. He taught literature at the University of Toronto and with his wife Zdena Salivarová established Sixty-Eight Publishers, a publishing house devoted to Czech exile and underground writers. It was Sixty-Eight Publishers that kept alive the writings of Milan Kundera, Ivan Klíma, and Škvorecký himself, all of whose works were unpublishable in Czechoslovakia. Škvorecký was quite prolific in exile, producing novels, short stories, dramas, and essays. His two most significant works in the novel genre are *The Miracle Game* (1972) and *The Engineer of Human Souls* (1977), both of which feature as the protagonist the author's alter ego Danny Smiřický.

The Miracle Game is a detective novel of sorts which begins in 1949 in which a parish priest is accused by the Communist authorities of fabricating a miracle in his own church. A statue of the Virgin Mary is made to move seemingly of its own accord, and the priest is arrested and ultimately dies during interrogation. In 1968 it comes to light that the police themselves produced the miracle, but in the end little is clear, and the author uses the event to draw parallels between the Communist interventions of 1948 and 1968. In *The Engineer of Human Souls* (1977) Danny, like Škvorecký himself, is now teaching literature at a university in Canada. The title refers to Stalin's famous designation of the role of writers in society, and the book abounds in literary references. Like *The Miracle Game,* the book shifts back and forth between two time periods—here, Czechoslovakia under German domination during World War II and Canada under democracy. The juxtaposition of two different ways of life gives rise to a host of misunderstandings, both disturbing and comedic.

Bohumil Hrabal (1914–1997)

When Bohumil Hrabal's books hit Czech bookstores in the mid-1960s, the author became an overnight sensation, and readers stood in line for each of his publications. His artistic method was a continuation Hašek's "pub tale," but Hrabal elaborated upon it by placing vulgarity side by side with extended poetic metaphors to create his own brand of graphic Surrealism—what he calls "Total Realism." According to Hrabal "a proper book is not one that allows a reader to sleep better, but one that makes him jump out of bed, run straight to the author in his long-johns, and punch him in the mouth."

Hrabal graduated from Charles University with a law degree but never practiced law. He grew up the son of a brewery owner, and his lifelong dream was to work in his father's brewery. When his father's business was nationalized in 1948, however, Hrabal fled to Prague, where he held a series of white- and blue-collar occupations: he was a toy salesman, a smelter, a waste paper compactor, a railway dispatcher—and all of his various jobs brought him into contact with people who would eventually populate his fiction. The novel *Closely Watched Trains* (1965) takes place at a small-town railway station during World War II, and the youthful hero Miloš Hrma (whose name translates as *mons veneris*) tries both to lose his virginity and destroy a German weapons transport. In both he succeeds. The director Jiří Menzel in collaboration with the author made the book into a movie, which won the Academy Award in 1967 for best foreign language film.

After 1968 the regime banned Hrabal's books, and existing editions of his works along with essays and interviews were pulped, but the author continued to publish underground. *I Served the King of England* (1971) also takes place during World War II and recounts the rise and fall of a dishonest waiter obsessed with money. Yet the hero is not a negative one, for he discovers "with money it is possible to buy not just a beautiful girl, but poetry too."[5] The book is filled with paradoxes and reversals, poetry and existentialist meanderings, which accompany the hero from his beginnings as a crooked hot-dog vendor to his end as a solitary philosopher. Of his novel *Too Loud a Solitude* (1977), Hrabal said, "I lived so that I could create this work; for it, I put off death."[6] The hero Haňťa works as a paper and book compactor, and over the years he has read an enormous number of books and become, as he says, educated against his will. He is the typical Czech barroom philosopher. Not much happens by way of action. The inefficient Haňťa, who spends rather a large amount of time reading, drinking beer, and decorating his bales of paper with reproductions of famous paintings, is to be transferred to work with an enormous modern hydraulic press where the work is efficient and impersonal. But rather than succumb to the modern world, Haňťa commits suicide by climbing into his press. In part, the book can be read politically—it was written at a time of censorship—but primarily it is a celebration of the life of culture over philistinism.

Milan Kundera (b. 1929)

Milan Kundera is the most famed and widely read Czech author outside of the Czech lands. With his novels *The Book of Laughter and Forgetting* (1981) and *The Unbearable Lightness of Being* (1985), he put Czech literature on the map of world literature. His reputation at home, however, is far

Presidents Bill Clinton and Václav Havel enjoy a beer and a laugh with Czech writer Bohumil Hrabal at the Golden Tiger Pub in Prague. © Corbis.

from unproblematic. Kundera began as a procommunist poet, the author of three collections of verse he refuses to have republished or translated, asserting the right of the author to exclude what he calls "immature" works from his *oeuvre*. According to Kundera he first "found himself" as an author in 1958 when working on a short story "I, the Mournful God," which, however, never made it into the definitive edition of his short-story collection *Laughable Loves* (1970). It is here that he discovered the art of irony, which seems to have at its base a radical distrust of everything, especially any strongly felt emotion. From this point, the heroes of Kundera's fictions are weary and wounded intellectuals, distrustful of any ideology or principles other than general condescension and irony. Kundera's first novel, *The Joke* (1967), paints a depressing picture of Czech society from February 1948 until the mid-1960s. The protagonist Ludvík Jahn posts a politically provocative postcard to a friend as a "joke." The postcard is intercepted by the authorities, and Ludvík is branded an enemy of the people, expelled from the Communist Party and the university, and sent into hard labor in a punitive battalion of the army. Years later Ludvík seeks revenge on the man responsible for his downfall by bedding his wife Helena. Husband and wife, however, have already been estranged for some time, and the upshot is, as is usual for Kundera, the utter humiliation of the woman.

After the 1968 Soviet occupation, Kundera emigrated to France and accepted a teaching post at the University of Rennes. Later he moved to Paris where he resides today. Kundera achieved worldwide fame with the two aforementioned novels written in exile, *The Book of Laughter and Forgetting* and *The Unbearable Lightness of Being*. Both books feature fashionable intellectualism uttered by a vocal authorial narrator who utterly overshadows the other characters, which function as mere ciphers for the author's philosophizing. With withering sarcasm, the narrator condemns totalitarianism, Western culture, rock music, and even sex. Readers are meant to identify with this detached ironic narrative persona floating above and mocking the rest of humanity. With his 1990 novel *Immortality*, Kundera began writing in French, and currently he is having all his Czech works retranslated from what he calls the French "original."

Kundera is not as much acclaimed at home as he is abroad. In the 1960s, he was a prominent public figure and intellectual each of whose articles and public statements was followed avidly by the public. When he fled abroad and achieved fame in the West, many Czechs and Slovaks looked forward to getting their hands on smuggled copies of his novels, which were forbidden in Communist Czechoslovakia. When they did manage to procure his works, however, most Czechs were sorely disappointed. Kundera's most acclaimed novels treat life under Communism and the Soviet invasion of 1968, but most Czechs and Slovaks did not recognize the version of their history presented by Kundera. For many, the author had simplified and theatricalized a complicated situation, and Czech and Slovak readers could not understand the West's fascination with his works. When the wall came down in 1989, Kundera undertook to have his books published in Czechoslovakia, but he planned to have them released one book at a time to keep readers eager for the subsequent work. The publishing house Atlantis published *The Joke* in 1991, but because the public's response was less than overwhelming, Kundera abandoned his plan. In the Czech Republic, there is still no official edition of *The Book of Laughter and Forgetting* or *The Unbearable Lightness of Being*.

Other novelists from Kundera's generation who came of age in the 1960s and continued to write and publish (either legally or illegally) in the 1970s and 1980s are Ladislav Fuks, Ivan Klíma, Ludvík Vaculík, and Vladimír Páral.

In the 1960s, Ladislav Fuks (1928–1994) became the Kafka-inspired spokesman for the fate of the Czechoslovak Jews, and his novels and short stories concentrate on the internal life of his protagonists rather than external events. *Mr. Theodore Mundstock* (1963) presents the situation of a Jew during the German occupation, but the presentation of the character's mental life could be that of anyone in an absurd or extreme situation. Mr. Mundstock prepares himself physically and mentally for his impending transport to a concentration camp, only to be run over by, ironically, one of the transport trucks when he arrives at the collection point. The narrative alternates between the real and the fantastic, and the reader is never quite certain if the protagonist's double, named Mon, is real or imaginary.

Ivan Klíma (b. 1931) published his works underground during totalitarian Communism, and his best works are in the short story genre, in which meditative and lyrical characters concentrate on their own inner worlds. He includes much biographical material and often returns to his experiences under Nazism and Communism. The collection *My First Loves* (1985) begins in the Terezín concentration camp where the author himself spent three-and-one-half years as a child. A boy falls in love with a girl named Miriam who gives him extra rations of milk, but the story ends without his ever speaking to her. The rest of the stories recount the narrator's loves and courtships up through the Communist era. Two other short story collections, *My Merry Mornings* (1979) and *My Golden Trades* (1990) give a picture of everyday life in Czechoslovakia under Communism during Normalization.

The Axe (1966) by Ludvík Vaculíks (b. 1926) was another novel examining Czechoslovakia's recent Stalinist past. It gives a harsh picture of life during collectivization. His Kafkaesque novel *The Guinea Pigs* (1970) explores Czechoslovak life in the 1970s. The protagonist purchases a guinea pig for his sons, but he himself becomes fascinated by its behavior and begins conducting experiments on it. The novel reflects upon human cruelty, manipulation, totalitarianism, and absurdity.

Vladimír Páral (b. 1932) was the most popular Czech author in Czechoslovakia under Communism. He wrote more than 20 novels, only three of which have been translated into English: *Catapult* (1967), *Lovers & Murderers* (1969), and *Four Sonyas* (1971). His works portray a new phenomenon—socialist consumerism. His characters seem devoid of any higher or more moral aspirations than racing for more money, better housing, and fresh sexual experiences. His novels are black comedies exposing the vacuous and philistine nature of much of society. After 1968 the Party banned his books, but rather than emigrate or go underground, Páral adapted his style to the new requirements and moved into the science fiction genre. Now writing in the freedom of post-1989, he seems to write about nothing other than sex.

Among the latest generation of writers, the two most popular with both the public and the press today are Michal Viewegh (b. 1962) and Jáchym Topol (b. 1962). Viewegh writes best-sellers and is the only Czech writer currently able to support himself by his own creative writing alone. His books are simply constructed, witty, and heavily autobiographical. The only one of his novels translated thus far into English, *Bringing up Girls in Bohemia* (1994), recounts the story of a young, quick-witted male high school teacher and novelist who sleeps with one of his female students. Viewegh, who was working as a high school teacher at the time of writing, and his wife divorced soon after publication.

Jáchym Topol's works by contrast are heavily symbolic and ambiguous with multiple stylistic levels. His long novel *Sister, City, Sliver* (1994) examines the tumultuous period of transition in Czechoslovakia from Communism to democracy. The novel is dark, violent, and disturbing, and although critics greeted it with acclaim, many readers had their reservations.

SLOVAK LITERATURE

Slovak literature is badly neglected by translators and hence very little recognized in the English-speaking world. One scholar compares it with Cinderella: "The beauty, ability, and potential for fame are there, but it is unknown, or at any rate less well known that it deserves to be." To be sure, one of the reasons for Slovak literature's obscurity is the small size of its nation—around five million inhabitants. But perhaps another partial explanation lies in the language's similarity to Czech, which worked against the creation of a written Slovak language in medieval times. The Czech written standard was often simply adopted, sometimes modified, and used alongside German, Latin, and Hungarian. Anton Bernolák (1762–1813) first codified the Slovak language, and Ludovít Štúr (1815–1856) finally standardized it. The first works published in modern Slovak did not see the light of day until 1840.

In poetry Pavol Hviezdoslav (1849–1921), Svetozár Hurban-Vajanský (1847–1916), and Ivan Krasko (1876–1958) are the Slovaks' most beloved writers. In prose, one of the few important authors translated into English is Jozef Cíger-Hronský (1896–1961). His novel *Jozef Mak* (1933) captures social conflicts in a Slovak village. Dominik Tatarka (1913–1989) was a Communist journalist and one of the few to join the dissident movement Charter 77. In his novel *The Demon of Conformity* (1963), he mocks Socialist Realism. After 1968 he was the leading Slovak dissident. Ladislav Mňačko (1919–1994) was imprisoned during World War II, and his first novel *Death Is Called Engelchen* (1959) was an attempt to demythologize the 1944 Slovak National Uprising. He later wrote against Stalinism in *The Taste of Power* (1967), the story of a leading Communist politician corrupted by power.

Martin Šimečka (b. 1957) is one of the few younger Slovak writers translated into English. His novel *Year of the Frog* (1985) is a fictionalized autobiographical account of his experience as the child of a dissident. A recent anthology by Picador Press entitled *Description of a Struggle* (1994) contains English translations of individual stories by several other contemporary prose writers.

On the whole Czech and Slovak literature is still trapped in a time of transition, as writers try to feel out their newly found freedom. After the collapse of Communism in 1989, the book market was flooded with previously banned Czech and Slovak authors, but readers quickly tired of reliving the past, and bestsellers and pulp fiction from the West soon displaced the literature of former dissidents and exiles. Czech and Slovak authors had to reorient themselves in the new atmosphere of freedom of expression and privatization, and many young writers are only now finding their voices. Furthermore, authors who were previously burdened with the tasks of educating the nation and keeping culture alive and vibrant now find themselves pushed increasingly to the side as merely another form of entertainment, competing with television, film, and video games.

NOTES

1. Karel Čapek, *Talks with T.G. Masaryk,* trans. Michael Henry Heim (North Haven: Catbird Press, 1995), 101.

2. Jaroslav Hašek, *The Good Soldier Švejk and His Fortunes in the World War,* trans. Cecil Parrott (London: Penguin Books, 1974), 18.

3. Jan Lehár et al., *Česká literatura od počátků k dnešku* (Prague: Lidové noviny, 1997), 566.

4. Ronald Hayman, *A Biography of Franz Kafka* (London: Phoenix Press, 2001), 17.

5. Bohumil Hrabal, *I Served the King of England,* trans. Paul Wilson (San Diego: Harcourt Brace Jovanovich, 1989), 16.

6. Monika Zgutova, *O životě a dile Bohumila Hrabala* (Prague: Mladá fronta, 1997), 174.

SELECTED BIBLIOGRAPHY

Novák, Arne. *Czech Literature,* trans. Peter Kussi. Ann Arbor: Michigan Slavic Publications, 1976.

Petro, Peter. *A History of Slovak Literature.* Montreal: McGill-Queen's University Press, 1995.

Porter, Robert. *An Introduction to Twentieth-Century Czech Fiction: Comedies of Defiance.* Brighton: Sussex Academic Press, 2001.

7

Media and Cinema

Journalists are scum!
—Former Czech Prime Minister Miloš Zeman[1]

You must remember always that of all the arts the most important for us is the cinema.
—V. I. Lenin[2]

SINCE THE FALL of Communism, cultural institutions in the Czech and Slovak Republics have undergone dramatic changes. In the areas of media and cinema, most of these changes have been for the worse. To be sure, the end of censorship has allowed voices of dissent to be heard; on the other hand, it has not necessarily led to the creation of a plurality of voices. Immediately after the Velvet Revolution, many experienced journalists were forced to leave the field to be replaced by inexperienced students, and many journalists simply switched sides, from uncritical support of the Communist regime to uncritical support of anything anti-Communist. Foreign investors immediately bought up most media outlets, and market share took precedence over serious journalism. The Czech and Slovak news markets were suddenly flooded with tabloid journals, pornography, and Western soap operas, all of which are of course a problem in the West, but Western countries, unlike the Czech and Slovak Republics, already have a journalistic tradition in place.

In cinema, state support immediately dried up. Filmmakers who were used to lavish government subsidies and the use of Prague's famous Barrandov Studios suddenly found themselves casting about for funding, and two-thirds of Barrandov employees were left looking for work. In 1992 the number of films made in the studios dropped from an average of 30 in the past years to six. On the up side, foreign filmmakers flocked to Prague to take advantage of the low prices of Barrandov, as well as employ Prague's gorgeous Gothic and Baroque architecture as backdrop scenery. They injected much-needed currency into the studios. But as prices rise and Prague's brilliant facades become covered over with billboards and disco lights, even these incentives may soon disappear.

MEDIA

The transition from totalitarianism to democracy has been a difficult one for the media throughout Central and Eastern Europe. Despite the emergence of hundreds of new media outlets—television and radio stations, newspapers, and magazines—since 1989, remnants of the old system remain in place, and the media still suffer from the totalitarian legacy of government control.

After the 1948 Communist coup in Czechoslovakia, the Communist Party strictly controlled all aspects of the dissemination of information through a censorship department. Party members replaced the heads of all media outlets, and all meaningful discourse was replaced by meaningless ideological cliché. In 1953 the Czechoslovak government created the Office for the Supervision of the Press to which all press materials were submitted for preliminary censorship. Each media outlet also had its own censor, and the government built banks of radio and television jammers to block foreign broadcasts.

On June 26, 1968 during the short-lived burst of freedom known as the Prague Spring, the Czechoslovak Parliament passed an amendment to the constitution, which read in part:

1. Censorship is inadmissible.
2. Censorship is understood to be any infringement whatsoever by state organs against freedom of the word and picture and their dissemination by the mass information media. This does not affect the authority of the public prosecutor or the courts.[3]

After the reimposition of hard-line totalitarianism rule, however, the so-called Normalization period, which lasted from 1969 to the end of 1989, the law was honored more in the breach than the observance. Twenty-four days after the Warsaw Pact invasion, an amendment was enacted creating the government Office for Press and Information, whose task it was "to uniformly regulate and control the activity of the periodic press and other mass information media."[4] Censorship was reinstituted, and the activities of the media directed from above.

At the end of 1989, the Communist government collapsed, and the Czechoslovak media freed itself from censorship within a week. Staff changes were made immediately in both Czechoslovak radio and television, and viewers and listeners were treated to live coverage of addresses by Václav Havel, the former dissident and future president, and Alexander Dubček, one of the prime movers during the Prague Spring who had been moved from the head of the Communist Party to an insignificant government post during Normalization. New periodicals sprouted up overnight throughout the country, and books and films banned under Communism were published and released.

CZECH REPUBLIC

PRESS

Problems with the Czech press arose from the very beginning. During the privatization period, many Czech newspapers, which had been owned by the government, were taken over by members of their staff, who established private companies and slightly altered the name of the periodical, so there would be no legal continuity. This allowed the new owners to keep both the subscribers and the trademarks of the original publications. The daily *Rudé právo* [*Red Rule*] became *Právo* [*Rule*], *Mladá fronta* [*Young Front*] became *Mladá fronta Dnes* [*Young Front Today*], *Večerní Praha* [*Evening Prague*] became *Večerník Praha* [*Prague Evening Paper*], *Zemědělské noviny* [*Agricultural News*] became *Zemské noviny* [*Country News*], and so on. Shortly thereafter, the owners of these new ventures sold their enterprises to Western countries, thereby reaping considerable profit.

In a similar manner, many journalists simply switched sides—from former propagandists for the Communist government to uncritical supporters of Prime Minister Václav Klaus' right-of-center ruling Civic Democratic Party. Of course, many of the more prominent journalists during Communism were forced to forsake the field altogether, and these were replaced by younger inexperienced journalists. Because of the absence of a journalistic tradition independent of government or political parties, journalists tended to support anyone who was anti-Communist.

Currently, there are four major daily papers that consider themselves "serious" publications: *Mladá fronta Dnes, Lidové noviny* [the *National News*], *Právo,* and *Hospodářské noviny* [*Economic News*]; the last is a financial paper similar to the *Wall Street Journal,* with a smaller circulation than the other three, but many consider its news analysis superior. *Lidové noviny* is the oldest Czech newspaper, founded in 1893 by a Moravian politician, Adolf Stránský. Its heyday was between the wars when writers such as Karel Čapek and Ferdinand Peroutka turned it into an organ of liberalism during a time of political extremes. It was banned under Communism, but dissidents began issuing a samizdat version and had a monthly subscriber list of around 400. It was reinstated after the revolution. *Mladá fronta Dnes* is politically slightly to the right-of-center. *Lidové noviny* and *Mladá fronta Dnes* have been competing with each other for the middle-brow reader with the result that both have been tending downmarket, replacing serious journalism with tabloid. *Právo* is slightly left-of-center, and its journalism and commentary tend to be of higher quality than those of *Lidové noviny* and *Mladá fronta Dnes,* but because under Communism the paper was the official voice of the Communist Party, many Czechs refuse to read it. The daily that outsells all these papers is the tabloid *Blesk* [*Flash*], which boasts a mostly nude page 3 girl. Of course, in Western countries, tabloid journalism competes with serious journalism as well, but the West has developed a tradition of serious news publications counteracting the flood of "infotainment." Such a tradition has yet to develop in the Czech Republic and Slovakia.

Except for *Právo,* all the daily newspapers are foreign owned. *Lidové noviny* and *Mladá fronta Dnes* are in the hands of the German company Rheinisch-Bergische Druckerei und Verlagsgesellschaft GmbH, the Swiss company Ringier owns *Blesk,* and the German-American firm Economia owns *Hospodářské noviny.* All regional newspapers were bought out by the German company Pol-Print GmbH & Co. Medien KG. The firm fired most of the journalists and replaced the individual papers with a centrally controlled and produced paper with only minor local variations. In general selling the ownership of Czech newspapers to foreigners was seen as a positive development. The foreign companies had money for new technologies and could ensure stability and independence.[5] On the other hand, foreign owners are primarily interested in market share, and for the most part serious investigative journalism has been sacrificed for profit. Furthermore, the owner's views dominate media coverage, and only articles with this viewpoint are accepted.[6] In the summer of 2003, for example, the management of *Mladá fronta Dnes* postponed publishing an article that criticized politicians who were attending the Karlovy Vary film festival, the largest in the country. The newspaper was a "business partner" for the festival, and the article alleged that business interests manipulated coverage of the festival. Several prominent journalists left the newspaper in protest.[7]

Television

Since the inception of Czechoslovakia as an independent country in 1918, radio and later television have been state owned and operated. Rather than dismantle the existing networks after 1989, however, the government decided to allow other independent radio and television stations to operate alongside them, according to the models in France and Germany.

The Czech Republic has two state-owned television stations, Czech Television 1 (ČT1) and a cultural channel, Czech Television 2 (ČT2). In 1993, the private channel, Nova Television (TV), owned by ČNTS (Czech Independent Television Station), which itself was headed by Vladimír Železný, began broadcasting. The station immediately went downmarket, with tabloid and even soft porn programs. Nova TV quickly outstripped its competitors, taking almost 70 percent of the Czech audience in its first year. An example of its programing is Nova's evening weather report, *Počasíčko,* during which an entirely naked, attractive buxom young woman delivers the forecast and gradually dresses herself according to the forecast. Needless to say, ratings went through the roof when the show aired. Later, Nova TV was compelled to alternate the nude female with an unclothed brawny male to keep in line with European Union sexual discrimination rules.

In 1994 an American-owned company CME sought to strengthen its hold on the station by buying out the interest of the original Czech and Slovak founders of ČNTS and making it possible for Železný to purchase the majority interest in a shadowy related firm. For several years the arrangement seemed to work smoothly. In 1999, however, a conflict arose between CME and Železný, who was fired from his post as chief executive. Seeking revenge, Železný found Czech financial backers to create his own company, CET 21. In August of 1999, he pulled the plug on the American-financed Nova TV and replaced it with his own Nova TV2, arguing that CME had not bought Nova TV but, rather, an insignificant service station. CME sued Železný, who was ordered to pay CME $28 million, and the Czech Republic was ordered to pay CME $500 million.[8]

The Czech public station has its own problems. Since 1998, there have been several failed attempts to professionalize the news and current affairs department of Czech TV. The most recent and most spectacular was in 2000 when the Council for Czech Television appointed Jiří Hodač, a BBC veteran, as chief executive of Czech TV. Hodač intended to introduce professional assessment procedures and open up Czech TV's finances to public scrutiny. Czech TV journalists and other employees, however, rebelled, alleging that Hodač had close ties to Klaus' ruling Civic Democratic Party. The journalists literally hijacked the station and broadcast their own propaganda inciting a populist rebellion that brought 100,000 citizens to Wenceslas Square on January 3, 2002 to protest the appointment, the largest public demonstration since November 1989. As popular support for the journalists grew, politicians backed away from Hodač, who finally stepped down.[9]

Following is a list of the main terrestrial, cable, and satellite television stations with market share of each (if available):

Public Service

ČT1: 20.61%

ČT2: 11.49%

Privately owned

Nova TV: 45.55%

Prima TV: 17.42%

Cable

UPC ČR

Intercable CZ

Satellite

HBO ČR

EastBox Digital

Internet

Czechoslovakia was officially connected to the Internet in February 1992, and since 1995, it has been possible to use the Internet commercially. Most government offices have Internet pages, and the Czech government has been introducing the Internet to schools. All of the major newspapers have Internet pages, as do several television and radio stations. Accessing the Internet, however, was prohibitively expensive for most individuals until an Italian cable company, Newtonlt, introduced access to about 55 Czech cities at reasonable rates. In 2005, however, the number of households with internet access was only 19 percent, a fairly low number. In Slovakia, it is 14 percent.

Book Publishing

Under Communism, Czechoslovakia had approximately 50 publishing houses, all government owned. Today, the Czech Republic alone boasts more than 3,000. When Communism fell in 1989, books by authors banned under the regime inundated the market. The public, however, soon grew weary of reliving the past, and thousands of copies gathered dust on bookstore shelves. Printruns that had averaged tens of thousands stabilized at around 3,000 copies. But while the average printrun has been decreasing, the number of titles has been increasing, from 11,738 in 1998 to 14,278 in 2002. Approximately one-third of all published titles are translations; English is the most common foreign language composing over half of all translated works. Around 25 percent of all books are fiction, a higher proportion than other countries, but this is slowly on the decline. The Czechs, it seems, are still trying to catch up on their previously banned dissident literature.[10]

SLOVAKIA

The media situation in Slovakia is similar to that in the Czech Republic. Even though Slovakia has been nominally free since 1993, under Prime Minister Vladimír Mečiar, who was finally voted out of office in 1998, the country was seen as a totalitarian state in a sea of democracy. Mečiar ran the country with an iron hand, and the press for the most part went along. Since his departure, direct political pressure on journalists has declined significantly, but it still exists. In a recent scandal at the beginning of 2003, the Slovak Information Service (SIS) was accused, and later convicted, of wiretapping journalists' phones.

The two most pressing problems among the Slovak media are a lack of qualified journalists and the tendency to write tabloid-like material. Most reporters are under 30 and have only a few years of experience. A politician once said that when he goes to a news conference, he sees before him a nursery school.[11] After Communism, just as in the Czech Republic, many journalists left the field to be replaced by young, inexperienced students whose idea of the media was strongly anti-Communist but not necessarily pluralist. Also similar to the Czech Republic is the fact that most newspapers are foreign owned, and the owners have gone predictably downmarket. The best-selling daily is the tabloid *Nový čas* [*New time*], which maintained a high-quality political section for some time, but when the paper was sold to a German company, the new owners decided to dispense with it. *Nový čas* is read by 26.9 percent of the population. The other best-selling dailies are *Pravda* [*Truth*] (9%), *Sme* [*We Are*] (8%), and *Šport* (5%).

The private station Markíza is the most widely viewed television channel, capturing 52.6 percent of the audience. It is followed by the public Slovak TV1, with 15.7 percent, and another private station, TV Joj, with 5.6 percent. Slovak Radio is a public service station with several channels: Rádio Slovensko (news and current affairs), Rádio Regina (regional), Rádio Devín (arts and culture), Rádio Rock FM (the name says it all), Rádio Patria (broadcast in seven national minority languages, mostly Hungarian), and Radio Slovakia (international broadcast in five languages). In 2002 there were approximately 25 private radio stations. Rádio Slovensko is by far the most popular station, with 46.8 percent of the listeners.[12]

Cinema

The First Republic

The period from the establishment of Czechoslovakia in 1918 to the Nazi takeover in 1938 is one of cultural efflorescence in Czechoslovak architecture, fine arts, literature, and cinema. At this time Bohemia was the most highly industrialized area in Central Europe, and three film companies were founded in 1918. Cooperation with neighboring Germany was established almost immediately, which brought film beyond the narrow confines of the new republic, as well as eased the transition to sound film, for it was not immediately apparent that creating Czech language films for a population of only thirteen million was a financially sound undertaking. In 1930, however, when the first sound films were made in Czechoslovakia, their success on the domestic market quelled any fears and encouraged further production.

In 1933 Václav Havel's uncle Miloš Havel built the modern film studio Barrandov in a suburb of Prague, which remains the center of Czech and Slovak film production today. Originally intended for foreign film production, the studios soon produced primarily Czech and Slovak films, between 30 and 40 a year. The first Czech film to achieve international acclaim (as well as contempt from many quarters) was Gustav Machatý's *Ecstasy* (1933), whose success had much to do with the full frontal nudity of Hedvige Kiesler who went on to Hollywood fame as Hedy Lamaar. The film was banned by Hitler, denounced by the Pope, and hailed at the 1934 Venice Film Festival. Kiesler's multi-millionaire Austrian husband unsuccessfully tried to buy up and destroy all the prints of the film. The protagonist of the movie—Kiesler—is newly married to an elderly dullard who ignores her sexual and personal needs. One day she is skinny-dipping, and her horse grazing nearby takes fright and gallops off with all her apparel, which gives rise to the infamous nude scene as Kiesler tramps off in the buff after her horse. Here she falls in love with a virile young man, the two shortly end up in bed, and the husband commits suicide. The film is extremely lyrical and burgeons with erotic symbolism. Henry Miller has written of the film:

> This is body rhythm, blood rhythm, as opposed to the masturbative rhythm of the intellect. The recognition of this rhythm involves not a new technique but a new way of living. Once again I repeat that the hostility provoked by Machaty's film arises not so much through dissatisfaction with a "weak ending," but through the silent menace, the challenge, of a new life mode.[13]

The film ends with a kitschy "hymn to labor" meant to suggest that the heroine's passion was misdirected and that the proper motive and objective of sexual fervor is childbirth and physical work. *Ecstasy* is one of the classics of world cinema.

The greatest comedy films of the interwar films were made by Jiří Voskovec and Jan Werich, a comic duo who founded the quasi-vaudeville Liberated Theater. The two performers were comparable to Laurel and Hardy, but, as author and critic Josef Škvorecký writes, "With all due respect to Stan and Ollie, Voskovec and Werich mean much more to Czech culture—they are the most revered symbol of a great era.... They moulded dadaism, circus, jazz, Chaplin, Buster Keaton, and American vaudeville into a new art form. They created a new form of intellectual-political musical."[14] The team's four films were screen adaptations of their plays: *Powder and Petrol* (1931), *Your Money or Your Life* (1932), *Heave, Ho!* (1934), and *The World Belongs to Us* (1937). The films utilize much slapstick, but social commentary is always close at hand. During the war, they fled to the United States and returned in 1945. When the world once again turned upside-down in 1948, Werich remained in Czechoslovakia, and Voskovec moved back permanently to the United States, where he became George Voskovec and a successful Broadway actor and film star.

After the war, the Czechoslovak government nationalized 60 percent of industry including film; this was in 1945, two years before the Communist takeover. After the war, nationalization was not associated exclusively with Communism. Those who advocated nationalizing the film industry argued that film was more than a consumer good; they wanted to free cinema from market forces. Nationalization ended the financial worries for most filmmakers and provided more opportunities than other regimes. Filmmakers no longer had to seek financial backing or worry about box office receipts because as employees of the studios, they received a permanent salary. According to one critic, conditions for Czech and Slovak filmmakers were potentially the best in the world.[15] The government also established the Prague Film School (FAMU) two years later in 1947. On the other hand, Czech and Slovak filmmakers were soon compelled to create their work according to Socialist Realist aesthetics, that is, movies were to portray the victory of socialism over capitalism in a conventionally realistic manner. Czechoslovakia gave birth to its share of films depicting the fulfillment of the Five Year Plan and successful battles against imperialist saboteurs, but an unintended result of Socialist Realist film was that Czechs and Slovaks stopped going to see these films and crowded into the few theaters running the latest foreign movies, especially those from the school of Italian Neorealism.

The New Wave

Khrushchev's denunciation of Stalin in 1956 began a process of self-examination throughout the Eastern Bloc, of coming to terms with the nightmare of Stalinist purges and show trials. In Czechoslovakia the process culminated in the Prague Spring and provided the impetus for the new film movement known as the Czechoslovak New Wave, one of the most important developments in world cinema. No other film industry received so much attention and so many awards as the Czechoslovak film industry of the 1960s.

Czechoslovak New Wave is usually defined by the output of a handful of directors who debuted in 1963—Jiří Menzel, Miloš Forman, Věra Chytilová, Jaromíl Jireš, and Ivan Passer. These directors espoused no official aesthetic program, but common elements include playful humor, irony, and especially eroticism in abundance. Despite the onomastic similarity, Czechoslovak New Wave had little to do with the concurrent cinematic school known as the French New Wave. The self-referentiality, long takes, and unpolished quality of directors such as Jean-Luc Goddard and François Truffaut was foreign to the Czech and Slovak directors who preferred standard takes and a more polished aesthetic. What the movements shared was an interest in "real" people and everyday concerns, as well as removing film from the studio and shooting on location.

Miloš Forman is the most prominent of the New Wave directors. Out of the country when the Russian tanks invaded in 1968, he remained abroad and emigrated to the United States, where he made the award-winning films *One Flew over the Cuckoo's Nest* (1975), *Amadeus* (1984), *The People vs. Larry Flynt* (1996), and many more. One of Forman's most notable talents is the ability to reflect the entirety of society in a small group of people, for example, in a firemen's ball. The results are often strikingly cruel and pessimistic, yet undeniably humorous. Forman has noted: "The first filmmaker who really touched me was Charlie Chaplin. All of his films. I don't know if I started liking his films because Chaplin was so good or if he touched something that was already in me that I didn't know about before. I was very moved by his mixture of laughter and tears."[16]

Loves of a Blonde (1965) was Forman's second feature film, and the first that made a name for the director abroad. It begins in a remote Czech village where an unusual problem has arisen—a dearth of men. Due to poor social planning, women vastly outnumber men. To rectify the problem, at least for a time, town officials decide to import a trainload of soldiers to attend a dance. Rather than dashing young recruits, however, the train transports to town a band of middle-aged dumpy reservists most of whom resemble the good soldier Švejk. The dance itself is pure screwball comedy as various incidents unfold on and off the dance floor between the sexes. Among the women is Andula, the blonde of the title, who dreams of marriage in the big city. After being seduced by the piano player in a scene that, for its time, was more candid than Western European film, Andula misinterprets the piano player's invitation to visit him in Prague, and much to his parents' surprise, she ends up on their doorstep. The final scene is both heartbreaking and hilarious.

In Forman's third film, *The Firemen's Ball* (1967), the local fire department organizes a ball to mark the retirement of a fire chief dying of cancer. The ball includes a beauty contest, with none of the contestants remotely beauteous, but all oogled by lecherous old men—the talent committee. The other event planned for the evening is a raffle, but all the prizes are stolen. Finally, when an actual fire breaks out, the firemen are caught completely off guard and unable to take any effective action. Czech firemen throughout the country were so outraged by the movie when it appeared that Forman undertook a national tour of apology.

Critics often compare Jiří Menzel to Forman. Both directors concentrate on ordinary people, employ humorous situations, and focus on similar themes—typically, love and the manner it plays out in society. Yet whereas Forman often employs non-actors and significant amounts of improvisation, Menzel prefers professional actors, and he painstakingly scripts his films, most of which are based on works of Czech literature. His most acclaimed work is *Closely Watched Trains* (1966) based on a novel of the same name by Bohumil Hrabal; it won the Best Foreign Language award at the Oscars in 1967. In short, the film is about World War II and premature ejaculation, or perhaps how an awkward young man overcomes his sexual frustrations and at the same time destroys a German munitions train. Throughout the movie, the hero, Miloš Hrma, is more preoccupied with losing his virginity than resistance or ideology. This, naturally, is one of the movie's chief subversive elements, and the Soviets banned the film for its mockery of the resistance.

When *Closely Watched Trains* won the Academy Award, it was suggested that Menzel was in league with Hollywood Zionists.

Most of the New Wave films are about sexuality, specifically, the awakening of young love. And because most of the filmmakers are men, New Wave films tend to involve a large measure of male voyeurism. One exception is the films of Věra Chytilová, the dame of Czech cinema. Most of her films are unavailable in the West, but the few that have been shown provoke strong viewer reactions, especially from the male members of the audience. *Daisies* (1966) is perhaps Chtytilová's signature work, and it is impossible to summarize. Chytilová herself has called it "a philosophical documentary in the form of a farce," and the intention was "to divert the spectator's attention from the psychology of the characters."[17]

The film begins with images of war (e.g., tanks and explosions) behind the opening credits. These are interlarded with shots of a flywheel relentlessly driving a piston. The film proper opens with two young women, both named Marie, sitting poolside against a fence and sporting two-piece swimsuits. They move like puppets and begin the following dialogue:

Marie I: I can't do anything.

Marie II:Nobody understands anything.

Marie I: Nobody understands us.

Marie II:Everything's spoiled in this world.

Marie I: If everything's spoiled …

Marie II:Well …

Marie I: We'll be spoiled too!

Whereupon both women tumble into a green field of daisies. From this ambiguous opening, the film launches into a fragmentary episodic series of events, without much of a plot. The girls flirt with older men who take them to fine restaurants expecting sexual favors in return; however, no relations materialize. In one scene the girls get drunk on beer in a nightclub and perform a perverse version of the Charleston. The movie concludes in a banquet hall the girls have come across overflowing with delicacies that have obviously been set out for an official delegation. They indulge in an orgy of ingestion and destruction.

Overall, Chytilová's social critique is wide-ranging, including jabs at male/female stereotypes, the destructive effects of consumption, the overall ideological nature of society. Yet Chytilová manages to swathe it all in playfulness, beauty, and childlike innocence. *Daisies* is highly entertaining, provocative irreverence.

Jaromil Jireš's *Valerie and Her Week of Wonders* also focuses on a woman; it is a parable of a woman's first menstruation, which involves vampires, lesbians, and lecherous priests. The narrative itself is often unclear, but the sexual symbols and imagery—alluding to the fantasies of a young girl experiencing the onset of puberty—are often "over the top" in their erotic suggestiveness. The result is unsettling and intoxicating. The title character, Valerie, is menaced by the Weasel, an odd, shape-shifting, vampire-like creature partial to the blood of chickens. The Weasel may be Valerie's father. In his attempt to deflower young Valerie, the Weasel enlists the help of the girl's grandmother, herself a vampire. On the side of good, we have a young man named Eagle, who may be Valerie's brother, but who also plays the role of suitor.

Valerie and Her Week of Wonders was adapted from a novel by the same name written by the Czech Surrealist poet Vítěslav Nezval, and Nezval's Surrealism is reproduced in the experimental nature of the film. It is unclear and lacks traditional narrative coherence. Yet the film's lack of clarity is nothing like that of *Daisies*. The individual scenes of *Valerie* are so rich with color, symbolism, and suggestiveness and the characters so imbued with the heritage of gothic folklore that the fragmented narrative does indeed possess some sort of coherence, not necessarily a logical one, but a coherence nevertheless.

The most popular movie among Czechoslovaks from the 1960s was Oldřich Lipský's *Lemonade Joe* (1964), a musical parody of the American western film. The novelist Karel May's westerns had popularized the American wild west in Central and Eastern Europe. The title character is a teetotaling gunslinger who comes to clean up the corrupt town of Stetson City. In the end he gets the girl and teaches the town to drink the soft drink Kola Loka instead of whiskey. The movie's most famous line expresses a typically Czech and Slovak sentiment: *Alkohol podávaný v malých dávkách, neškodí v jakémkoliv množství* ["Alcohol taken in small doses is not harmful no matter what the amount"].

After the Warsaw Pact invasion in August 1968, the government was slow to reform the film industry. Finally, during the second half of 1969, the reorganization took place, affecting several completed films and several in mid-production. In 1973 the government issued a list of banned films, concluding with a list of four that were "banned forever."[18] Chief literary advisor Ludvík Toman issued a statement in which he said: "We are interested in art which rejects and criticizes skepticism, feelings of alienation, desperation, inconsiderate sexuality, egoistic bourgeois individualism. We want to support by our films those properties which strengthen our society and not those which break it up."[19] Film was to return to the aridity of the socialist realist aesthetic. Many directors fled abroad, and many remained in Czechoslovakia but without work, including Chytilová and Menzel.

In general during the 1970s and 1980s films were made not to cause offense. Many filmmakers retreated into history or fairly tales, a popular genre among the Czechs. Most of these fairy tales were upbeat and positive. An exception was the films of Jan Švankmajer, the Dark Lord of Czech Cinema. Švankmajer began making films in 1964 and has made over 50 of them, most of them shorts. Among them are four full-length feature films—*Alice* (1988), *Faust* (1994), *Conspirators of Pleasure* (1996), and *Little Otík* (2000). Švankmajer calls himself a "militant Surrealist." Although Surrealism for the most part died out in the West after World War II, it continued underground in Nazi and Communist Czechoslovakia during and after the war, and seems to have assumed new life after the end of totalitarian rule. Švankmajer is one of the school's foremost practitioners. His cinematic technique is to employ a combination of stop-motion animation, or "claymation," puppets, and real actors. His themes, however, are far from those usually associated with puppets and claymation. Švankmajer's films are interior psychic journeys that summon and parade inner demons in a disgusting physicality. From the 1960s to 1980s, Švankmajer infuriated the authorities with his mesmerizing films and was unable to work for extended periods. In *Alice,* for example, which is based on Lewis Carroll's *Alice in Wonderland,* the censors were perhaps under the impression that Švankmajer's version would be as psychically innocuous as the original. But in Švankmajer's hands the story becomes an exploration of the morbid terrors of childhood. His *Faust* reworks Goethe's and Marlowe's versions, but it takes place in the center of Prague. The story is simultaneously read by a puppet and acted out by the performer Petr Čepek, who died shortly after filming. *Conspirators of Pleasure* explores the bizarre and erotic fixations of four characters: a mail carrier who inhales balls of bread through her nose, a man obsessed with a female television news anchor and constructs a contraption to provide erotic stimulation as he views the evening newscast, a policeman who embeds nails in a rolling pin, which he slides up and down his naked flesh, and a dominatrix pursuing a mannequin through her apartment and terrorizing it with a whip. The mannequin comes to life, and the audience cringes as the whip cuts into the vivified doll.

Little Otík is Švanmajer's longest film, coming in at over two hours. It is based on a fairy tale by Karel Jaromír Erben in which a childless couple adopts a tree stump and attempts to raise it. It soon comes to life and develops a voracious appetite culminating in cannibalism.

Švankmajer has developed a sizable following outside of the Czech Republic—see, for example, the tribute by the Brothers Quay, *The Cabinet of Jan Švankmajer*—which has allowed him to continue with his bizarre film experiments in the post-Communist period when state funding has dried up completely.

After the Velvet Revolution, the Czechoslovak film industry underwent a dramatic transformation: not only was censorship abolished, but so were state subsidies, and film became subject to market pressures like any other industry. Filmmakers were now in the reverse position of unlimited freedom but severely limited funding, and domestic film production dropped immediately. Unlike American films, Czech and Slovak films cannot cover their costs, not to mention make a profit, from domestic box office receipts alone. The country is simply too small, and filmmaking is too expensive. Moreover, only a few Czech and Slovak films are likely to be successful internationally.

In 1991, Barrandov Studios were stripped of all state support. The managing director, Václav Marhoul, immediately laid off more than one thousand employees, and the studios now cater primarily to foreign filmmakers. The number of Czech films produced by Barrandov was reduced from 20–30 a year to two–three a year. Domestic films are a luxury.[20] The government has recognized the need for film subsidies and established the State Fund for the Development of Czech Cinematography. The fund receives no money directly from the government but instead from the sale of pre-1990 Czech films, and a surcharge of one crown (five cents) on each cinema ticket sold in the country. The fund, however, provides only 2.5 million euros (US$3,184,000) a year, while the average budget for a Czech film is between 500,000 (US$636,800) and one million euros (US$1,274,000). Michal Bregant, dean of the internationally renowned Prague Film School FAMU, says the government is uniquely unsupportive of the film industry:

In the Czech Republic we have little support compared to for example Hungary, which got 13 million euros [US$16,557,000] from the state budget into the film industry just recently. But it's very, very far away from what we are experiencing here because the Czech government isn't giving a single cent into the film industry…. There is this state fund for the support of Czech film, but it is state by name only. The state is not putting anything into it.[21]

In 1990 Czech public television became the chief financial support for Czech film, which has a commitment to support the cultural identity of the Czechs. It has had a hand in the production of nearly all Czech feature films created since 1990, but in 2004 it was compelled to reduce its co-production activities significantly. Yet even without certain funding, Czech films continue to be made—through compromise and accommodation. Filmmakers, for example, will charge a lot to shoot a commercial and then very little for a film. And because the studio is too expensive, filmmakers tend to shoot a lot on location, thereby unintentionally duplicating an aspect of the New Wave aesthetic.

The most successful recent Czech film, both domestically and internationally, was Jan Svěrák's *Kolya* (1996), starring Jan's father Zdeněk Svěrák, who also provided the screenplay. The film is a somewhat sentimental, backward glance at the period of Normalization, involving a young Russian boy and a hardened but essentially sweet middle-aged womanizer named Louka. Even the portrayal of the occupying Soviet forces emphasizes their "common humanity" with the Czechs. Louka grows up by having to care for the Russian boy, and the movie ends with his own fathering of a child and settling down. The film is touching and gently ironic. It pokes fun at Czechs who played at being dissidents but who in truth put themselves at almost no risk. *Kolya* won the Academy Award for Best Foreign Language Picture in 1997.

In 2000 Jan Hřebejk made the astonishing *Divided We Fall,* a World War II film depicting the moral ambiguities and ironies of sheltering a Jew during the German occupation. It was nominated in 2001 for Best Foreign Language Picture but lost to Ang Lee's *Crouching Tiger, Limping Dragon.* *Divided We Fall* is often compared to Roberto Benigni's *Life Is Beautiful* for its combination of pathos and humor in a Holocaust film, but unlike Benigni's film, Hřebejk's never descends to melodrama. His latest film *Up and Down* (2004) is a socially conscious black comedy with multiple storylines. One of the movie's primary targets is racism, an especially vitriolic target in the former Eastern Bloc.

The most recent films of Petr Zelenka have become cult objects in the Czech Republic and Slovakia. *Buttoners* (1997) comprises six vignettes from the mundane to the bizarre to create a surreal picture of society, from social deviance to suicide to the Holocaust. His *Year of the Devil* is a "mockumentary" of the Czech folk-rock band Čechomor. Zelenka mixes the real with the fictitious to create a "musical adventure" in which people come to hear the music within themselves. The film was wildly popular when it premiered in March 2002 and was the Grand Prize winner at the Karlovy Vary film festival.

Slovakia has not been as fortunate. The end of state funding, which came upon the heels of the breakup of Czechoslovakia, seemed to spell the end for Slovak filmmaking. In 1999, however, the Slovaks attempted with some success to breathe life into their industry with the Bratislava International Film Festival. Vladimír Adásek's film *Hana and her Sisters* was the only new Slovak feature film, an independent, low-budget movie made with some difficulty. The main character is confused about his sexual orientation and keeps both straight and gay porn beneath his bed, along with a collection of old LPs by the Czech singer, Hana Hegerová. In a series of cabaret episodes, the director himself appears as the red-headed singer playing to the audience. Besides the gender confusion, the film focuses on a range of odd family members and local inhabitants. Adásek is now planning a contemporary version of Saint-Exupéry's *The Little Prince*.

NOTES

1. Jan Čulík, "Press Freedom Under Threat," *Central European Review* 1, no. 3 (July 12, 1999), http://www.ce-review.org/99/3/culik3.html.

2. *Sovietskoye Kino,* 1–2 (1933): 10.

3. *Sbírka zákonů* 84 (1968): 238. Cited in Frank L. Kaplan, "Czechoslovakia's Press Law: Shaping the Media's Future," in *Revolutions for Freedom: The Mass Media in Eastern and Central Europe,* ed. Al Hester and L. Earle Reybold (Athens, GA: The James M. Cox, Jr., Center for International Mass Communication Training and Research, 1991), 41.

4. Kaplan, "Czechoslovakia's Press Law," 42.

5. Jan Jirák, "The Czech Republic: Media Accountability Systems—An Unknown Concept," *European Journal Center,* http://www.ejc.nl/hp/mas/jirak.html.

6. Josef Schrabal, "Europe v. USA Freedom of the press," *Newyorkske listy* (Winter 1997), http://www.columbia.edu/~js322/nyl/melantrich/freedom-of-the-press. html.

7. "2004 World Press Freedom Review, Czech Republic," International Press Institute, http://www.freemedia.at/wpfr/Europe/czech.htm.

8. Jan Čulík, "Czech Media: 2002," http://www2.arts.gla.ac.uk/Slavonic/Czech_ Media.doc.

9. Jan Čulík, "Czech Republic," *Censorship: A World Encyclopedia,* 4 vols. ed. Derek Jones (London: Fitzroy Dearborn Publishers, 2001), vol. 1, 630.

10. "Knižní produkce v ÈR v roce 2002—základní fakta," Union of Czech Booksellers, http://www.sckn.cz/ckt/index.html.

11. Samuel Abraham, Roundtable discussion in *Eurozine,* http://www.eurozine. com/article/2003–06–20-abraham-en.html.

12. "The Slovak Media Landscape," European Journalism Centre , http://www. ejc.nl/jr/emland/slovakia.html. See also the media overview poll by the *Slovak Spectator,* http://www.slovakspectator.sk/clanok?cl=18474.

13. Henry Miller, "Reflections on 'Extasy,'" *Selected Prose,* 2 vols. (London: MacGibbon & Kee, 1965), vol. 2, 403.

14. Josef Škvorecký, *All the Bright Young Men and Women: A Personal History of the Czech Cinema,* trans. Michael Schonberg (Toronto: Peter Martin Associates Ltd., 1971), 23–24.

15. Antonin Liehm, *Closely Watched Films: The Czechoslovak Experience* (New York: International Arts and Sciences Press, 1974), 413.

16. Peter Hames, *The Czechoslovak New Wave* (Berkeley: University of California Press, 1985), 131.

17. Hames, *Czechoslovak New Wave,* 211.

18. The four film's were Forman's *Loves of a Blonde* (1965), Menzel's *Larks on a String* (1969), Jan Němec's *Report on the Party and the Guests* (1966), and Vojtěch Jasný's *All My Good Countrymen* (1968).

19. Hames, 258.

20. Angus Finney, *The State of European Cinema: A New Dose of Reality* (London: Cassell, 1996), 73–75. See also Peter Hames, "Czech Cinema: From State Industry to Competition," *Canadian Slavonic Papers,* Vol. XLII, no. 1–2, March–June 2000, 63–85.

21. Kate Barrette, "Czech Film Industry: Beloved and Beleaguered," *Czech Radio 7, Radio Prague,* January 21, 2005, http://www.radio.cz/en/article/62575.

SELECTED BIBLIOGRAPHY

Hames, Peter. "The Velvet Generation." *Central European Review* 2, no. 41 (November 2000), www.ce-review.org/oo/u1/kinoeye41_Hames.html.
———. *The Czechoslovak New Wave.* Berkeley: University of California Press, 1985.
Hester, Al, and L. Earle Reybold, eds. *Revolutions for Freedom: The Mass Media in Eastern and Central Europe.* Athens, Georgia: The James M. Cox, Jr., Center for International Mass Communication Training and Research, 1991.
Liehm, Antonin. *Closely Watched Films: The Czechoslovak Experience.* New York: International Arts and Sciences Press, 1974.
Škvorecký, Josef. *All the Bright Young Men and Women: A Personal History of the Czech Cinema,* trans. Michael Schonberg. Toronto: Peter Martin Associates, 1971.

WEB SITES

Central European Review: http://www.ce-review.org.
Eurozine: http://www.eurozine.com.
Freedom House: http://www.freedomhouse.org.

8

Performing Arts

The history of the National Theater is really the history of our national life in this new period.

— František Adolf Šubert, the first director of the Czech National Theater[1]

I have the feeling that if absurd theater had not existed before me, I would have had to invent it.

— Václav Havel[2]

Someone told me that in Prague rock and roll could be heard. It was a daring word, and at that time was pronounced in the same breath as the word imperialism.

— Miroslav Horníček, Czech actor, writer, and director[3]

THE HISTORY OF THEATER in the Czech and Slovak lands is like that of no other nation. During the nineteenth-century National Revival, playwrights and puppeteers such as Josef Kajetán Tyl and Matěj Kopecký roamed the countryside performing plays in Czech to raise the national consciousness. It was the founding of the National Theater in the 1880s that finally gave the Czechs their own permanent stage. Instead of a play, it was an opera, Smetana's *Libuše,* that was performed upon the theater's grand opening, demonstrating that the most significant achievement of Czech dramatic art was opera rather than drama. Music has a rich history in the Czech lands, and Czechs style themselves as a nation of musicians; *co Čech, to muzikant,* every Czech is a musician, is an old proverb. In fact, a Czech song was voted "Song of the Millenium" in an international poll. *Škoda lásky*—known as the "Beer Barrel Polka" in English and *Rosamunda* in German—was written by the Czech polka king Jaromír Vejvoda in the 1930s. During the Austro-Hungarian Monarchy, two-thirds of the musicians and half of the band leaders in the Austrian Military Orchestra were Czechs. Today, an excellent music education begins early, and most Czechs can sit around a campfire and sing the night away to the accompaniment of a guitar. Rock music, known as *bigbít,* came from the West in the 1950s much to the exasperation of the Communist authorities, who alternately banned and tolerated the imported music. It was rock music that led Václav Havel and other dissidents to form the human rights movement Charter 77.

THEATER

The National Theater

The development of Czech theater is intimately bound up with Czech national consciousness. It was one of the most powerful manifestations of the rebirth of the Czech nation in the nineteenth century. Because it was a shared experience, the theater was an ideal place to transmit to an often illiterate public Czech national history, folk songs, and legends, as well as the Czech language itself. For Czechs, theater had a definite political meaning, as the first announcement by the Committee to Build the National Theater made clear in 1851:

> The Czech patriot can now view with inspiration and hope the progress which our fresh national spirit has already made in education and culture … yet we are still lacking something without which Europe will hardly regard us as an educated and cultured nation. We mean an independent *national theater* … which will testify to the world of our national culture …
>
> We cherish the pleasant hope that through cooperation and unified support of all the friends of art and of the Czech nation a National Theater will soon be built—as a monument to our constitutional rights of equality and as an adornment for the capital of our Czech nation.[4]

The purpose of the announcement was to enlist the Czech population of Bohemia and Moravia in a project to construct a national cultural institution. The National Theater was conceived as nothing less than the symbol of the rebirth of the nation and an announcement to the rest of the world that culturally the Czechs could go toe-to-toe with any nation in Europe. Before the construction of the National Theater, a permanent stage for Czech theater did not exist in Prague. Small troupes and companies often performed in improvised outdoor settings or halls and sometimes in the Estates Theater when it was not being used by the regular German company.

Funds for the building of the National Theater were collected by subscription beginning in 1851. Contributions came from all quarters—the nobility, the intelligentsia, the bourgeoisie, villagers, workers, and students. Events were sponsored to raise money, and artists provided proceeds from the sale of their works. In 1862, a Provisional Theater was built exclusively for Czech productions. Constructed in six months, it was built on the site of the future National Theater with the understanding that it would eventually be incorporated into the larger theater. In May of 1868, the foundation stone was laid at the greatest national celebration the Czechs had ever had. It was a political and cultural exhibition. The foundation stone itself came from Říp, a mountain to the north of Prague, a veritable holy site where, according to legend, Father Čech, the founder of the nation, first established his rule in the fifth century. When other Czechs from around Bohemia and Moravia learned of the origin of the foundation stone, "Stone Fever" set in, and Czechs from all over Bohemia and Moravia sent in their own stones to demonstrate their national solidarity. The first stone to arrive in Prague was greeted with fanfare by hundreds of students at the train station, and from there they accompanied it to the building site. One hundred riders on horseback escorted the foundation stone from Říp, and when it arrived, an estimated 80,000 people were on hand. On May 16, 1868, 19 stones were laid at the foundation stone ceremony.

Only Czech workers were employed in the construction of the theater, and only Czech artists were allowed to decorate its walls. Moreover, all the stones used in the construction came from Bohemia and Moravia. After several financial and political setbacks, the theater was finally completed and opened in June of 1881. Smetana's opera *Libuše* was chosen for the grand opening. Soon after, however, disaster struck. At 6:20 P.M. a fire broke out on the roof due to worker negligence, and by 7:20 P.M. the roof had collapsed. The National Theater burned to the ground only two months after its inauguration. Yet in an unparalleled display of patriotism, once again Czechs from all over opened their pocketbooks and donated to the cause. Sufficient funds were raised, and in November of 1883, the Czech National Theater once again opened its doors, and once again the main hall resounded with the strains of Smetana's *Libuše*. Above the proscenium arch is inscribed the theater's motto: *Národ sobě* (The Nation['s gift] to Itself]. The National Theater symbolized the triumph of a nearly century-long struggle for the independence of Czech national life. It was an inspirational symbol of national identity.

Czech theater of the nineteenth century provided a popular venue for emphasizing and championing the Czech language through dramatizations of idealized versions of Czech history. It fostered a sense of culture and furthered the national striving for autonomy. But nineteenth-century playwrights did not restrict themselves to reliving, or more often "inventing," the past glories of the Czechs; they also tried to show them how they *should* be. Josef Kajetan Tyl (1808–1856), whose drama *Fidlovačka* (Spring Festival [originally of Prague shoemakers] 1834) gave the Czechs their national anthem "Where Is My Home?" stated, "Elsewhere people may wish theater to show them as they already are, but we must want a theater to show us as we ought to be."[5] Unwittingly, Tyl was foreshadowing one of the tenants of twentieth-century Socialist Realism.

The Twentieth Century

Much Czech theater of the late nineteenth century was concentrated around historical dramas imitative of French and German models with elaborate scenic displays. At the beginning of the twentieth century, and especially upon the establishment of Czechoslovakia in 1918, Czech theater broke away from these foreign influences and became one of the leaders in innovative European theater. Not only were the Czechs perfectly placed geographically to imbibe the theatrical avant-garde from France, Germany, and the Soviet Union, they also had an enormous burst of vitality and confidence due to their sudden freedom after centuries of Austrian rule. During the final years of the Empire, Czech culture was going through decades of catching up with European culture; there was a sense of making up for lost time.

Two directors dominated Czech theater in the early part of the twentieth century, Jaroslav Kvapil (1868–1950) and Karel Hugo Hilar (1885–1935). Kvapil began at the National Theater and Hilar at the Vinohrady Theater, which had opened in 1907. These two men saw theater directing as the work of an artist, and through their efforts Czech theater and Czech playwrights advanced to the forefront of European theater. Kvapil, an adherent of the Russian theatrical director Konstantin Stanislavsky (1863–1938) and the Modern school of psychological acting, acquainted Czech theatergoers with Chekhov, Gorky, Oscar Wilde, and especially Henrik Ibsen. During World War I, in 1916, he produced his magnificent Shakespeare cycle. Hilar was against Kvapil's psychological theater and produced much more Shaw, as well as plays by Eugene O'Neill and Luigi Pirandello.

The playwright who overshadows all others during the First Republic is Karel Čapek (1890–1938). We came across Čapek in the chapter of this volume on literature, and it was indeed his prose works that brought him to the attention of the Nobel Committee. His plays, however, drew the largest audience. Čapek's dramas are primarily plays of ideas rather than of emotions or characters. The play that first drew the world's attention to Čapek, as well as to this newly created Central European country, was *R.U.R.: Rossum's Universal Robots* (1920; see Chapter 6, "Literature," for a plot summary). A common theme in Čapek's works is a human invention that gets beyond the control of its creator, wreaking havoc and destruction. Čapek, who held a doctorate in philosophy from Charles University, was skeptical of technology, but the resolution of *R.U.R.* and his early works in general reveal an enduring faith in human goodness. A similar conceit forms the basis of *The Makropulos Affair* (1922), in which a woman has lived 300 years because of a formula her father had discovered for eternal life. The end of the play reveals Čapek's point: eternal life is undesirable; the limitations of life are what provide its meaning.

Čapek's other two plays from the 1920s are Expressionistic comedies written in collaboration with his brother Josef. *From the Life of Insects* (1922) displays the foibles of humans by embodying them in the insect world where they are observed by a tramp. It was the first Czech play to be performed over one hundred times at the National Theater. *Adam the Creator* (1927) is entirely fantasy. Adam destroys God's creation, and the latter allows him to create it anew with disastrous results. Čapek did not write another play for ten years, until world events seemingly galvanized him to once more write for the theater. *The White Plague* (1937) and *Mother* (1938) are responses to the growing and inexorable threat posed by neighboring Nazi Germany.

Music hall entertainment and cabaret, or dinner theater, were also popular in Prague from the turn of the century. Jaroslav Kvapil opened the first professional Prague cabaret in 1910, and others soon followed. The writer Jaroslav Hašek (again, see Chapter 6 of this volume, "Literature") was a prominent figure in Prague cabarets and pubs, where he acted out his well-known improvisations. During one such performance Hašek founded his political party, The Party of Moderate Progress Within the Boundaries of the Law, which satirized Austrian political life.

Alongside the official, state-sponsored theaters, avant-garde theaters sprang up during the First Republic and developed their own style usually in a spirit directed against established conventions. They provoked audiences with wordplay, allusion, and juxtaposition. Playwrights abandoned literary texts and took inspiration from cinema, music halls, carnivals, and street demonstrations. The most popular of the avant-garde theaters was the Liberated Theater founded in 1925 by Jindřich Honzl and Jiří Frejka. In 1927 Honzl invited the student actors Jiří Voskovec and Jan Werich (who became known by the conjugate symbol V+W) to stage a production of their *Vest-Pocket*

Revue (the title was in English), and it became an immediate and long-running success. Full of wordplay and jokes, the *Vest-Pocket Revue* poked fun at traditional theatre and even the self-conscious sententiousness of the avant-garde with loosely connected skits, songs, and dances. When Hitler came to power in 1934, and Germany's power and influence throughout the region was on the rise, V+W's productions became topical, attacking fascism both within Czechoslovakia and beyond.

At the beginning of the German occupation, which lasted from 1939 to 1945, theater life went on relatively undisturbed, and theater attendance reached an all time high. Czechs demonstrated their national solidarity not by rebellion, but by massive attendance at Czech theater and opera. Naturally, anti-fascist plays such as Čapek's *The White Plague* were banned by the Nazis, as were plays by authors of those countries who had declared war on Germany (Shakespeare was, however, a frequent exception). As time went on, the works of Jewish authors were forbidden as well. Theater performances were briefly suspended immediately after the assassination of the Reichs Protector Reinhard Heydrich, Hitler's deputy, in 1941, and representatives of all Czech theaters were beckoned to the National Theater to pledge their allegiance to the Third Reich.[6] Finally, all theaters in the Protectorate of Bohemia and Moravia were shut down permanently on September 1, 1944. The Slovaks had their own fascist coup during the war, and all Czech theater workers were driven from Slovak theaters.

One paradoxical theater venue during the war was concentration camps. Inmates performed plays, cabarets, and even operas during their imprisonment. The most surreal of these camps was Terezín (known to the Germans as Theresienstadt), a former military garrison town in the north of Bohemia. It was not a death camp itself but, rather, a holding station for Jews on the way to death camps in Poland. The paradox of Terezín was that it was a ferment of cultural activity. The camp had its own newspapers, elementary schools, as well as an orchestra and theater. Twenty-five theatrical productions took place in the Terezín concentration camp, often with very large and intricate stage sets. One was Smetana's *The Bartered Bride,* whose premier took place in 1942.

The 1960s

After the war, Czechoslovakia came under Communist control, and although there were attempts at quality drama, the overall result in the 1950s was the dullest and most sterile theater imaginable. Communist authorities banned experimental and avant-garde theater, and drama was saddled with the responsibility of presenting unambiguous moral imperatives by depicting the building of socialism and the overcoming of bourgeois morality. Theater output became pure propaganda controlled by official Party guidelines. Many theaters were closed, and many actors and directors were suspended.

When the thaw began after Krushchev's 1956 denunciation of Stalin, the centralized monolithism of Czech theater gave way to a burgeoning of small, often experimental theaters; moreover, dramatists in general turned away from broad social themes and focused on the individual and his or her private problems. By 1963, Prague alone could boast of around 50 theater companies.[7] The most important new theaters were Jiří Suchý's and Ivan Vyskočil's Reduta, founded in 1957; Semafor founded by Suchý and Jiří Šlitr in 1959; the Ballustrade Theater, led by Jan Grossman; the Drama Club founded by Jan Kačer and Alena Vostrá in 1965; and Theater Beyond the Gate founded by Otomír Krejča in 1965. The most prominent playwrights of the period were Josef Topol, Václav Havel, Ivan Klíma, and Milan Kundera.

Beginning in the 1960s, however, playwrights begin to move away from the individual and the personal toward the social. The stage became an alternative social model—an absurd and grotesque one. In general, drama became more experimental, constructed around philosophical ideas and concepts. The Theater of the Absurd had an enormous impact at this time, not only in Czechoslovakia, but throughout the Eastern Bloc in general. In the West, Theater of the Absurd was seen as primarily apolitical, especially in comparison with theater as practiced by the followers of Brecht. In the Eastern Bloc, however, the plays of Beckett and Ionesco became the model for a certain type of political theater. As one theater critic puts it:

> When *Waiting for Godot*—a totally apolitical play in Britain or American—was first performed in Poland at the time of the thaw of 1956, the audience there immediately understood it as a portrayal of the frustration of life in a society which habitually explains away the hardships of the present by emphasizing that one day the millennium of plenty is bound to come. And it soon became clear that a theatre of such concretized images of psychological dilemmas and frustrations which transmuted moods into myths was extremely well suited to deal with the realities of life in Eastern Europe, with the added advantage that, concentrating on the psychological essentials of the situation in a setting of myth and allegory, it had no need to be openly political or topical by referring to politics or social conditions as such.[8]

Václav Havel (b. 1936) was the most important playwright of Czech Absurd drama. After his success at home, his name swiftly rose to international prominence, and after 1968 he began his dissident activities, which would make him the most well-known dissident in the countries of the Eastern Bloc, as well as pave his way to the presidency in 1989. Havel worked first as a stagehand and then became the dramaturge, or literary advisor, for the Theater on the Ballustrade, where he worked from 1960 to 1969. His first full-length play at the Ballustrade was *The Garden Party* (1963), a satire of modern bureaucracy. It was an immediate success both at home and abroad and initiated Theater of the Absurd in Czechoslovakia. Havel's method is to employ dramatic techniques to make situations and characters appear ridiculous. In *The Memorandum* (1965), an artificial language is introduced, Ptydepe, which is supposed to allow for greater precision in office communications. The result, however, is a complete collapse of human communications and relationships. This theme is developed further in *The Increased Difficulty of Concentration* (1968) in which a machine is used to analyze humans. The scene, however, is shifted from the workplace to the home, and the mechanisms of private life come to the fore. These three plays are social satires of life in contemporary Czechoslovakia, but their relevance to any bureaucratic system is clear.

In the 1970s Havel wrote a series of one-act plays, *Audience* (1975), *The Unveiling* (1975), and *Protest* (1978), in which the protagonist, Vaněk, is Havel's alter ego, a dissident playwright in trouble with the authorities and who faces the absurd realities of Czech life. Other playwrights who tried their hand at Absurd theater in the 1960s and 1970s were Ivan Klíma with his *The Castle* (1964), Milan Kundera in *The Owner of the Keys* (1962) and *Balderdash* (1968), and Pavel Kohout in *Poor Murderer* (1972).

The events of August 1968 eventually plunged Czechoslovak theater into two decades of compelled insipidness, but not right away. The authorities had other, more pressing concerns than fractious thespian activity. The number of plays performed in Czech and Slovak theaters remained high, but the repertoires were notable for the absence of any plays or operas from the Warsaw Pact countries that invaded Czechoslovakia. This was how the Czechs expressed their dissatisfaction with the regime. In March of 1969, however, massive demonstrations broke out in Prague's Wenceslaus Square celebrating the defeat of the Russians by the Czechoslovaks at the World Hockey Championships.[9] During the demonstrations, celebrants shattered the windows of the Russian Aeroflot offices. At this point, the officials imposed Normalization with a vengeance, and theater repertoires were purged of anything slightly subversive, initiating 20 years of mediocrity. Havel, Kohout, Klíma, and Kundera continued to compose plays critical of socialism, which were performed abroad, but at home they were silent.

In the mid-1980s, the Soviet leader Mikhail Gorbachev began his *glasnost* and *perestroika* reforms in the Soviet Union. Ironically, it was contemporary

Soviet dramas from this period performed on Czech and Slovak stages that signaled a less oppressive atmosphere in Czechoslovakia. Because of the relaxed censorship in the Soviet Union, Soviet plays could be more liberal and critical than Czech plays.[10]

Here we should mentioned one wildly popular theater troupe that began in 1967 and rose to prominence under Normalization—the Jára (da) Cimrman Theater. The theater was the brainchild of Ladislav Smoljak, Jan Svěrák, and Jiří Šebánek, and like many typically Czech organizations, it was established in a tavern. The foundations of the theater are mystification and pseudo-scholarliness, and its immediate impulse was the desire of the men to gather once a week without the company of women. The theater is devoted to "discovering" and "rescuing" the legacy of the nineteenth-century Czech genius Jára Cimrman who was born to an Austrian mother and a Czech father in Vienna in 1857, 1864, 1867, or 1894—the exact date is unknown since the parish priest who recorded the birth was in a state of inebriation at the time. Cimrman was a little known inventor (he invented the CD or "Cimrman Disk"), an explorer (his Arctic expedition missed the North Pole by a mere seven meters), and a dramatist (he suggested to Anton Chekhov that two sisters were not enough for a full-fledged play and personally fertilized the cherry orchard), yet his activities and inventions found little response in his day.

The performances of the Jára Cimrman Theater follow the same pattern. The first half is devoted to "scholarly" lectures on Cimrman himself presented by "Cimrmanologists," that is, the members of the troupe dressed in formal attire who deliver lectures on such topics as Cimrman's method of musical notation (in which all the notes are written upside-down) or his concept of absolute rhyme (whereby rhymes consist of one and the same word). The second half showcases a performance of one of the master's productions—a play, fairy tale, detective story, or even an operetta. The performances are ironic, tongue-in-cheek, but performed absolutely seriously and deliberately amateurishly. One of the primary points of Cimrman is a critique of Czech history and the Czech character.

From the beginning, the public's response to Cimrman has been overwhelming. During the theater season, the troupe performs six to eight shows a week, and performances are sold out months in advance. Moreover, in a 2005 poll taken by Czech Television, Cimrman was voted the "Greatest Czech of All Time."[11] The contest was based on a British reality show that has been repeated in five other countries. Whereas the voters elsewhere chose statesmen, scholars, and scientists, it was the fictitious Jára Cimrman that led the pack in the Czech Republic, that is, until Czech Television ruled that a fictional character could not win the contest. Cimrman was excluded from the running but was eventually presented with his own award as the "Greatest Fictitious Czech of All Time," just ahead of Jaroslav Hašek's creation the good soldier Švejk.

Post-1989

Even though the events of 1989 brought a playwright to the presidency, Czech and Slovak theaters have faced considerable downsizing. Censorship is gone but so are the lavish subsidies of yesteryear. The monopoly of the theaters was abolished, the operation of theaters was open to the private sector, and the existing network of theaters was transferred from the national to the local authorities. Government subsidies have decreased every year since 1990. Moreover, theater attendance has dwindled significantly due to competition from video games, film, and commercial television. Yet it is perhaps too early to sound the death knell for Czech theater.

In some ways, the Czech theater scene resembles that of the 1920s and 1930s during the First Republic. The old oppressor is gone, and playwrights and theater directors have no monolithic enemy against which to direct their creative efforts. The result is a highly unusual mixture of different forms and styles, often consciously playful with no sense of cultural mission.

CLASSICAL MUSIC

Smetana—Dvořák—Janáček compose the Holy Trinity of Czech classical music. Classical music has a rich, if somewhat uneven, history in the Czech lands. At the center of Europe, Prague has been well placed to absorb influences from the great European music centers of Vienna and Berlin over centuries.

The beginnings of Czech music go back to the religious hymn or song. The earliest preserved sheet music dates from the eleventh century, *Hospodine pomiluj ny!* ("Lord, Have Mercy"), a paraphrase of the Kyrie Eleison, and derives from the Roman church service, but the hymn contains many Old Church Slavonic elements. Its deep choral melody is indeed breathtaking. The Czechs can boast of several world-class composers during the Renaissance and Baroque periods, but after 1620, many musicians fled abroad. Of those who settled and continued working in Vienna were Jan Hugo Voříšek (1791–1825), Jan Leopold Koželuh (1747–1818), and Pavel Vranický (1756–1808). Beethoven chose the last to conduct the premiere of his First Symphony. Josef Mysliveček (1737–1781) settled in Italy where the locals referred to him as *Il divino Boemo,* [the divine Bohemian]. His work is often compared to Mozart's.

Despite this musical exodus from Bohemia, Prague's music culture blossomed. Mozart was more welcome in Prague than Vienna, and every famous composer was greeted in Prague with open arms. In 1772 the British musical historian Charles Burney visited the capital and wrote that he had heard that the Czechs were the most musically talented nation in Germany, and perhaps all of Europe. J. C. Bach had assured him that if conditions for the Czechs were as favorable as those for the Italians, they would surely eclipse them.[12]

It was not until the Romantic period and the National Revival, however, that Czech composers started looking for native Czech themes. Bedřich Smetana (1824–1884) rose to prominence at this time and today is esteemed as the Czech national composer even though he was never able to write error-free Czech. It was Smetana who helped realize the creation of an independent Czech national opera, and in 1868 he laid the foundation stone of the National Theater on behalf of all Czech artists. His opera *Libuše* was performed on the opening night. Several of Smetana's operas—*The Brandenburgers of Bohemia, Libuše,* and *Dalibor,* for example—are fiercely patriotic verging on bombastic, and the composer was often accused of an excessive Wagnerianism. In response, Smetana composed the comic opera *The Bartered Bride* ("sold bride" is perhaps a better translation), a beloved, lively picture of rural Bohemian life with appealing melodies, folksy humor, and copious beer drinking. A peasant's daughter outwits her parents in order to marry the man she loves rather than his half-brother. Smetana wrote in his diary in 1865, "That year I concluded my first comic opera and I myself gave it the title, 'The Bartered Bride' because Sabina, the writer of the text, did not know what to call it. It was in two acts with prose additions. I determined to try and see whether, if I succeeded in writing in a lighter style, I could not prove to all my opponents that I knew my way about very well in the minor musical forms, a thing they disputed, considering me to be too confirmed a Wagnerian to manage it."[13]

Smetana's most famous work is the orchestral cycle *My Homeland,* which he wrote after going deaf. Each movement celebrates a different aspect of Czech culture, history, and mythology. It opens with the majestic *Vyšehrad,* solemnizing the heroic battles of the distant past, then *The Moldau,* the most frequently performed piece and the one tourists associate with Prague, follows the river from its source to the Prague Castle. *Šárka* evokes a Bohemian myth of an Amazonian love story. *From Bohemia's Fields and Groves* presents a series of folkloric portraits. *Tábor* harks back to the fallen Hussites, and *Blaník* concludes the cycle with the hope that one day the Blaník Knights will awaken when the nation's need is greatest.

Antonín Dvořák (1841–1901) supported himself by playing second viola in Smetana's orchestra in Prague's Provisional Theater. He quit the orchestra in 1871 to devote himself to composition. Dvořák was quite successful abroad, which is something that eluded Smetana during his lifetime. In

1891 the New York Symphony offered Dvořák the post of Director, and his three years in America resulted in his most popular work, Symphony No. 9, *From the New World* (1893). At the time, Dvořák claimed he had employed American folk music and spirituals, but this he later denied. Music scholars generally agree that the work has more in common with Bohemian folk music than American. The best examples of Dvořák's interpretation of Bohemian folk music are his two sets of *Slavonic Dances*.

Leoš Janáček (1854–1928) is the most renowned Czech composer of the twentieth century. His challenging operas are perhaps his most important contribution to the history of music. Much of his music derives from dissonant and unexpected harmonies, which are related to general trends in early twentieth-century music. While composing the opera *Jenůfa*, from 1894 to 1903, Janáček developed his theory of the "speech melody," which was based on the rhythms and inflections of the spoken Czech language. His most famous operas are *Kát'a Kabanová* (1921), *The Cunning Little Vixen* (1924), and *The Makropulos Case* (1926).

Bohuslav Martinů (1890–1959) was one of the first composers to incorporate jazz elements into his compositions. He was extremely prolific, composing over 400 works. His music is notable for its mixture of classical and avant-garde elements to create a completely new sound. Martinů left his homeland for Paris in 1923, and when the German army approached Paris, he fled to the United States, where he settled in New York. Later he moved to Switzerland and never returned to his homeland. Martinů's most frequently performed works today are the opera *Juliette* and the ballet *Spalíček*.

THE POLITICS OF ROCK

In 1990 just after Václav Havel was elected president of a newly free Czechoslovakia, Frank Zappa arrived in Prague at his invitation. Five thousand fans, by Zappa's own estimate, were waiting at Prague's Ruzyně airport to greet the musician. Coincidentally, the American Ambassador to Czechoslovakia, Shirley Temple Black, was at the airport as well awaiting departure. A Czech TV news crew collared the ambassador and asked her to comment on Zappa's historic visit. Temple Black was speechless but finally managed to recall that she had, in fact, heard of Zappa's daughter, Moon Unit; however, she knew nothing about the father. Now it was the Czechoslovak public's turn to be speechless: they were aghast at the ambassador's cultural ignorance. How could the American ambassador know nothing of this American cultural icon, a musician who had inspired thousands of Central Europeans to dissident, if not revolutionary, activity?

Frank Zappa had come to Prague to advise Havel on ways to improve the Czechoslovak economy, and Havel had planned to make the musician his

Special Ambassador to the West on Trade, Culture, and Tourism. Havel knew that the county needed foreign investment, but he was also aware of the ugliness that often accompanies it. By appointing someone whose primary concern was culture, he hoped things would go differently in Czechoslovakia. Zappa welcomed the invitation and immediately began setting up meetings with corporations interested in investing in Czechoslovakia. He told *The Nation* magazine, "You don't have to know about international financing. You just have to know about composition."[14] Bush administration officials quickly dissuaded Havel from the appointment, but he made Zappa an unofficial cultural attaché nevertheless.

Frank Zappa's visit is indicative of the role rock music played in the cultural and political underground from which Václav Havel arose. Havel served as president of Czechoslovakia from 1989 to 1992 and then president of the Czech Republic from 1993 to 2003. Rock musicians and underground poets were well represented in his cabinet because during the totalitarian regime underground culture was the place in which artists and philosophers attempted to, in Havel's phrase, "live in truth."

Rock music, or "Big Beat" as it was called, came to Czechoslovakia the same way it did to other countries of the Eastern Bloc, through the songs of Chuck Berry and Elvis Presley in the 1950s. In the late 1950s countless Czech and Slovak groups emerged performing covers of western tunes, which they sang in English or recast into Czech. For example, Jiří Suchý's version of "Rock Around the Clock" became *Tak jak plyne řeky proud* ["How the River Flows"], and Viktor Sodoma of the group Mefisto sang Elvis's "Don't be Cruel" as *Co je to láska?* ["What Is Love?"].[15] By 1964 there were over one hundred amateur rock bands in Prague alone.[16] The most popular were Mefisto, Komety (the Comets), and Olympic. The last is still performing today. The rock phenomenon quickly became an alternative way of life, whereby young people expressed their dissatisfaction with the pseudo values expressed by the regime. Attempts by the authorities to confine and restrict this western cultural phenomenon failed miserably.

It was Beatlemania that really stirred things up in Czechoslovakia. It swept through the country like a tornado. A reporter for the Prague paper *Svobodné slovo* attended a concert by a local Czech band and was outraged by the behavior of the fans: "They wriggled, they fell off the platform and crawled back onto it, they gasped for air hysterically. I expected them to bite each other any minute. And then the destruction began."[17] Beatlemania was soon followed by Allen Ginsberg who arrived in Prague for two months in 1965. The American beat poet and free love guru attended countless rock concerts and festivals, read his own poetry at specially arranged public readings, and conducted yoga seminars. On May 1, 1965, Charles University students elected

Ginsberg King of May, elevated him onto their shoulders, and transported him throughout Prague. Ginsberg's outspoken criticism of the Communist regime brought unwelcome attention from the authorities. He was arrested three times and finally ejected from the country as an American homosexual narcotic hippie, a poor role model for Czechoslovak youth.

To a large extent, the popularity and acclaim of Ginsberg's visit exposed the disaffection experienced by much of the youth of Czechoslovakia. Membership in Communist youth organizations had been dropping, and now teenagers all over Czechoslovakia were gathering in illegal underground clubs where they met to listen to music, read poetry, and create "happenings."

In January 1968, Alexandr Dubček became head of the Czechoslovak Communist Party and undertook a series of reforms culminating in the historic Prague Spring. Rock bands flourished in the new freedom. Groups such as the Matadors, Flamengo, the Beatmen, and Karkulka played their own versions of songs by the Kinks, the Who, and the Yardbirds. The shows themselves were not that exciting in terms of musicianship, but the enthusiasm of the audience made up for weak performances. The most original of these early bands was the Primitives Group. They were the first to experiment with the psychedelic sound of Jimi Hendrix, the Doors, the Grateful Dead, and Frank Zappa's Mother's of Invention. Moreover, their performances were more like "happenings" than ordinary concerts. In shows such as Fish Fest or Bird Fest, the band members would dress up in animal costumes and pelt the audience with fish and fowl.

After the collapse of the Prague Spring and the institution of Normalization, measures were taken to wipe out rock music and its pernicious influence on youth. Hippies were arrested and forcibly given haircuts. Bands were prohibited from taking foreign names, from performing songs by British and American groups, and from wearing outlandish attire. Repertoires had to be approved beforehand, and under no circumstances could men wear long hair. Many bands stopped playing altogether; some, such as Olympic, cooperated and changed their sound, and several musicians left the country.

As the official music scene treaded water in a sea of watered-down pop, several alternative underground bands emerged such as DG 307,[18] *Hever a Vazelína*, and *Umělá hmota* [Artificial Matter]. The most important underground group, however, was The Plastic People of the Universe, named after a Frank Zappa tune. The Plastics, as they are commonly called, formed shortly after the Warsaw Pact invasion and briefly held professional status. Their primary influences were the Velvet Underground, the Fugs, and of course Frank Zappa. Following the lead of the Primitives Group, the Plastics employed visual techniques to enhance their performances, which became part concert, part "happening." Paul Wilson, who sang for a brief time with the group, describes his first Plastics' concert:

> The stage was decorated with gigantic inflated polyethylene cigars. Just as it was getting dark outside the Plastics came on wearing white satin sheen gowns that looked as though they had slept in them, and dark, sinister makeup.... At the climax of their [first] song, a fellow with no eyelashes or eyebrows ignited two Bengal fires, which filled the room with a choking, acrid smoke, then he squirted an ampoule of lighter fluid into his mouth and did a fire-breathing act right on the dance floor.[19]

In its beginnings, the band performed covers of Western tunes, but then realized that contemporary music should speak to its audience in a language they understood. The Plastics began working with the underground poet and philosopher Egon Bondy and set his poems to music. Bondy's poetry deals with the most basic aspects of mankind—and these aspects are often obscene. Even during the Prague Spring, Bondy's poems were too "realistic" for publication. The collaboration of the band and poet resulted in the Plastics' first LP in 1974, *Egon Bondy's Happy Hearts Club Banned.*

The Plastics became the cynosure of the Czechoslovak underground movement. The Czech underground was not simply a group of people who conglomerated simply to defy Communism by playing forbidden music. After a time, counter-cultural intellectuals, such as Václav Havel, Ivan Martin Jirous, and Václav Benda, began to "theorize the underground," and it became a truly alternative culture. Jirous was the Plastics' artistic director and an art historian by training. He designated the culture of the underground the "second culture." In his definition the second culture is not only music, "it is a mental attitude of intellectuals and artists who consciously and critically determine their own stance toward the world in which they live. It is a declaration of a struggle against the establishment."[20] This second culture seeks not to displace or destroy official culture, but to establish a realm of existence not dependent upon the hierarchy of values laid down by the official culture.

After the loss of their professional status, the Plastics continued to perform, but rarely. In 1973 they were asked to play in southern Bohemia in a small town near České Budějovice. News of the event spread like wildfire through the country, and hundreds of youths descended on the town. The police intervened before the Plastics had a chance to perform. Truncheon-wielding cops broke up the gathering, spilling much blood and breaking several limbs. The event became known as the Budějovice massacre.

From then on the police hounded the Plastics and other underground groups. In 1976 after a music festival honoring Jirous' wedding, the Plastics were arrested, interrogated, and put on trial. The day after the arrests, Western news agencies picked up the story, and Czech rock and roll suddenly became the focus of human rights advocates. A group of Czech intellectuals, including Václav Havel, came to the defense of the band. Havel and the philosopher Jan Patočka wrote an open letter to the West German novelist Heinrich Böll in an attempt to enlist his support. Böll responded positively, and his letter initiated a discourse with other European intellectuals on Eastern Bloc dissidence.

The trial of the Plastics was a farce reminiscent of the 1950s Stalinist show trials. Havel managed to attend the hearings, and his essay *The Trial* was widely circulated in Czechoslovakia and included along with the Plastics' first album. This was no mere trial:

[It was] an impassioned debate about the meaning of human existence, an urgent questioning of what one should expect from life, whether one should silently accept the world as it is presented to one and slip obediently into one's prearranged place in it, or whether one has the strength to exercise free choice in the matter; whether one should be "reasonable" and take one's place in the world, or whether one has the right to resist in the name of one's own human convictions.[21]

The Plastics' trial was the initial impetus for the Czech human rights movement Charter 77, a manifesto issued by a coalition of Czech writers and intellectuals on January 1, 1977. The announcement of the charter came out in various Western newspapers a few days later on January 6. Communist authorities arrested several of the signatories the following day and began cracking down on dissident activities. Charter 77 details the violations of the 1975 Helsinki Human Rights Accord. The government saw the Charter as a threat and quickly circulated a "voluntary" Anti-Charter condemning Charter 77, which state employees were required to sign. The manifesto eventually landed Havel in jail and was a precursor to the Velvet Revolution twelve years later.

Several of the band members were sentenced to jail from eight to twelve months. Ivan Jirous was sentenced for 18 months. After their release, the band continued to perform clandestinely throughout the 1970s and 1980s. Václav Havel's summer house was the site of more than one concert.

After the Velvet Revolution and Frank Zappa's historic visit, another momentous meeting took place between Václav Havel and Lou Reed, the founder of the Velvet Underground, who had traveled to Prague in 1990 to interview Havel. In Prague Castle, Reed presented Havel with a copy of his latest album, and Havel related the tale of the Plastic People to an obviously awestruck Lou Reed, explaining how influential the Velvet Underground and rock music had been in the Velvet Revolution. Later that night, Havel took Reed to a club where a band was playing. As Reed recalled, "I suddenly realized the music sounded familiar. They were playing Velvet Underground songs, beautiful, heartfelt, impeccable versions of my songs. To say I was moved would be an understatement."[22] The band was Půlnoc [Midnight], which contained several former members of the Plastic People. Reed joined them on stage. After the concert, Havel introduced Reed to his friends, many of them former dissidents, and they told Reed of reciting his lyrics in prison for comfort.

In July 1988, the Plastics performed in New York City, and on September 16, 1998, Milan Hlavsa, the band's founder, played a dinner show in Washington, D.C., for Presidents Clinton and Havel. He was accompanying his old hero, Lou Reed.

Today, the music scene in the Czech Republic and Slovakia is as alive and vibrant as anywhere else in the free world. Although Anglo-American groups dominate the market, many Czech and Slovak groups have not abandoned their native tongue. Some formerly banned groups playing today are *Psí vojáci* [Dog Soldiers] and *Garáž*. New bands include

Shortly after the Velvet Revolution in 1989, President Václav Havel invited the Rolling Stones to perform in Prague. Havel himself introduced the band, saying the Stones were "messengers of freedom" to the Czechs who had just freed themselves from Communist rule. © Corbis.

MIG21 (named after a cold war era combat fighter), Lucie, *Žlutý pes* [Yellow Dog], Support Lesbiens, and the Plastic Beatles of the Universe. The most well-known Slovak pop group is the perennially popular Elán, legendary in both republics.

Notes

1. Stanley Buchholz Kimball, *Czech Nationalism: A Study of the National Theatre Movement, 1845–83* (Urbana: University of Illinois Press, 1964), 170.

2. Václav Havel, *Disturbing the Peace: A Conversation with Karel Hvížďala,* trans. Paul Wilson (New York: Random House, 1990), 54.

3. Jirí Suchý, ed., *Semafor* (Prague, 1965), 200.

4. Kimball, *Czech Nationalism,* ix.

5. Jarka M. Burian, *Modern Czech Theatre: Reflector and Conscience of a Nation* (Iowa City: University of Iowa Press, 2000), 12.

6. Burian, *Modern Czech Theatre,* 61–62.

7. Paul I. Trensky, *Czech Drama Since World War I* (Armonk, NY: M. E. Sharpe, 1978), 13.

8. Martin Esslin, *The Theatre of the Absurd,* 3rd ed. (London: Penguin Books, 1980), 317.

9. The Soviet journalist Evgenii Rubin describes what occurred after the match:
The Czech captain, Iosef Golonka, approached the Soviet team, pointed his stick forward like a machine gun, and shot the players. Those in the stands sang, cried, kissed one another, and prayed. Even the Czech coach, Vladimir Kostka, a perfectly loyal Party member said at the press conference that the result of the game far exceeded the bounds of a sports victory. Lawrence Martin, *The Red Machine: The Soviet Quest to Dominate Canada's Game* (Toronto, 1990), 95.

10. Burian, 155.

11. Coilin O'Connor, "Jára Cimrman—the 'Greatest Ever' Czech?" Radio Prague February 16, 2005, http://www.radio.cz/en/article/63467.

12. Charles Burney, "Of the Progress of Music in Germany, During the Present Century," in *A General History of Music, from the Earliest Ages to the Present Period. To Which Is Prefixed, A Dissertation on the Music of the Ancients,* 4 vols. (London, 1776–1789), 4: 587–616.

13. František Bartoš, ed., *Smetana, Letters and Reminiscences* (Artia: Prague 1955), 96.

14. Interview with David Corn, *The Nation,* March 19, 1990.

15. Timothy W. Ryback, *Rock Around the Bloc: A History of Rock Music in Eastern Europe and the Soviet Union* (Oxford: Oxford University Press, 1990), 25.

16. Sabrina Petra Ramet, ed., *Rocking the State: Rock Music and Politics in Eastern Europe and Russia* (Boulder: Westview Press, 1994), 56.

17. Ryback, *Rock around the Bloc,* 58.

18. DG 307 is a psychiatric diagnostic code the band chose under the mistaken impression that it designated schizophrenia. When the band members discovered that it actually referred to "temporary situational disturbances," they were thrilled since this description seemed to them more representative of their band.

19. Paul Wilson, "What's it Like Making Rock'n'Roll in a Police State? The Same as Anywhere Else, only Harder, Much Harder," *Views from the Inside: Czech Underground Literature and Culture (1948–1989),* ed. Martin Machovec. In press.

20. Ivan Martin Jirous, "Report on the Third Czech Musical Revival," in *Views from the Inside.*

21. Václav Havel, *Open Letters: Selected Writings 1965–1990,* ed. Paul Wilson (New York: Random House, 1992), 105.

22. Joseph Yanosik, "The Plastic People of the Universe," March 1996. http://www.furious.com/PERFECT/pulnoc.html.

SELECTED BIBLIOGRAPHY

Burian, Jarka M. *Modern Czech Theatre: Reflector and Conscience of a Nation.* Iowa City: University of Iowa Press, 2000.

Kimball, Stanley Buchholz. *Czech Nationalism: A Study of the National Theatre Movement, 1845–83.* Urbana: University of Illinois Press, 1964.

Ramet, Sabrina Petra, ed. *Rocking the State: Rock Music and Politics in Eastern Europe and Russia.* Boulder: Westview Press, 1994.

Ryback, Timothy W. *Rock around the Bloc: A History of Rock Music in Eastern Europe and the Soviet Union.* New York, Oxford: Oxford University, 1990.

Trensky, Paul I. *Czech Drama Since World War I.* Armonk, NY: M. E. Sharpe, 1978.

9

Painting

Be yourself, and you will be Czech.

—Manifesto of Czech Modernism[1]

THE CZECH AND SLOVAK LANDS have a rich history in the visual arts from thousand-year-old sculpture to twenty-first-century Surrealism. The emphasis of this chapter will be on the present, but to make any sense of the present, we cannot ignore the past, for the past masters have become part of any educated Czech's cultural knowledge. Hence, a historical overview of Czech and Slovak art will precede a discussion of the present.

THE PAST

Except for a few outstanding examples of Romanesque wall paintings and illuminated manuscripts, Czech and Slovak painting did not achieve the level of other European countries until the second half of the fourteenth century under King Charles IV (reigned 1346–1378) and Wenceslas (1378–1400), when a notable school of painting emerged under the influence of Italian and French art. By 1400, painting was already fully developed in Prague. After the Battle of White Mountain, however, the Czech lands fell behind their neighbors culturally and artistically. During the Baroque period, Czech Sensualism emerged in Baroque art to become a characteristic feature of Czech painting in general throughout the period. Art declined precipitously at the end of the eighteenth century but emerged powerfully during the nineteenth-century National Revival.

Astronomical clock on the town hall on the Old Town
Square in Prague. It was rebuilt in 1490, and according
to legend the town councilors were so afraid the clock-
maker Hanuš would recreate this masterpiece that they
put his eyes out. Courtesy of Getty Images/Photodisc.

Romanesque Art (1100–1230)

Czech and Slovak art from the Romanesque period is exclusively religious
and both stylistically and thematically homogenous. Wall paintings of holy
figures and well-known legends adorn Romanesque churches throughout
the two republics. Artists borrowed their themes primarily from Italy and
the alpine lands, but in addition we find depictions of local Czech legends
whereby the artist was apparently trying to demonstrate that the Czechs and
Slovaks had entered the society of cultured European nations.

The basis of the Romanesque image is the drawing. Because the subject matter of Romanesque art is exclusively religious, the artist sought maximum expressiveness rather than imitation of external reality. The abstractness and symbolism of much Romanesque art brings it close to the aesthetics of modern art.

The illuminated manuscript is a remarkable art form of the Romanesque era. Before the invention of the printing press by Johann Gutenberg around 1450, books were copied by hand and decorated with illustrations that "illuminated" the contents of the text. Among the oldest preserved Czech-illuminated manuscripts is the Gumpold legend of St. Wenceslas, written upon the order of Princess Emma, the wife of Boleslav II. It dates before 1006. The number of preserved manuscripts from the entire eleventh century is so small, however, that it is difficult to trace the development of this artistic branch. Under King Vratislav (r. 1061–1092), however, we have evidence of an active artistic workshop in Prague, and it was most likely for Vratislav's coronation in 1085 that the famous Vyšehradský Codex was created. The oldest preserved Romanesque wall paintings reside in the Rotunda of St. Catherine in Znojmo. Other examples are in the St. Peter and Paul Church in Albrechtice from the third quarter of the twelfth century and in the Church of St. Peter in Prague. In Slovakia we find remnants of Romanesque wall paintings in a rotunda in Bíni from the twelfth century, in a rotunda in Dechtice from 1172, and in a church in Krušovice from the end of the twelfth century.

Gothic Art (1230–1530)

Gothic art and architecture arose in France and has nothing to do with the tribe of the Goths, who during the so-called Great Indo-European Migrations descended from northern Europe and took possession of the eastern part of Europe in 600 B.C. The term in fact dates from the sixteenth century, coined as a pejorative term by a French art historian who considered the style barbaric. The Gothic visual aesthetic is characterized in art and architecture by linear and restless forms. It reflected the scholasticism, mysticism, and religious intensity of the Middle Ages.

Czech and Slovak painting from the Gothic period remained faithful to the Romanesque style until the end of the thirteenth century. The Gothic style first appears in manuscript illumination and only later in wall painting. The earliest Gothic illuminated books are hymnals made upon the order of Elizabeth Richenza, the widow of King Wenceslas II. From 1340, we have the unfinished Velislav Bible with illustrations of contemporary life.

Gothic art reached its peak during the reigns of Charles IV and Wenceslas when the Czech lands became one of the main centers of European culture.

Western influences from England intermingled with the domesticated Italian tradition. Paintings by court artists such as Master Theodoric, Master Oswald, Nicholas Wurmser, and others were used to decorated Karlštejn Castle, the Emmaus monastery, and Wenceslaus Chapel in St. Vitus Cathedral.

The so-called fine style was also introduced around 1400 and can be seen in several of the so-called fine Madonnas. A six-volume bible and the Golden Bull were illuminated for Wenceslas IV, a great collector of books. The Hussite wars interrupted the development of art, and the Gothic tradition continued only in southern Bohemia and Moravia. Two noteworthy works from the Hussite period are the Göttingen Codex (after 1460) and the Jena Codex (beginning of the sixteenth century)

After 1470 the quality of Czech paintings began to improve but did not reach the European standard as it did during the second half of the fourteenth century. Dutch painting was introduced through Germany, and wall paintings began to adorn castle halls depicting hunting, tournament, and dancing scenes. The first depiction of a Czech landscape scene appears in the background of a picture of a chase in Blatná near Rožmitál.

Renaissance Art (1530–1620)

By the end of the Middle Ages, scholastic scholarship and learning were mired in fruitless dialectics that brought no real progress. This was in part due to the fact that the subject matter was the sophistic exegesis of the bible and the writings of the holy fathers, which paid little regard to practical problems of society and everyday life. New scientific methods based on empirical evidence provided new knowledge of the world and was not based on "revealed truth." This new thinking penetrated all areas of life, especially mathematics, physics, geometry and optics, anatomy, and finally the plastic arts.

Perhaps the three most famous Italian Renaissance artists are Leonardo da Vinci (1452–1519), Michelangelo Buonarotti (1475–1564), and Tiziano Vecellio (1490–1598). Their art is based on symmetry, harmony, balance, and unity, which were principles Renaissance artists derived from nature. Artists were consciously searching for a new concept of beauty. Technical developments important to the movement were the development of oil paints, the study of optics and anatomy, and the development of perspective. Observation of the real world became primary, and artists undertook the careful study and depiction of the human body, especially naked, the beauty of which Renaissance artists could fully appreciate. In the Renaissance worldview, man, rather than God, became the center of the universe.

Compared to Italy, the Czech lands were saturated with the traditions of Gothic learning and art, which lasted well into the sixteenth century and amounted to an almost national style. Furthermore, much of the work of domestic and foreign Renaissance artists in the Czech and Slovak lands was looted and carried off by the Swedes during the Thirty Years War (1618–1648).

One of the foremost Czech painters of the Czech Renaissance was Master of Litoměrice Altar, creator of the wall paintings in Wenceslas Chapel in St. Vitus Cathedral, as well as of the first Czech Renaissance portrait, Albrecht of Kolowraty in 1506. From 1514, we have the Litoměrice hymnbook with illustrations of the burning of Jan Hus, and a wall painting from after 1510 in Švihov Castle depicts "St. George's Contest With the Dragon."

Italian artists brought with them to Prague the technique of graffito, which became nearly a necessary component of the ornamentation of castles, palaces, and especially burghers' homes—both on the exterior and interior—in the second half of the sixteenth century. The wall is covered completely with dark plaster and then with another thin layer of light plaster. Decorative patterns or motifs are then etched into the damp upper layer. Graffiti in the Czech lands are remarkable for their variety of forms and themes. Frescoes appear in Renaissance interiors, for example, in the main hall of Bechyně Castle and the ceiling of Bučovice Castle, which is also decorated with painted paneling.

Baroque and Rococo Art (1620–1780)

At the end of the sixteenth century, the court of Rudolf II became an international Center of Mannerism. Rudolf invited artists such as Giuseppi Arcimboldo, Bartholomaeus Spranger, Josef Heintz, Hans von Aachen, Aegidius Sadeler, and others to work for him in Prague. Mannerism was influential until the first quarter of the sixteenth century. After the Czech defeat at White Mountain in 1620 by the Catholic Hapsburgs, a reaction ensued against the rationalism of the Renaissance. In general the Baroque aesthetic reflects a longing to understand the secrets of religious truth, to penetrate and explore the depths of the human soul and release it from the material world via mystic ecstasy. Baroque art is characterized by striking and powerful forms, which are often convoluted, exaggerated, and amplified, leading the viewer into a realm of fantastic dream-like images.

In wall painting and frescos, artists worked closely with architects to create the greatest effect possible. Among the most significant works of Baroque art are ceiling frescos on church vaults and cupolas, entertainment halls, and loggias. At first, ceiling painting was used as decoration, but it later became a means to create space. Painting emphasized the rhythm of the architecture and later would be used to create the illusion of opening up into the heavens to reveal complex scenes of heavenly events, both religious and mythological.

In canvas paintings, new subjects appeared due to fresh influences, especially from Holland—genre painting, landscape painting, hunting scenes, still lifes. The figures are presented in complex contrasts and movements, vertiginous rotations, contrasting colors and light and shadow. Particularly popular is the technique of "chiaroscuro," whereby the color creates a play of light reflections and shadowy half tones.

The influence of Italian Baroque entered Bohemia in the eighteenth century. Karel Škréta Šotnovský ze Závořic, Petr Brandl, and Václav Vavřinec Reiner are the greatest representatives of the Czech Baroque painting of the eighteenth century. Chiaroscuro is introduced by Michal Václav Halwachs and fully developed in the expressive compositions of M. L. Willmann. The period of the Josephine Enlightenment in the nineteenth century means the interruption of the painting tradition; its continuation is ensured only by a narrow stream of wall painting done by craftsmen.

Neoclassicism, Romanticism, Realism, and Impressionism (1780–1900)

The fundamental conditions of spiritual and societal life changed due to the French Revolution in 1789, the transformative forces of which were aimed primarily at the destruction of the feudal system. The battle between those who were attempting to preserve the old order and those calling for a new organization of society formed the substance of public life, primarily in France, but it also created powerful reverberations elsewhere, even in the Czech and Slovak lands.

One of the pillars of revolutionary thought was the eighteenth-century rationalism of the French encyclopediasts. Reason and the rules of logic were elevated to the status of a source of knowledge, and it was according to these rules that society was to be organized. The first sign of the victory of rationalism was the removal of religious thought and the Catholic Church from its monopoly position, a place it had occupied in Europe throughout the Middle Ages and up to the eighteenth century.

At the other end of the cultural spectrum during this period is Romanticism. Against the cold schematics of dull reason, Romanticism used intuition to plumb the unknowable depths of the human soul. It was a movement of irrationalism based on powerful emotion, which bore some resemblance to religious faith. On the other hand, it was an inward search based on individual abilities, and the movement developed the cult of the individual, his extraordinary abilities and often heroic feats (Titanism). Regarding the organization of society, Romanticism depended on tradition, and much Romantic art attempted to understand the past (Historicism). It also, however, recognized the natural rights of the individual. "Man is born free, and everywhere he is in chains," wrote Jean Jacques Rousseau (1712–1778), one of the intellectual fathers of Romanticism.[2] The Romantics preached a return to nature, to its multifarious and inexhaustible sources. Moreover, it was Romanticism that was the impetus for the National Revival. Many Romantic artists began looking to the countryside and to folk culture, an area of study artists had previously neglected.

Neoclassical artists by contrast looked back to the art of the ancients. Obviously there were no paintings for them to imitate, so ancient reliefs and sculpture served as inspiration. The Neoclassicists also continued the traditions of the Renaissance and of certain classicizing tendencies in Baroque and Rococo art. The Romantic artist studied medieval styles, especially the Gothic, which the Classical painters scorned as barbaric. It found hitherto unknown worlds in the heroic past of its own nation. Romanticism was, however, rather eclectic in its achievements and did not create a distinctive style. On the other hand, the school became a point of departure for Modernism.

The Prague Academy was founded in 1800 upon Neoclassical artistic principles. Among the younger generation were František Tkadlík, Antonín Mánes, and Václav Mánes. Tkadlík went from Neoclassicism to Romanticism, and several of his students concentrated on Romantic-historical subjects for the better part of a half century. Tkadlík became director of the Academy in 1836. Josef Navrátil emerged from his Rococo roots to become one of the foremost Czech Romantic painters. His late works manifest elements of Realism.

Realist artists avoided poetically charged images and literary themes. Theirs was an attempt to capture unmediated nature. The subjects of Realist paintings are unaffectedly objective, whether they be landscapes, interiors, or still lifes. The Realist employment of colors to build forms owes something to Baroque painting, but the Baroque monumentality found its antipode in Naturalism, which presented "slices of life" without regard to societal standing. This unmediated contact with nature elicited new thematic impulses, such as human labor, especially of agricultural workers and peasants. On the other hand, the development of methodological elements while observing natural phenomena led to a rejection of the "objectness" of the painting subject and thus to Impressionism, essentially a French art movement associated with Renoir, Degas, and especially Monet. Impressionists worked mostly outdoors and tried to capture the play of light and shadow. They preferred bright colors, quick brushwork, and inattention to detail. Claude Monet noted that he preferred enjoying his bad eyesight, and renouncing painting altogether if necessary, as long as he could see a bit of what he liked. Antonín Slavíček and Jan Preisler are two of the foremost Czech Impressionist painters. Their work is distinguished from French Impressionism by more natural colors and symbolic combinations of reality as perceived by sense and a strong internal experience. Their work led directly to Symbolism.

Art Nouveau and Alfons Mucha

Alfons Mucha was born in Moravia at the end of the nineteenth century, and his style of painting personified the style of art called Art Nouveau, a decorative art movement begun in Western Europe around 1880 and lasting until World War I. Artists associated with Art Nouveau attempted to eradicate the dividing line between art and audience. There was to be no distinction between high and low art; *everything* could and should be art. Art Nouveau is characterized by an ornamental asymmetrical style of whiplash linearity, and its themes are symbolic and often erotic. The ornamentation is alive and restless, but at the same time balanced. Mucha studied for a while in Vienna and then moved to Paris. His work was wildly popular, so much so that it was often imitated and referred to as *le styl Mucha*. His work is based on a strong composition, sensuous curves derived from nature, refined decorative elements, and natural colors. The renowned French actress Sarah Bernhardt commissioned Mucha to create a poster for a theater production of *Gismonda.* The poster, a full-length picture of the actress, was quite unusual for its time. Bernhardt launched her protégé into society and signed him to a six-year contract to design posters, costumes, jewelry, and set designs. At the age of 34, Mucha was an overnight sensation.

The Art Nouveau poster was a new type of print, made to decorate walls and not lie around in dusty museums. Color lithographs could be printed in large quantities and sold at reasonable prices. This seems to have corresponded with Mucha's own ideas of art. He says: "I was happy to be involved in an art for the people and not for private drawing rooms."[3] The works were inexpensive, accessible to the general public, and found a home among poor families as well as in more affluent circles.

Mucha's style is unique. The center of all his works is a sensuous, spellbinding, beautiful woman radiating a seemingly natural sexual energy. Her hair is usually unfurled, and the dresses descend complicated folds. She is often adorned with jewels, and the artist always inscribes his figures within a circle, which frames the design. Mucha composed advertisements for cigarettes, liqueur, cookies, bicycles, beer, and much more. The posters, however, were only a means to an end. Mucha's goal was to earn enough money to allow him to paint recreations of historic events important to his native country, the Czechs, and to donate his work and services to his people. His idea was to create a series of 20 oversize paintings depicting those moments in the history of the Slavic people that had a decisive impact in the development of Europe. To raise money, Mucha went to America where he assumed he would receive handsome fees painting portraits of the rich and famous. After living in the United States for eight years, he realized that he would not achieve his goal; however, he did finally locate a patron, a millionaire by the name of Charles Crane, who provided Mucha with the money to allow him to undertake his epic.

In 1910 Mucha returned to Bohemia and over the next 18 years painted 20 enormous canvasses, measuring approximately 24' wide x 30' high. He presented the paintings to the city of Prague in 1928. The paintings illustrate the history of the Slavic people from prehistory to the nineteenth century, but they turned out to be somewhat of an embarrassment. No one knew what to do with the series. The canvases were too large to be housed in a museum, and no one wanted to construct a special facility for them. Moreover, Mucha's message seems to have lost some of its urgency. When he conceived the project, the Czechs and other Slavic countries were, for the most part, under Austrian rule. Mucha's idea was to demonstrate the fact that the Slavs contributed significantly to European culture. By the time the paintings were ready for display, however, the issue had already been resolved politically. The Slavs were free of their Austrian overlords and were establishing new republics with full equality. Outside of Bohemia, however, the response to the paintings was positive overall. When the series came to New York in 1921, over 600,000 visitors attended the exhibit, and the reaction was ecstatic.

In addition to his Slav Epic, Mucha worked assiduously and without commission on a large number of projects for the newly created Czechoslovak government. He designed everything from bank notes and stamps to the national emblem and the police uniforms.

THE TWENTIETH CENTURY

In general the nineteenth century was a backward-looking time for the Czechs. Throughout their National Revival, they were attempting to create a modern Czech culture based on indigenous Czech ancient culture, which to a large extent blinkered them to cultural developments elsewhere. At the turn of the century, however, several artists came together renouncing old trends in art and ridiculing Czech nationalistic slogans, songs, and art. To them, Mucha's Slav Epic epitomized the provincial and bourgeois nature of Czech art and culture. In 1895 several writers and critics organized themselves into a cultural group, calling themselves Czech Modern, and they published a "Manifesto of Czech Modernism" in which they wrote: "In no way do we accentuate Czechness: be yourself, and you will be Czech…. We do not know national maps."[4] The Czech Modern group urged Czechs to look beyond their borders and take note of the cultural worlds thriving in other countries. One of the impulses for Czech modern art was the same as modern art everywhere—to reject tradition and develop new forms and original means of expression that would transcend the relativity of time and history. As the Czech artist Emil Filla put it, "to create new values and redeem oneself."[5]

Cubism

As early as 1910, Cubism became the dominant tendency in Czech art, and Prague was the most important center of Cubism after Paris. But an understanding of Cubism requires a knowledge of a few earlier artistic trends, namely Symbolism, and Expressionism.

The Symbolists turned inward and upward, away from the external world. The movement was supposed to be suggestive, reflecting a journey of the imagination and emphasizing sensual experience and the other world. Dreams are important for the Symbolists, but not in the sense of the Freudian subconscious (i.e., the realm of the Surrealists). For the Symbolists, the dream is a waking reverie triggered by a sensual experience, which lifts the mind from mundane preoccupations. Expressionism is a German art movement in which the representation of reality is distorted to express an inner vision. It is much more emotionally charged than Impressionism or Symbolism. The spiritual father of Expressionism was the Norwegian painter Eduard Munch, but the most famous practitioners were the German Max Beckmann and the Austrian Egon Schiele.

Cubism originated in Paris around 1907. Its practitioners professed an intellectual revolt against the sensual and emotional art of Expressionism and Symbolism. In Cubist art, three-dimensional subjects are fragmented and redefined from several different points of view simultaneously. The originators of the movement were Pablo Picasso and Georges Braque. In the Czech lands, Cubism became mixed with Expressionism. In 1905 a retrospective of Eduard Munch was held in Prague, and the psychological aspect of the artist captured the public's imagination. For the first time, Czech artists such as Emil Filla, Bohumil Kubišta, and Josef Čapek witnessed the expression of psychological alienation through emotionally charged aesthetics. Munch demonstrated art's potential to plumb the depths of the modern psyche. Between 1905 and 1907, the expression of internal states rather than immediate perceptions came to dominate Czech art. This was the contribution of Prague to the European avant-garde movement—the confrontation of the spiritual atmosphere of Central Europe with the pictorial structure of the

Paris Cubists.[6] The movement is often referred to as Cubo-Expressionism. Jan Zrzavý, Emil Filla, Josef Čapek, and Václav Špála, are perhaps the most renowned practitioners of Cubo-Expressionism. These artists were fascinated with existential anxiety and a loss of faith.

The still life was the traditional Cubist theme in the work of Braque and Picasso, but it appeared rarely in Prague before 1912. The depiction of charged existential states was typical for Czech Cubists, moments when man is torn out of the common course of events and becomes intensely conscious of himself and his relation to exterior reality.[7]

Devětsil

During World War I, Cubism, Expressionism, and Cubo-Expressionism gradually died out in the Czech lands. Many of the artists of these groups were living abroad or serving at the front. By the time the Czechoslovak First Republic was established in October 1918, a group consisting of former Cubo-Expressionists including Josef Čapek, Václav Špála, and Jan Zrzavý assumed the artistic sobriquet the *Tvrdošíjní* or the Stubborn Ones. Their art was a restrained or subdued version of their earlier Cubo-Expressionism in which much of the existential anxiety was suppressed. After World War I, a crisis of faith afflicted the Western world—faith in progress, in democracy, in humanity. For many, the war had revealed the feeble foundation of human civilization and humaneness, and after the war Expressionism came to dominate the avant-garde. But not in Czechoslovakia. After the war, the Czechs and Slovaks came into the possession of their own independent state for the first time in three hundred years; hence, their outlook on the world was much less pessimistic, and this of course is reflected in their art. The Czechs downplayed the anxiety of their Cubo-Expressionism. In many works, we see how the artist is less concerned with the anxiety of modernity than with the social issues of lower class urban characters—prostitutes, beggars, and alcoholics. The Stubborn Ones did away with anguished self-portraits and the mystical religiousness and symbolism of Cubo-Expressionism to focus on the optimistic emotional climate of post-war Czechoslovak life.

On the other hand, some artists attacked the Cubists for a lack of revolutionary zeal. The artist and theorist Karel Teige advocated a politically engaged aesthetics, in other words, a Communist aesthetics, and to this end he founded a new artistic group called Devětsil, which became the ideological center of Czech avant-garde art throughout the 1920s. It is unknown how or why the group chose its name. The word Devětsil is a pun on its literal meaning, the butterbur, and the two words *devět* and *sil* meaning "nine forces." The name might refer to the nine Muses of

Parnassus, or perhaps the euphony of the word itself attracted the members of the group.

Regardless of how Devětsil got its name, the group was founded in Prague on October 5, 1920, and it attracted painters, architects, photographers, writers, actors, critics, journalists, and musicians, those for whom progressive aesthetics and social ethics constituted what Teige called an "art of the present time."[8] Over the course of its existence (1920–1931), the organization had more than 60 members. They preached Marxism and revolution, and the new art was to be class based, proletarian, and Communist. Teige repudiated Expressionism as a "cadaver" from a dead era. In his view, Expressionism was an "area of vague shadows," an exaggerated literary art obsessed with mystical symbolism, decadent barbarism, and "convulsive sickly expression." Expressionism focused on individualism and lacked self-control, which, in Teige's view, led to nihilism and degeneration. He believed that art should play a positive social role and evoke an optimistic mood. In general, Devětsil believed social engagement and "pure aesthetics" could revolutionize not only art, but mankind as well. They rejected the –isms of the past and began anew to create an original concept of the world based on primary, unmediated experience.

The most prominent members of Devětsil included Karel Teige (theoretician and organizer), the writer Vladislav Vančura, the poets Vítěslav Nezval and Jaroslav Seifert, and the painters Jindřich Štyrský and Marie Toyen. Not only did they promote a new artistic style, but they also experimented with new materials and techniques that modern technology had made available— film, photography, photomontage, and new printing methods. Teige's early work was inspired by the work of the Stubborn Ones—Josef Čapek, Václav Špála, and Jan Zrzavý. Along these lines, he developed something he called "spiritual realism," a style he thought suggested an objective characterization of modern life. His works did not receive the acclaim the artist had expected, leading Teige to decamp to Paris, a city he considered free of the overheated emotionalism of German Expressionism.

In Paris, Teige relinquished his earlier "spiritual realism," and his works assumed an objectivism and rationalism that he had found in French art. Teige sought a combination of dynamism and control, which reached its culmination in a reconfiguration of the alphabet. In one of his most celebrated projects, Teige collaborated with the poet Vítěslav Nezval and the dancer Milča Majerová to create choreographed letters. They emphasized playfulness and the poetic, which began to replace Devětsil's obsession with politics and Communist ideology.

This attempt to replace traditional forms of art and redefine the very means of visual communication led Teige and Devětsil to the concept of "pictorial-poems." In the 1920s, Prague was home to the Prague Linguistic Circle headed by the Russian linguist Roman Jakobson. The group comprised linguists interested primarily in modern poetry and avant-garde art in general. Teige was fascinated by Jakobson's idea that poetry came into being "when the word is felt as a word and not as a mere representation of the object being named ... when word and their composition ... acquire a weight and value of their own instead of referring indifferently to reality."[9] Thus the word, the ink on the page, has something intrinsically poetic itself. It is not merely a stand-in for an object.

Pictorial poems were the first original contribution of Devětsil to the European avant-garde. Pictorial poems were an example of democratization in art; they were accessible to all and easily understood. Teige synthesized word and image in his "Postcards from Utopia"—collages of cutouts from maps, travel brochures, labels from foreign shipping lines, which suggest metaphorical travel. In several articles, Teige wrote that the pictorial-poem was a way station between the verbalized ideal of the motion picture and his projected avant-garde films, through which he envisioned poetically and abstractly the beauty of the modern world. None of Teige's film ideas were ever realized.

Another aspect of Devětsil as envisioned by Teige was the purely Czech artistic movement called Poetism. In general, Poetism was a joyful celebration of modernity. It was playful, spontaneous and did not hide its enthusiastic belief in progress. In part, it functioned as a reaction against the pessimism and melancholy following the war. Poetism was intoxicated with life, with its sensuality and lyricism, and for the most part poetism ignored life's darker aspects. In his "Second Manifesto of Poetism" (1928), Teige conceived of a higher unity of all art forms, which he called a "poetry of the five senses," to include pictorial, poems, photomontages, abstract film, as well as other, still unrealized art forms such as olfactory poetry.

The first real book of Poetism was Vítěslav Nezval's volume of poetry *Pantomime* (1924), illustrated by Jindrich Štyrský who used drawings, photographs of clowns, neon signs and Hollywood actors, and reproductions of paintings and pictorial poems. In "Modern Trends in Poetry" (1937), Nezval placed Poetism within concurrent artistic trends:

> It is related to Futurism by its liking of cities and speed, to Cubism by its demand for independence from restrictions on freedom of expression, to Surrealism by its inclination towards spontaneity and its emphasis on the free associations of images.[10]

The gradually worsening economic situation of the 1920s somewhat dampened the unbridled optimism of the Poetists, and by the 1930s, the movement had moved inward, from the external to the internal world, and closer to Surrealism.

Eventually two of the members of Devětsil, Jindřich Štyrský and Marie Toyen, grew weary of what they called the geometric abstraction of Czech modernism since Cubo-Expressionism. They moved to Paris in 1925 to regroup and refocus their energies. They called their new movement Artificialism, and this movement lasted from 1926 to 1931. Toyen and Štyrský claimed they were giving poetic form and color to an emotional image. They wrote:

> Cubism turned to reality instead of giving way to the imagination. When it reached the essence of reality, it found that it had no wings.... Artificialism arrives with an opposite perspective.... Letting reality remain as it is, Artificialism tends to maximize the imagination.... Artificialism makes identical the painter and the poet. Its interest is concentrated on poetry.... [Artificialism] renders poetic emotions ... and excites sensibilities that are not only visual. It leads the spectator out of the carousel of his customary imagination, it breaks the system and mechanism of connected images.... [It does not] deny the existence of reality, but neither does it build its arguments from it.... Artificialism concentrates on poetry that fills the gaps between real forms, and that radiates from within reality.[11]

Poetry for the Artificialists was not just the literary form. What they had in mind was a form of communication that stirs the emotions and liberates the imagination. To this end, the Artificialists employed different techniques to suppress the materiality of paint or pencil. Their colors were brighter, and the transitions between colors and forms were subdued. In Artificialist works, colors fade into each other to create a dreamy atmosphere that lacks any fixed boundaries, freeing the imagination and leading the mind to free association based on the titles of the work. The works were intended to create a new "artificial" reality and produce in the viewer a welter of memories and associations, a lyrical atmosphere akin to Poetism. Štyrský writes:

> My eyes need to be thrown food constantly. They swallow it crudely and voraciously, and then at night, in sleep they digest it.... Childhood is my native land. Dreams are my native land, where black snow falls from the clouds.[12]

This emphasis on free-association and the dreamlike quality of the works of the Artificialists appear to link them up to Surrealism, which exploits the erotic possibilities of the Freudian subconscious. To the Artificialists, however, the Surrealists exaggerated the estimation of the subconscious. Artificialism is akin to Poetism. Both are predominantly free artistic forms of expression. When they returned to Czechoslovakia in 1929, however, Toyen and Štyrský served as the founders of Czech Surrealism.

Surrealism

The founder of European Surrealism was the Parisian André Breton. In his *First Surrealist Manifesto* of 1924, Breton defined Surrealism as

pure psychic automatism, by which one proposes to express ... the actual functioning of thought. Dictated by thought, in the absence of any control exercised by reason, exempt from any aesthetic or moral concern, ... Surrealism is based on the belief in the superiority of certain forms of previously neglected associations, in the omnipotence of dreams, in the disinterested play of thought.[13]

The *surreal*, claimed the Surrealists, had always existed and was apparent in earlier works by Hieronymous Bosch (1450–1516), Francisco Goya (1746–1828), and Giuseppe Arcimboldo.

Freud's *Interpretation of Dreams* (1899), hypnosis, and automatic writing were primary influences on Surrealist aesthetics. By inducing trance states, the Surrealists found they could obliterate the outside world and, unhampered by reason, inhabit a marvelous realm of heightened reality denied the conscious mind. The Surrealists sought to reveal the collective subconscious and explore the archetypal myths of mankind. Their ultimate aim was the "future resolution of these two states, dream and reality, which are seemingly so contradictory, into a kind of absolute reality, a *surreality*."[14]

In Prague, modern artists were somewhat skeptical of Surrealism, partially because in the early stages, Czech modernists suspected that French Surrealism was not sufficiently revolutionary. Karel Teige, who later became the primary exponent of Czech Surrealism, claimed French Surrealism was too passive and undisciplined to respond to the socialist needs of the present day. Surrealism stressed the unconscious and extremely individualistic creativity based on psychic automatism, which was opposed to his own aesthetic ideology of collective action. Teige believed that modern art must be carefully controlled and intentionally willed. Imagination must be organized, harmonized, and directed. Only by being subject to the artist's rational control might a poetic vision be employed for universal good. Teige's reservations with Surrealism were probably similar to those he harbored with respect to

Expressionism: it was too vague, too shadowy, too emotional. It had nothing to do with communism or the "common good." But as the economic depression wore on, the optimism of Poetism began to fade, and increasingly the rumblings of Thanatos and Eros emerged. Furthermore, in his *Second Surrealist Manifesto* (1929), Breton expressed his support for dialectical materialism, which brought the movement closer to the aesthetics of the Czech Modernists.

The first Surrealist exhibit in Prague took place in 1932 showcasing works by Štyrský, Toyen, Filla, and the sculptor Vincenc Makovský, which appeared alongside works by Arp, Dalí, Ernst, De Chirico, Miró, and Tanguy. It was the largest Surrealist exhibition yet to have taken place anywhere in the world outside of France. Largely due to this show, Surrealism dominated the Czechoslovak art scene in the 1930s. The popularity of the movement in Czechoslovakia was unprecedented outside of France. In 1935 André Breton traveled to Prague to give a lecture entitled "The Surrealist Situation of the Object." Breton claimed that Prague was the ideal site for Surrealism, for the city was

> wrapped in its legendary magic [and] is truly one of those cities that has been able, in a magnificent way, to fix and retain the poetic idea that is always more or less drifting aimlessly through space.... Seen from afar ... it appears to us as the magical metropolis of old Europe. If only because Prague has nurtured within itself all the imagery and enchantment of the past it seems that it is possible to be heard from this point in the world with less difficulty than from any other point.[15]

Officially the Czech Surrealist Group was formed in 1934, with Teige, Štyrský, Nezval, and Toyen forming the center. Teige was its spokesman, who consistently tied Czech Surrealism to dialectical materialism. By the end of the 1930s, Czech Surrealism was a divided movement between those who supported Stalinism and Socialist Realism and those who battled against both Stalinism and Fascism and insisted on freedom of creation. The result was an overall condemnation of the movement from both the left and the right.[16] All arguments came to naught, however, when the Nazis marched into Prague in March of 1939. Surrealism was declared *entartete Kunst* (degenerate art). The members of the Czech Surrealist group continued to meet secretly, however, and even managed to put out several underground publications. After the war, several Surrealists moved to Paris, and in 1947 an exhibition entitled "International Surrealism" took place in Prague, organized by some of the displaced Czech Surrealists.

Surrealism was pushed underground after the 1968 Prague Spring, but it reemerged as vibrant as ever in the 1990s, perhaps most distinctively in the work of the Czech artist and director Jan Švankmajer. Švankmajer's films have shocked, mesmerized, repulsed and delighted audiences, amassing international cult-like followings and inspiring countless other artists and even imitators (see Chapter 7 of this volume, "Media and Cinema").

Post–World War II

After World War II and the installation of Communist rule, Socialist Realism became the official aesthetic doctrine of Czechoslovakia. The government determined what would be considered as acceptable art. Many artists realized that the potential for the artist to somehow express his own vision and have an effect on society was virtually nil. Artists began to turn inward and direct their powers toward creating an inner spirituality. Vladimír Boudník (1924–1968) was one such inwardly oriented artist. The basis of Boudník's art was direct contact with reality, with the concrete process of production. Steel scraps and splinters became "artifacts" that Boudník would transfer to his abstract graphic sheets. As a character in a short story by his friend Bohumil Hrabal, Boudník states, "When I draw in the street, people begin to reveal themselves. I unleash the same thing in them that the Surrealists uncovered in themselves. Even in a spot on the wall there exists a trembling Rembrandt… and then it's the viewer's picture. What the Surrealists have in their books, I have in my little finger. Today's artists don't have experience, they only repeat, they make use of formulas that are now dead."[17] In his "Manifesto of Explosionism" written in 1949 Boudník suggested that everyone could create art by realizing and externalizing his own personal visions and experiences, "If you are a manual laborer, don't try to make excuses because your hand shakes. Today's art demands living truth and not the superficial school-taught elegance!"[18] Boudník is best known for his prints, "active" and "structural" graphics. He would hammer irregular cuts of metal into flat sheets upon which he would place materials such as fabric, sawdust, and string to create printing plates. These abstract prints are surprisingly subtle and delicate.

Mikuláš Medek (1926–1974) was one of the most persecuted artists in Czechoslovakia. His highly refined and exquisitely structured canvases betray the influence of existentialism and Surrealism and depict the deplorable and painful situation of man in the modern world. The paintings are pervaded with complex structures of symbols and visual metaphors, which he uses to express the grotesque, absurd, and painful dimensions of humanity's existence. In 2004 the film director Aleš Kisil made a documentary film of Medek entitled *I Don't Paint, I Vomit My Paintings Out.*

In 1963 a group of artists came together emphasizing an art that would have the potential to become integrated into society. They suggested an "objective" approach to art as against the subjective styles dominant at the time. They called their group Crossroads *(křižovatka)*, and their movement New Sensibility *(nová citlivost)*. Jiří Kolař (1914–2002), one of the founders, created "objective forms" through different types of collages, which he called *roláž, chiasmáž, muchláž,* and *proláž.*[19] He would place scraps of a picture upon another to create an integrated work of art. The effectiveness depended on the amount of contradiction between the two images. Kolař managed to turn the art of collage into his own original artistic discipline. Hounded by the police, he was forced to emigrate to Paris where he lived from 1980 to 1999.

In the 1970s, several artists surrendered to the pessimism of the era. Jiří Sopko (b. 1942) created unsettling mocking and sarcastic images of people using odd color combinations and bizarre figures to create minimalist depictions of powerless human beings trapped in an abnormal society. Jiří Načeradský (b. 1939) was one of the most original practitioners of the "new figural" style, a revival of classical figural painting. He was also influenced by pop art, comic books, and the mass media. His figures resemble machines, insects, or even monstrous beings from science fiction and create a grotesque commentary on the individual in socialist society.

The latest generation of Czech and Slovak artists are the first to be entirely free of the political pressures that accompanied totalitarianism. Artists such as Tomáš Vaněk, Pavel Kopřiva, and Michal Pěchouček produce work that is less visually arresting than their immediate predecessors and which often incorporates cheap, everyday materials such as potatoes, string, and tram ticket stubs.

NOTES

1. "Česká Moderna," *Rozhledy sociální, politické a literární* (Prague: 1896), 1.

2. Jean-Jacques Rousseau, *Du Contrat Social et autres œuvres politiques* (Paris: Garnier Frères, 1975), 236.

3. Jack Rennert and Alaine Weill, *Alphonse Mucha: The Complete Posters and Panels* (Boston: G. K. Hall & Co. 1984), 10.

4. "Česká Moderna," 1.

5. Emil Filla, "Cesta tvořivosti" in *Uvahy o výtvarném umění* (Prague: Karel Brož, 1948), 380.

6. Miroslav Lamač, "Czech Cubism: Points of Departure and Resolution," in *Czech Modernism 1900–1945,* ed. Josef Anděl et al. (Houston: Museum of Fine Arts; Boston: Bulfinch Press, 1989), 56.

7. Lamač, "Czech Cubism," 56.

8. S. A. Mansbach, *Modern Art in Eastern Europe: From the Baltic to the Balkans ca. 1890–1939* (Cambridge, England: Cambridge University Press, 1999), 61.

9. Mansbach, *Modern Art in Eastern Europe,* 64.

10. František Šmejkal, "Devětsil: An Introduction," in *Devětsil: Czech avant-garde art, architecture and design of the 1920s and 30s,* ed. Šmejkal et al. (Oxford: Museum of Modern Art; London: Design Museum, 1990), 20.

11. Mansbach, 70–71.

12. Šmejkal, "Devětsil," 73.

13. André Breton, *Manifested u Surréalisme,* 1924, http://www.geocities.com/lmc2124/breton.html#manifesto.

14. Breton.

15. František Šmejkal, "From Lyrical Metaphors to Symbols of Fate: Czech Surrealism of the 1930s," in *Czech Modernism,* 65.

16. Mansbach, 82.

17. Bohumil Hrabal, "Legenda o Egonu Bondym a Vladimírkovi," *Morytáty a legendy* (Prague: Mladá fronta, 2000), 19. Originally published in 1968.

18. Vladimír Boudník, "Manifest explosionalismus č. 2," in *České umění 1938–1989,* ed. Jiří Ševčík et al. (Prague: Academia 2001), 111.

19. These terms are nonce words all based on the Czech word for collage, *koláž. Roláž:* cutting a picture into strips or squares and then putting them back together according to various principles. *Proláž: roláž* using more than one picture. *Chiasmáž:* arranging a number of cutouts from the same text into odd geometrical forms. *Muchláž:* crumpling up pictures of well-known people or objects and using them in a collage.

SELECTED BIBLIOGRAPHY

Anděl, Josef et al. *Czech Modernism 1900–1945.* Houston: Museum of Fine Arts; Boston: Bulfinch Press, 1989.

Mansbach, S. A. *Modern Art in Eastern Europe: From the Baltic to the Balkans ca. 1890–1939.* Cambridge, UK: Cambridge University Press, 1999.

Pečinková, Pavla. *Contemporary Czech Painting.* Australia: Gordon and Breach Arts, 1993.

Sayer, Derek. *The Coasts of Bohemia: A Czech History.* Princeton: Princeton University Press, 1998.

Šmejkal, František et al. *Devětsil: Czech avant-garde art, architecture and design of the 1920s and 30s.* Oxford: Museum of Modern Art; London: Design Museum, 1990.

10

Architecture

I have no proof, but I am convinced that the Czechs would not have survived the last half century with their sanity reasonably intact without the sheltering function of their *zlatá Praha* (golden Prague) to tide them over the horrors and provide the citizens with a chance to be free, civilized, and worldly again.

—Eric Dluhosch, Professor Emeritus of Architecture, MIT[1]

NEARLY THREE HUNDRED CASTLES and châteaux are scattered throughout the Czech and Slovak lands, and more than 70 historic town centers have been designated conservation areas. The capital of the Czech Republic itself, Prague, is justifiably regarded as the best place to see Czech architecture. No other European city possesses such a wealth of unspoiled historic structures from so many different periods. Four particular styles of architecture stand out and set something of a European standard: Gothic, Baroque, and two Modernist styles, Cubism and Functionalism. In the early twentieth century, Prague became one of the great (if not the greatest) display of early Modern architectural trends. Unlike many other Central European capitals, Prague was never destroyed by invading armies or occupiers and, hence, never underwent overall fundamental reconstruction. Today, it stands as a showcase of ten centuries of architecture with Baroque fortresses standing alongside Gothic houses and Renaissance gardens adjacent to Art Nouveau bungalows. The focus of this chapter is primarily the architecture of the twentieth century, but the rich historical styles of Prague—"city of a hundred spires"—cannot be ignored.

Built by the father and son architecture team Christoph and Kilian Ignaz Dientzenhofer at the beginning of the eighteenth century, St. Nicholas' is one of the finest examples of Baroque architecture in Europe. Courtesy of Getty Images/Photodisc.

THE PAST

Romanesque (1100–1230)

The Romanesque style was a pan-European movement that began in France. Its name, derived from ancient Roman structural basis, had nothing to do with the classical unities of Roman construction but, rather, was based on the Roman vault. Romanesque architects were obsessed with security, and much of their work was strongholds and fortresses. Romanesque architecture is characterized by round arches and vaults, and strong, simple, massive forms.

St. Georges Basilica is the oldest surviving Romanesque building in Prague. Bořivoj's son, Prince Vlastislav (915–921), founded the basilica before 920 and is buried here along with other members of the Přemyslid dynasty.

Three Romanesque rotundas have survived intact in Prague, all quite small: the Rotunda of the Holy Cross in the Old Town, from the early twelfth century, the Rotunda of St. Martin from the second half of the eleventh century, and the Rotunda of St. Longinus from the end of the eleventh century.

Gothic (1230–1530)

During the Gothic period, the pointed arch replaced the round Roman arch, which provided a much more efficient transfer of weight, permitting a higher opening with the same width. Another prominent aspect of Gothic architecture was the flying buttress on the exterior of the structure, which transmits the thrust of the vault to the ground, neutralizing the lateral pressure from vaults and ceilings and making it possible to abandon massive block-like construction. Unlike Romanesque architecture, walls were no longer structures holding things up and could be used as panels to hold stained glass and sculpture. The soaring arches and the light permitted in through the stained glass were meant to evoke the mystery of God. The greatest construction boom in Prague came under Charles IV (reigned 1346–1378) when the city became the seat of the Holy Roman Empire and the cultural and political center of Europe. Charles invited two important architects to Prague, Matthias d'Arras of France and Peter Parler of Germany. Czech patriots in the nineteenth century later Bohemized the latter's name into Parléř. The slim spires of Gothic architecture became the dominant feature of the Prague skyline, and the city became known as "100-Spired Prague," *Stověžatá Praha.*

When Charles came to Prague, the Castle District lay in ruins, and he undertook its reconstruction, beginning in 1353, at great expense. Part of the reconstruction was the building of St. Vitus Cathedral, the largest of Prague's churches. d'Arras designed the structure, and Parler and his sons made it into one of Europe's greatest Gothic buildings. Now the cathedral serves as a mausoleum for the kings of Bohemia, a gallery of their sculptures and portraits, and a treasure-vault storing the country's crown jewels.

Bethlehem Chapel in the Old Town is a tall, two-gabled building built in 1391, especially for sermons delivered in Czech rather than Latin. From 1402 to 1413, Jan Hus made it the center of the Czech Reformation and preached up to seven sermons a day here on holidays. Bethlehem Chapel became the most important church in Prague. The structure features plain architectural forms meant to proclaim the new teachings of the Church. The interiors are plain and decorated with texts from Hus' writings. Charles

The Malá Strana (Lesser Town) Bridge Tower guards one end of Charles Bridge. It was built in the second half of the fifteenth century to help guard the Old Town against northern invaders. Courtesy of Getty Images/Photodisc.

Bridge—originally called Prague Bridge but renamed in 1860—is perhaps Prague's most famous monument. Spanning 520 meters (1,706 feet) and 16 arches, it is the longest bridge in Central Europe. According to legend, Charles wanted to make the bridge as strong as possible and thus mixed egg in with the mortar. Czech citizens sent in hundreds of eggs from all over the country.[2] The bridge had no sculptural decorations until 1683 when the citizens of Prague erected a statue of Jan Nepomuk, and from 1698 to 1713, another 21 sculptures were added. Now the bridge is mobbed with tourists during the day and peddlers who cater to them. In the evening, young people sit atop the bridge belting out American pop songs to the gentle twanging of a guitar.

Other notable Gothic constructions are the Old-New Synagogue, the oldest surviving synagogue in Europe, the Týn Church on the Old Town Square, and the Old Town City Hall. Charles also established Central Europe's first university, Charles University, in 1348. Hungarian and Slovak nobles also fell in love with the Gothic and constructed several grandiose cathedrals, such as the Cathedral of St. Elizabeth in Košice and the Church of St. James in Levoča. Another late Gothic work is the chapel Spišský Štvrtok.

Renaissance (1530–1620)

Italian architects brought the Renaissance style to Prague in the sixteenth century, and the vertical, dynamic spires of the Gothic gradually gave way to horizontal and static spaces. Man, rather than God, became the measure of all things during the Renaissance, and a rational harmony became the fundamental architectural principle: the beauty of a building depended on the rational integration of the proportions of all the parts, where nothing could be added or taken away without destroying the harmony of the whole. Straight lines and right angles replaced Gothic spires and curves, and ribbed vaults were abandoned in favor of tunnel vaults and other plain vaults that provided large surfaces for artistic decoration with frescos or graffiti.

One of the greatest examples of Renaissance architecture is the Royal Summer Palace, or Belvedere, near the castle begun in 1535 under Ferdinand I by Italian architects. The ground floor is surrounded by a typical airy arcade carried by tall columns and adorned with rich reliefs. An Italian gardener created a geometrical garden conceived in harmony with the work of architecture simultaneously with the construction of the palace. A large bronze singing fountain was installed later in 1573, which ranks among the most important Renaissance sculptures in the Czech and Slovak lands. Swedes plundered the palace in 1648 during the Thirty Years War, and Josef II converted it into a military laboratory.

A singularly striking structure is the Hvězda (Star) Hunting Lodge. Built from 1555 to 1557, the lodge is in the form of a six-pointed star, thereby following the Renaissance principle of a centralized structure above a regular geometric figure. The layout of the interior is elaborately articulated with abundant architectural detailing. It now houses a museum devoted to the Czech author of historical fiction, Alois Jirásek (see Chapter 6, "Literature").

In 1541, a massive fire destroyed a large part of the Castle District and the New Town, and much of the area was rebuilt in the Renaissance style. The Italian architects, however, were strongly influenced by Prague's Gothic environment, which resulted in a special type of Bohemian Renaissance style. Narrow plots of land necessitated taller, more vertical structures than is usual for Renaissance structures. Schwarzenburg Palace is the most beautiful Renaissance building in Prague, built from 1545 to 1563 for Jan of Lobkowicz.

Týn Church on the Old Town Square in Prague. Established in 1185, its present appearance dates from the 1300s. It is a marvelous example of Prague Gothic architecture. The astronomer Tycho Brahe is buried here. © Corbis

Ornamental graffiti adorns the façades, and the interior is decorated with tremendous mythological paintings. (The astronomer Tycho Brahe died of uremia during a banquet at Schwarzenburg Palace because he thought that going to the restroom before the host was bad form.) Other impressive Renaissance buildings are the Town Hall in the Castle District and the House at the Minute. The origin of the latter's name is unknown. It was originally built in the Gothic style in the late sixteenth century and then rebuilt in 1564. After 1603, the House at the Minute was gradually decorated with graffiti, which was later covered over with a late-Baroque façade. During a renovation in 1905, the graffiti was discovered, and the Baroque façade was removed.

Renaissance was also popular in Slovakia, especially in the town of Bardejov. Its town hall is a masterwork of Renaissance construction. Other examples are the restored church in Bratislava and the church and surrounding houses in the eastern Slovak city of Fričovce.

Prague buildings and street scene. Courtesy of Corbis.

Baroque (1620–1780)

Baroque throughout Europe is associated with the Counter-Reformation. After the Czech defeat by the Catholic Hapsburgs in 1620, Prague lost its status as a royal residence and became a secondary seat of the Hapsburgs, a provincial town. Many Prague citizens fled the country and sold their houses at bargain prices. Many of the house were demolished to make room for Baroque constructions. The word "Baroque" is Italian, and its meaning was originally derogatory. Baroque meant "strange, peculiar, contorted" and designated deviations from the Renaissance style. Baroque architects grew tired of the strict, rational ordering of buildings associated with the Renaissance. The quest for the ideal, for perfect equilibrium no longer seemed significant. A new generation of architects began to overthrow established boundaries

The Baroque Troja Summer Palace was built in the late seventeenth century by Jean-Baptiste Mathey for Count Sternberg. It is one of the most striking summer palaces in Prague and now houses two permanent art exhibits—Czech Painting of the nineteenth century and Czech sculpture 1900–1970. © Corbis.

and conventions and created monumental and massive constructions. The Baroque is meant to evoke an emotional state by appealing to the senses: the sensuous richness and hyper-rational grandeur overwhelms the spectator making him feel small. The Catholics wanted to push back the logical clarity of Protestantism, which was associated with the Renaissance. According to the new thinking, God was supposed to be a mystery beyond the logical comprehension of man. Unlike Renaissance architects, Baroque architects had no desire to instruct and no moralistic desire to judge. All they sought was to carry away the viewer by emotion. Baroque architects experimented with new and vigorous massing and abandoned the static form of the square and the circle for shapes that swirl and move—s-curves, undulating façades, and plans based on ovals. In fact, the Council of Trent in 1545 declared that the square and circle were too pagan for Christian churches; they became essentially excommunicated shapes.

Wallenstein Palace is the first and largest Baroque palace in Prague, built in the Lesser Quarter without any regard to the surrounding streets and fortifications. Twenty-three houses, three gardens, and a brick factory were demolished to clear space for its construction. The palace is concentrated around a landscaped garden and five courtyards, and the garden itself is populated with bronze statues of ancient gods. The façade is composed of three unvarying strips of windows and dormer windows on the roof. Inside, a large fresco adorns the ceiling glorifying Count Wallenstein's military victories. He was in fact a war profiteer.

Humprecht Jan Černín created his own similar palace near the Castle. The façade of the Černín Palace is 135 meters (443 feet) long, covered by a long line of 30 half-columns. In 1851 it was sold and turned into a military barracks. The Clementinum stands in the Old Town near the Charles Bridge. It was one of the first Jesuit colleges in the country, which was a result of Ferdinand I's inviting the Jesuits to Prague in 1556 to support his Counter-Reformation policy. The building is strangely massive in the surrounding medieval environment. Its fortress-like conception became a symbol of the hard Counter-Reformation line of the Jesuits.

St. Nicholas Church in the Old Town is perhaps the most famous Baroque building in Prague. A church was being erected here, and then in 1702 a new bold design appeared based on curved lines, which determined the character of both the main façade and the nave. The façade is 40 meters (131 feet) long, composed of both convex and concave curves. The plan of the church was a Baroque experiment in Europe. The architect, Christoph Dientzenhofer, built the dynamic façade and the large nave with intricate vaults over the intersection of three ovals. The interior of the church is full of Baroque illusionism.

In Slovakia, the best example of the Baroque is the stunning University Church of St. John the Baptist in Trnava, with its magnificent stucco decorations built in 1635. The early-Baroque exterior is somewhat spare, but the interior boasts a host of Baroque masterpieces created over two centuries. The delicately carved altar is 20 meters high and 15 meters wide.

Nineteenth-Century Historicism

The nineteenth century was one of "neos": Neo-Classical, Neo-Gothic, Neo-Baroque, and Neo-Renaissance. During this period, the National Revival, the Czechs were seeking to reinterpret their history and project a distinct view of themselves as a national entity separate from the Germans and Austrians. The deliberate use of individual historical styles was meant to suggest a certain political attitude. Thus, the Neo-Classical style expressed democratic and republican ideals and was applied to government buildings. Gothic, on the other hand, reminded Czech citizens of the glorious reign of Karel IV in the Middle Ages when Prague stood at the center of European art and culture. Neo-Baroque was in fact rare in Prague, and oddly enough it was the Renaissance era that formed the primary source of inspiration for the nineteenth century, odd because the Renaissance itself was the least-represented style in Prague. Neo-Renaissance was applied to administrative buildings, museums, banks, theaters, and concert halls. One specificity of Czech Neo-Renaissance architecture was the incorporation of traditional domestic forms such as folk and rustic architecture. The constructions lost their monumentality, and excess decoration was removed from the façades. The National Theater, completed in 1881 (see Chapter 8 of this volume, "Performing Arts") is a distinctly nationalistic form of the Neo-Renaissance.

THE TWENTIETH CENTURY

In the twentieth century, a younger, more progressive generation of architects and artists influenced by avant-garde developments in the rest of Europe rejected the historicizing culture of the previous century in favor of a new modernism. Prague was booming economically and culturally, providing these new architects the opportunity to experiment and express their vision of modernity. Historicism was abandoned for new, more practical and technically innovative forms, and science, technology, and political progress left their mark on architecture. Modernist architects saw the use of nature in both constructive and decorative elements as an appropriate alternative to the use of past styles. Art Nouveau and Viennese Secession were the first two new Czech artistic movements of the twentieth century. In Prague, typical features were decorative vegetable and figural motifs, large windows, stained glass, exposed masonry, molded plaster, and unarticulated façades. A subsequent development was Functionalism, a style suggesting functional logic and an almost complete lack of ornamentation. New building materials, especially reinforced concrete, enabled a more open layout without the necessity of supporting structures such as pillars. Functionalism is considered one of the finest trends in Czech architecture and was used on large administrative buildings and some private dwellings. The third architectural movement of the first decades of the twentieth century is Cubism, an exclusively Czech trend theorized and practiced by a small group of artists who sought to turn it into a national Czechoslovak style. Even though some buildings were constructed in this manner, it never achieved mass popularity. Socialist Realism arrived from the Soviet Union in the 1950s, but only two hotels—the International and the Jalta—were constructed in this style. Most building efforts in the 1950s and 1960s were concentrated on creating mass housing developments of monotonous, prefab buildings referred to as *paneláks*.

Art Nouveau

In its early years, Art Nouveau represented a reaction against the contemporary preference for emphasizing historical forms. Columns and pilasters gradually disappeared, giving way to new "naturalistic" motifs, such as vegetable and fruit ornamentation. Architects also employed intricate patterns emphasizing geometry. Curved roofs began to top buildings, and natural stone and colored glass were used abundantly. Art Nouveau architects tried to bridge the crafts and the arts; they saw the building as an artistic totality and concentrated their attention on the smallest architectural details, such as grille work and door handles. At the same time they would make visible some of the most fundamental structural features of the building. The Art Nouveau artist sought to strike a balance between man and nature using artistic symbols to add a spiritual dimension to personal experience.

Prague is one of the foremost cities in Art Nouveau architecture, and its primary theorist was Jan Kotěra (1871–1923), pupil of the Viennese architect Otto Wagner and known as the father of modern Czech architecture. More than anyone else, Kotěra presided over the break with the past and was the primary influence over the the next generation of architects, such as Pavel Janák and Josef Gočár. Kotěra's originally naturalistic style evolved toward a strong geometric and constructionist style. He designed house No. 12/72 on Wenceslas Square (originally called Peterka House). It has an unusual early Art Nouveau façade with stucco and plastic decoration by Josef Pekárek and Stanislav Sucharda.

Originally conceived by Josef Fanta in a Neo-Renaissance style, Prague's main train station (built from 1901 to 1909) was gradually altered in the style of Art Nouveau around a massive ticket hall and departure area. The main hall has a wide semicircular window above the main entrance flanked by two slim towers adorned with allegorical figures and topped with crystal glass cupolas.

Prague's population boom at the beginning of the century necessitated the construction of social facilities and buildings referred to as community houses. From 1905 to 1911, a Community House for the City of Prague was built in the Old Town next to the Power Tower. Antonín Balšánek and Osvald Polívka based their design along the diagonal of a rhomboidal site. The structure was built around a central ballroom and concert hall, the Smetana Hall, which has a capacity of 1,500 people. The building houses several restaurants, six ballrooms, and several exhibition halls. A dome sits atop the building, and the main façade displays a mosaic by Karel Špilar entitled "Homage to Prague." The ground-floor rooms of the building are decorated with paintings by Alfons Mucha, František Ženíšek, and Max Švabinský and with statues by Josef Václav Myslbek and Emanuel Hallmann. All of the rooms have stained-glass windows, inlaid floors, and marble- and wooden-polished wall linings. In January 1918, Czech and Moravian Ministers of Parliament met in the Smetana Hall and adopted the so-called Epiphany Declaration, demanding an independent Czechoslovak State.

Other examples of Art Nouveau architecture in Prague are the Koruna House on Wenceslas Square, the steel Palace of Congress in the Exhibition and Trade Fair Park, and the Hotel Paříž, which was made a national monument in 1984.

Art Nouveau is not as abundant in Slovakia as it is in the Czech Republic, but here we find some magnificent work as well. The Blue Church in Bratislava is a stunning structure built from 1909 to 1913 and designed by the Budapest architect Edmund Lechner. It is named for the blue color of its plaster, blue mosaic, and blue glazing. The façade displays a mosaic of St. Elisabeth holding roses.

Cubism

The other notable Czech architectural movement from the beginning of the twentieth century is Cubism, with the offshoot Rondocubism becoming a national style. Art Nouveau was the dominant design at the beginning of the century, which included furniture and wall paintings as well as architecture. The sparseness of Kotěra's style, however, soon elicited opposition from a younger generation of architects who found it too sterile, materialistic, and utilitarian. In 1910, Pavel Janák formulated a program to enhance Kotěra's style with more expressive elements. This new style had its origin in the French Cubism of Picasso and Braque. In 1911, Emil Filla and Otto Gutfreund formed the Group of Plastic Artists *(Skupina výtvarných umělců)*, which was soon joined by the architects Pavel Janák, Josef Gočár, Josef Chochol, and Vlastislav Hofman. Geometrical shapes and horizontal lines began to replace Art Nouveau's vegetable and flower motifs. Objects were "splintered" and depicted as conglomerations of oblique lines and contrasting areas of light and shadow. Architects drew on Cubism in painting to create unusual façades with multiple planes and broken surfaces articulated by radiating and diagonal lines. These artists avoided rectangles and squares and replaced them with triangles, diagonals, rhythmical grids, and jagged forms, which they thought expressed the more active nature of the human spirit. In some sense Cubism was a reaction to the naturalistic qualities of Art Nouveau: the Cubist architect wanted to demonstrate his ability to dominate, prevail over, and transform matter. He wanted to reshape it by means of indentations and fractures. Cubist construction, however, was not simply an application of the latest trend in painting to architecture. Cubist-minded architects argued that Cubism was a trend that could be integrated harmoniously into the rich historical traditions of Prague. They became experts in urban renewal but at the same time rejected the reproduction of historical styles. Instead, they sought an understanding of universal laws of architecture, which would inform their work.[3]

The most famous Cubist structure is the House of the Black Madonna, designed by Josef Gočár in 1912. The building was originally a department store. Its four stories are topped with two mansard stories. Reinforced concrete made it possible to open up the façade with large windows, and the structure fits into the Baroque environment surprisingly well. The building now houses the Museum of Czech Cubism.

Josef Chochol designed the most radical Cubist structures from 1911 to 1913. They include the Tenement House in Vyšehrad, a group of three residences in the Old Town, and the astounding Kovarovic Village in Vyšehrad. The surface of the façades on these structures is further broken down to create a dynamic play of light and shade.

The outbreak of World War I had a disastrous effect on Czech Cubism, primarily due to a powerful resurgence of Czech nationalism. Art audiences began to favor traditional elements of folk art and architecture over originality. At this time Janák and Gočár began experimenting with color, rounded forms, and especially decorative elements, which they had rejected previously. With ornamentation they managed to garner public approval, and their works began to display national and folkloric elements. This tendency developed into Rondocubism, a trend Gočár and Janák presented as a national Czechoslovak style. In the new state, Rondocubism completed with Neoclassicism and was applied to several ministries, apartment blocks, and bank buildings, such as Gočár's Czechoslovak Legiobank in the New Town. The four stories above the ground floor present a mosaic of cylindrical supports topped with a projecting cornice. A long frieze by Gočár depicts the exploits of the voluntary Czechoslovak Legion, which fought in France, Italy, and Russia.

From 1922 to 1925, Janák, in collaboration with Josef Zasche, built the Adria Building on Jungmanovo Square. The building somewhat resembles a Renaissance structure topped with massive battlements and rich relief. Otakar Novotný's apartment building in Holešovice is another fine example of Rondocubism.

Functionalism

A more productive branch of modern architecture was called Functionalism. Functionalist architects famously declared that "form follows function"; they rejected ornamentation and began to display the structural materials of buildings in their designs: structural steel, exposed brickwork, and plaster. The result was that the "functional" design of the structure came more and more to the fore. At its most extreme, its architects denied that art had any place in architecture. In part, the architects were motivated by a rejection of the monumentalist historical structures throughout Prague, which they saw as catering to the rich. The goal of many Functionalist architects was the creation of mass housing for workers with little or no aesthetic amenities. Functionalism was also applied to large administrative buildings, as well as publishing houses and other art institutions. As early as 1908, Jan Kotěra designed a house for the publisher Jan Laichter in the Vinohrady district in Prague, a harbinger of modern rationalist architecture. The store front is segmented into cubic volumes that correspond to the purpose of the interior rooms. Sculptural decoration has vanished and has been replaced with different types of brickwork, the only ornamentation on the surface.

It was after World War I that Functionalism became widespread throughout Czechoslovakia. In the 1920s, Modern architecture was associated with the avant-garde group Devětsil (see Chapter 9 of this volume, "Painting"). According to the members of Devětsil, the working class would become the focus of the new art, a class of people, they theorized, that looked for beauty in the simplest things. On the other hand, modern life was inseparable from modern technology. In 1922, Devětsil's primary theorist, Karel Teige, advocated a purge of the old forms of architecture of the nineteenth and early part of the twentieth century and approved of only the simplest, most rationalist creations of the modern style. Josef Chochol wrote in 1921 that the new architectural form should be "an empowered expression of the purpose whose face it is," it should "stop at the precise function of this purpose and be free of anything that is superfluous," it should be "liberated at last from all the archaic influences, epigony, and eclecticism and never be touched by the poisonous stench of the decaying corpses of yesterday's styles."[4] This was Functionalism at its most radical, often referred to as Scientific Functionalism. It was almost a purely mathematical result of functional requirements. Architects began to rethink the social function for architecture and to apply modern construction materials and structures. In the early 1930s, a group of radical young architects came together around the magazine *Stavba* and created a common program of Functionalism, which was largely a program emphasizing aesthetic minimalism. Ludvík Kysela was one of the most prominent architects of the Stavba circle, and his buildings left a lasting mark on Prague. He designed three major buildings on Wenceslas Square based on the same simple ground plan: the Lindt Department Store, 1925–1927, composed of five wide, horizontal bands and topped by a curved and rounded roof; the Alfa Building, 1927–1929; and finally the Baťa Shoe Store, the most representative of his works. The store is composed of seven stories and has a mini-mum of corridors in the sales areas. The reinforced concrete frame is divided into traditional modules of 6.15 meters (20 feet), and the columns are filled with cast iron with the smallest possible cross section (50 cm [20 inches]), identical in each story. The façade is entirely of glass with the floors distin-guished with narrow white strips of glass. Tomáš Bat'a himself, the founder of Bat'a Shoes, was a devotee of the rational methods of Functionalism. He encouraged a Modernist approach to both shoe manufacture and architec-ture, and after making a fortune selling shoes to soldiers during World War I, he decided to reconstruct his hometown of Zlín employing a Functionalist design centered around his shoe factory. Bat'a invited Le Corbusier to design the layout for the whole town, but he later decided to employ a student of Jan Kotěra, František Lydia Gahura. The city is still dotted with simple, box-like red-brick houses that Bat'a constructed to house his workers, and the unadorned brick, steel, concrete and glass surrounded by greenery in this garden city make Zlín a model for urban planning.

The economic boom of the 1920s brought the first stores devoted exclu-sively to retail sales, many of which were constructed according to Functionalist design. The first full-service, European-style department store, *Bílá labut'* [The White Swan] was constructed in the Functionalist style from 1937 to 1939 in the New Town of Prague. The building is composed of six floors and two base-ments, and the enormous façade is made of glass divided into square grids.

František Libra designed the Edison Transformer Station in the New Town of Prague in 1926. Its asymmetrical construction is composed of sev-eral large, box-like structures divided by horizontal banks of windows and topped with a glass sculpture by Zdeněk Pešánek. Müller's Villa in Střešovice (1928–1930) is a remarkable work by Adolf Loos, a Viennese architect who became a Czechoslovak citizen in 1920. It is a stark, compact block with sharply carved out windows. The interior, however, destroys any impression of austerity. Loos employed a wide spectrum of colors from blood-red radia-tors, to pink linoleum, to blue ceilings, and the multi-leveled, high-ceiling rooms penetrate one another rising up in a spiral along staircases.

As the 1920s progressed, architects began to express their reservations about the extreme, almost unattainable ideal of Functionalism. The require-ments were too restrictive, placing excessive constraints on the architect's creativity. According to the critics, the architects of Scientific Functional-ism had an extremely narrow view of man, a person who only ate, slept, and worked. They failed to take into account a person's psychological and aesthetic needs. These considerations led to Emotional Functionalism, whereby an intentional beauty would be incorporated into the Functionalist structure. Scientific Functionalists had rejected entirely the traditional unity of architecture, painting, and sculpture. Emotional Functionalists, on the other hand, returned to the practice of decorating their buildings with sculpture and painting. The most vivid example of Emotional Functionalism is Richard Podzemný's Zemská Bank on Freedom Square (1936–1937); with its rounded corners and gleaming white ceramic tiles, Zemská Bank soon received the nickname "Glass Palace."

Post–World War II

After the Communists took over Czechoslovakia, left-wing architects thought they could begin to design more purely Functionalist architecture, but this was not to be. Stalinist Neoclassicism was foisted upon Czechoslovakia, but only two hotels were built in the style—the International and the Jalta. The design of the Hotel International was inspired by Historicist architecture. A central tower dominates the structure, and the entire building is rigorously symmetrical. The Jalta is not as monumental as the International and is, in fact, somewhat decorative with geometrical ornamentation on balconies and windows. After Khrushchev's denunciation of Stalin in 1956, architects were restricted to designing and assembling prefabricated apartment buildings known as *paneláks,* created for hundreds of thousands of Czechoslovak citizens who were forced to live in a tasteless, monotonous wasteland of gigantic housing complexes, a vulgarized version of Functionalism. Czechoslovakia industrialized rapidly in the 1950s and 1960s, driving herds of villagers to the cities and creating a massive housing shortage. The simplest, quickest, and cheapest way to accommodate them was to construct enormous apartment blocks clumped together so densely that services could be provided to them as efficiently as possible. *Paneláks* were built throughout the Soviet Bloc and were not only a cheap source of housing; they were also meant to integrate home, work, and social life. Schools, factories, clinics, and cultural centers were all built nearby. Nevertheless, the poor construction, bad heating, and general monotony of the buildings were an unwelcome solution to the country's housing shortage. Today, these *paneláks* house approximately one-third of the Czech population and are showing signs of aging. Nearly every Czech and Slovak city is ringed by monotonous jungles of these towering blocks. The buildings themselves seem uninspired, but often the apartments within belie the drab exterior.

The Velvet Revolution

Foreign investment and tourism has turned Prague into a prospering city. Much money went into restoring buildings that had fallen into disrepair during Communism, and the architectural system has diversified tremendously. One of the city's most striking and publicized buildings is the Rašin Building, 1993–1994, also called the "Fred and Ginger" or the "Dancing Building." Frank Gehry and Vlado Milunic created a startling building composed of two towers, one concrete and one glass. The latter billows out and twists toward the former, and the entire structure resembles a dancing couple. A twisted metal cupola sits atop the building, and the façade facing the river fits in with the nineteenth-century contours of the neighboring buildings.

Notes

1. Eric Dluhosch, "Preface," in Rostislav Švacha, *The Architecture of New Prague,* trans. Alexandra Büchler (Cambridge, MA: MIT Press, 1995), xii–xxxi.

2. Erhard Gorys, *Czechoslovakia* (London: Pallas Athene, 1991), 56.

3. Švacha, *The Architecture of New Prague,* 102.

4. Švacha, 237.

Selected Bibliography

Gorys, Erhard. *Czechoslovakia.* London: Pallas Athene, 1991.

Margolius, Ivan. *Prague: A Guide to Twentieth-Century Architecture.* London: Ellipsis, Konemann, 1996.

Pavitt, Jane. *The Buildings of Europe: Prague.* Manchester: Manchester University Press, 2000.

Sedláková, Radomíra. *Prague: An Architectural Guide.* Stoccarda, Italy: Hatje Verlag, 1997.

Staňková, Jaroslava et al., *Prague: Eleven Centuries of Architecture,* trans. Zdeněk Vyplel and David Vaughan. Prague: No Publisher, 1992.

Švacha, Rostislav. *The Architecture of New Prague,* trans. Alexandra Büchler. Cambridge, MA: MIT Press, 1995.

Index

About the Author

CRAIG CRAVENS is a Fellow of Czech Studies at the University of Texas, Austin.